AMERICA'S
PRISONS
OPPOSING VIEWPOINTS®

Other Books of Related Interest in the Opposing
Viewpoints Series:

A M E R I C A ' S
PRISONS
OPPOSING VIEWPOINTS®

David L. Bender & Bruno Leone, *Series Editors*

Stacey L. Tipp, *Book Editor*

OPPOSING VIEWPOINTS SERIES ®

Greenhaven Press, Inc.   PO Box 289009   San Diego, CA 92198-0009

Library of Congress Cataloging-in-Publication Data

America's prisons : opposing viewpoints / Stacey L. Tipp, book editor. — 5th ed.
    p.   cm. — (Opposing viewpoints series)
    Includes bibliographical references and index.
    Summary: Presents opposing viewpoints about prison issues. Includes critical thinking skill activities and a list of organizations to contact.
    ISBN 0-89908-178-9 (lib. bdg.) — ISBN 0-89908-153-3 (pbk.)
    1. Prisons—United States.   2. Criminals—Rehabilitation—United States.   3. Punishment—United States.   [1. Prisons. 2. Prisoners.]   I. Tipp, Stacey L., 1963-   .   II. Series: Opposing viewpoints series (Unnumbered)
HV9471.A49   1991
365'.973—dc20
                                                    91-12661

"Congress shall make no law . . . abridging the freedom of speech, or of the press."

First Amendment to the U.S. Constitution

The basic foundation of our democracy is the first amendment guarantee of freedom of expression. The Opposing Viewpoints Series is dedicated to the concept of this basic freedom and the idea that it is more important to practice it than to enshrine it.

Contents

Why Consider Opposing Viewpoints?

"It is better to debate a question without settling it than to settle a question without debating it."

Joseph Joubert (1754-1824)

The Importance of Examining Opposing Viewpoints

The purpose of the Opposing Viewpoints Series, and this book in particular, is to present balanced, and often difficult to find, opposing points of view on complex and sensitive issues.

Probably the best way to become informed is to analyze the positions of those who are regarded as experts and well studied on issues. It is important to consider every variety of opinion in an attempt to determine the truth. Opinions from the mainstream of society should be examined. But also important are opinions that are considered radical, reactionary, or minority as well as those stigmatized by some other uncomplimentary label. An important lesson of history is the eventual acceptance of many unpopular and even despised opinions. The ideas of Socrates, Jesus, and Galileo are good examples of this.

Readers will approach this book with their own opinions on the issues debated within it. However, to have a good grasp of one's own viewpoint, it is necessary to understand the arguments of those with whom one disagrees. It can be said that those who do not completely understand their adversary's point of view do not fully understand their own.

A persuasive case for considering opposing viewpoints has been presented by John Stuart Mill in his work *On Liberty*. When examining controversial issues it may be helpful to reflect on this suggestion:

9

The only way in which a human being can make some approach to knowing the whole of a subject, is by hearing what can be said about it by persons of every variety of opinion, and studying all modes in which it can be looked at by every character of mind. No wise man ever acquired his wisdom in any mode but this.

Analyzing Sources of Information

The Opposing Viewpoints Series includes diverse materials taken from magazines, journals, books, and newspapers, as well as statements and position papers from a wide range of individuals, organizations, and governments. This broad spectrum of sources helps to develop patterns of thinking which are open to the consideration of a variety of opinions.

Pitfalls to Avoid

A pitfall to avoid in considering opposing points of view is that of regarding one's own opinion as being common sense and the most rational stance, and the point of view of others as being only opinion and naturally wrong. It may be that another's opinion is correct and one's own is in error.

Another pitfall to avoid is that of closing one's mind to the opinions of those with whom one disagrees. The best way to approach a dialogue is to make one's primary purpose that of understanding the mind and arguments of the other person and not that of enlightening him or her with one's own solutions. More can be learned by listening than speaking.

It is my hope that after reading this book the reader will have a deeper understanding of the issues debated and will appreciate the complexity of even seemingly simple issues on which good and honest people disagree. This awareness is particularly important in a democratic society such as ours where people enter into public debate to determine the common good. Those with whom one disagrees should not necessarily be regarded as enemies, but perhaps simply as people who suggest different paths to a common goal.

Developing Basic Reading and Thinking Skills

In this book, carefully edited opposing viewpoints are purposely placed back to back to create a running debate; each viewpoint is preceded by a short quotation that best expresses the author's main argument. This format instantly plunges the reader into the midst of a controversial issue and greatly aids that reader in mastering the basic skill of recognizing an author's point of view.

A number of basic skills for critical thinking are practiced in the activities that appear throughout the books in the series. Some of the skills are:

Evaluating Sources of Information. The ability to choose from among alternative sources the most reliable and accurate source in relation to a given subject.

Separating Fact from Opinion. The ability to make the basic distinction between factual statements (those that can be demonstrated or verified empirically) and statements of opinion (those that are beliefs or attitudes that cannot be proved).

Identifying Stereotypes. The ability to identify oversimplified, exaggerated descriptions (favorable or unfavorable) about people and insulting statements about racial, religious, or national groups, based upon misinformation or lack of information.

Recognizing Ethnocentrism. The ability to recognize attitudes or opinions that express the view that one's own race, culture, or group is inherently superior, or those attitudes that judge another culture or group in terms of one's own.

It is important to consider opposing viewpoints and equally important to be able to critically analyze those viewpoints. The activities in this book are designed to help the reader master these thinking skills. Statements are taken from the book's viewpoints and the reader is asked to analyze them. This technique aids the reader in developing skills that not only can be applied to the viewpoints in this book, but also to situations where opinionated spokespersons comment on controversial issues. Although the activities are helpful to the solitary reader, they are most useful when the reader can benefit from the interaction of group discussion.

Using this book and others in the series should help readers develop basic reading and thinking skills. These skills should improve the reader's ability to understand what is read. Readers should be better able to separate fact from opinion, substance from rhetoric, and become better consumers of information in our media-centered culture.

This volume of the Opposing Viewpoints Series does not advocate a particular point of view. Quite the contrary! The very nature of the book leaves it to the reader to formulate the opinions he or she finds most suitable. My purpose as publisher is to see that this is made possible by offering a wide range of viewpoints that are fairly presented.

David L. Bender
Publisher

Introduction

"The Law, like a good archer, should aim at the right measure of punishment."

Plato, *Laws*, XI

Prisons have become the central component of America's criminal justice system. While all societies have felt compelled to punish those people who violate the law, the United States has extensively developed and relied upon its prison system to perform this function. Indeed, according to a 1991 research report prepared by the Sentencing Project, a national nonprofit organization that promotes sentencing reform, the United States now imprisons more of its citizens than any other nation in the world. Although America has always relied heavily on incarceration as a sanction for criminal behavior, an examination of the nation's history reveals considerable variation in public attitudes toward convicted felons. While periods of liberal reform appear to be correlated with support for the enlightened treatment of prisoners and the upgrading of prison conditions, in less liberal times, the opposite is true.

In Colonial America, prison systems employed barbaric techniques whose main purpose was clearly revenge. Corporal punishments were swift, painful, and supposedly corrective. Public degradation was a common chastisement for minor offenses, while hanging, burning at the stake, and breaking on the rack were among the principal punishments applied for more serious crimes. These harsh punishments clearly reflect a society which believed in the innate evil of the criminal. They also exemplify a tendency to use punishment for its own end, with no regard for potential rehabilitation.

However, progress and change, so obvious in other aspects of everyday life, also affected the penal system. The first predecessor of the prisons we know today was erected in 1790 in Pennsylvania. Built mainly through the reform efforts of the Quakers, its goal became not punishment but correction, and as such was far ahead of its time. Consistent with the Quakers' ethics, the method called for solitary confinement without work. It was assumed that offenders would be more quickly repentant and ultimately reformed if they could reflect on their crimes unham-

13

pered by distractions.

The idea that criminals could be "corrected" and that reforms in the prison system would enable criminals to return to a normal life eventually became the criteria for determining the state of prisons and the treatment of inmates. After 1870, prisons began to employ such practices as prisoner education, vocational training, indeterminate sentencing, and parole. These new methods and the growing faith in prisoner rehabilitation clearly reflected a radical change from the inhumane treatment and fatalistic attitudes of earlier times.

Another factor significantly affected modern attitudes toward prison conditions and the treatment of inmates. During the 1940s, increased reliance upon and respect for the social science of psychology essentially changed the way criminologists viewed the criminal mind. Oral and written psychological tests were employed in an effort to determine the factors motivating criminal behavior. The upbringing, environment, and conscious and subconscious motives of criminals were examined to help determine not only why criminals behave as they do but also how best to deal with them.

Belief in rehabilitation gradually waned after the mid-1970s, however, as major evaluations of rehabilitation programs cast doubt on their ability to improve recidivism rates among convicted felons. Indeed, the findings of one prominent investigator, Robert Martinson, were widely accepted as proof that nothing works in the treatment of offenders. Declining faith in efforts at rehabilitation coincided with increased public intolerance for crime and criminals. This intolerance is reflected in the harsher prison sentences meted out to offenders in recent years. As incarceration rates have increased, living conditions in prisons and jails have deteriorated badly. Furthermore, the availability of rehabilitation programs has decreased as the system struggles simply to accommodate the increased prisoner volume.

America's Prisons: Opposing Viewpoints debates five important questions: What Is the Purpose of Prisons? How Do Prisons Affect Criminals? How Can Prison Overcrowding Be Reduced? Should Prisons Be Privatized? and What Are the Alternatives to Prisons? The materials included are drawn from a wide spectrum of sources and individuals. Judges, psychologists, prisoners, and others are represented in this volume. Each of the debates revolves around these related issues: How, if at all, can society make prisons effective? Or more to the point, how can prisons control future criminal behavior and protect society? As readers explore these topics, the complexity and necessity of dealing with prisons make it clear that the debate will continue.

What Is the Purpose of Prisons?

Chapter Preface

One of the fundamental disagreements in the debate over the purpose of prisons is whether prisons should punish offenders or attempt to rehabilitate them. Allan C. Brownfeld, a syndicated columnist whose editorials appear frequently in such conservative publications as *Human Events*, *Washington Inquirer*, and *Conservative Chronicle*, makes a cogent case for punishment. Brownfeld argues that society has lost sight of the fact that criminals are responsible for their actions and thus deserve punishment. Indeed, he rejects most efforts at prisoner rehabilitation because they dilute the principle of personal responsibility for wrongdoing. As Brownfeld puts it, American society does not require "psychological theories of 'rehabilitation,' . . . but a concept of responsibility for the results of one's actions and punishment for serious violations. It is high time that the concept of punishment was rediscovered."

On the other hand, Warren Burger, a former chief justice of the United States Supreme Court, believes that society has an obligation to rehabilitate those it imprisons. If prisons are merely warehouses, Burger argues, inmates will almost certainly return to crime when released. Burger contends that prisons should become "factories with fences," in which offenders are rehabilitated through productive work programs. Putting prisoners to work would provide them with marketable skills to obtain work in the world outside prison and would instill in them the discipline they need to remain employed, Burger concludes.

Should prisons punish or rehabilitate offenders? The following chapter addresses this question and explores the broader debate about the proper purpose of prisons.

"The most desirable penal policy is that of just punishment, the swift punishing of blameworthy behavior."

Prisons Should Punish

Francis T. Murphy

Prisons were constructed as a humane alternative to the public floggings and executions that were originally used to punish criminals. They were to be havens where prisoners could do hard labor and repent their crimes in solitude. Francis T. Murphy, the presiding justice of the New York Supreme Court Apellate Division First Judicial Department, argues in the following viewpoint that prisons have lost this original purpose. Criminals have broken society's moral rules, he concludes, and prison should effectively punish them for this infraction.

As you read, consider the following questions:

1. What factors does the author cite to prove the public no longer believes that criminal behavior can be changed?
2. Why, according to Murphy, should punishment be the goal of prison?
3. What standards must people hold themselves to, according to the author?

Francis T. Murphy, "Moral Accountability and the Rehabilitative Ideal," *New York State Bar Journal*, January 1984. Reprinted with permission. Copyright 1984, New York State Bar Association.

When a man is sentenced and led from courtroom to prison, two statements have been made as the door closes behind him. The judge has spoken to his crime, and society has spoken of how it will deal with him. Embedded in these statements is a fascinating complex of ideas about the nature of man, morality, law and politics.

Prior to the 1800's, the prison system was unknown. Society's answer to the felon was usually given at the end of a rope or the swing of an axe. In imposing sentence, a judge was virtually a clerk, for he had no discretion in the matter. He simply sent the defendant to a death commanded by law.

During the first half of the 1800's, however, a confluence of ideas and political events produced the prison in America. So unusual was the idea of the prison that Europeans came to America in order to visit prisons and record what they saw.

The Idea of Prisons

How did the idea of the prison originate? In part, the prison was a humane answer to the criminal. Hanging a man for stealing a spoon or forging a note seemed immoral. In great part, the prison was an economic indulgence, for prior to the Industrial Revolution society could not have afforded prisons. Yet, lying behind humane motives and the new economy was a belief that included much more than the prison. The first half of the 1800's was an age of reform. Belief in the perfectibility of human beings and in the improvement of their social institutions was prevalent. In America and Europe a liberalism traceable to thinkers like Locke and Erasmus, to the Renaissance and ancient Greece, had as its central principle that to every question there was a rational answer, that man was able to discover rational solutions to his problems, and when thus enlightened he could live in a harmonious society. It was natural that a belief of that magnitude, infused into economic and social problems of every kind, and joined with a humanitarian spirit and the new, industrial wealth, would inhibit the tying of the rope and the swinging of the axe. Thus it was that the first half of the 1800's introduced in America not only the prison as a place for punishment and deterrence, but the prison as a place for the rehabilitative ideal, today condemned by many as the right idea in the wrong place.

The Rehabilitative Ideal

A usable definition of the rehabilitative ideal is that a primary purpose of penal treatment is the changing of the character and behavior of the prisoner in order to protect society and to help him. It is an idea that has attracted groups who march to the beat of very different drums. It has attracted those who think of

18

crime as an individual's moral failure, or as an evil caused by corrupt social institutions, or as an entry in the printout of a prisoner's genetic program. Accordingly, the rehabilitative ideal has elicited different means—extending from the early 1800's imposition of absolute silence upon all prisoners in New York, and the unrelieved solitary confinement of all prisoners in Pennsylvania, to the twentieth century's faith in therapeutic interventions, such as the promoting of literacy, the teaching of vocational skills, the use of psychotherapy, and the less popular surgical removal of brain tissue. All of these means have one thing in common. Each has failed as a reliable rehabilitative technique and each, ironically, has today drawn public anger not upon those working in the rehabilitative disciplines, but upon very visible judges few of whom, if any, purport to be competent in any rehabilitative skill. Indeed, it is an anger that has a sharp edge, for though judges observe a traditional silence when accused of failing to rehabilitate the imprisoned, judges nevertheless have legislatively or constitutionally been drawn within the range of public attack in other areas of the rehabilitative ideal—sentencing discretion, the indeterminate sentence, probation, parole, and prison conditions.

From Rehabilitation to Punishment

Our corrections system is built on the concept of rehabilitation. Clearly, it doesn't work. The recidivist rate, billions of wasted dollars and the failure of countless prison job-training programs have left little room for argument. Perhaps it's time to change the premise of corrections from one of rehabilitation to simple punishment.

Kent W. Perry, *Newsweek*, March 13, 1989.

Notwithstanding that the rehabilitative ideal never actually dominated the criminal justice system as a value prior to punishment and deterrence, it was generally believed by the public and the Bench that it had that primacy. In any case, substantial defections from that ideal began about twenty years ago, not only among editorial writers and politicians but among scholars as well. Today, the ideal is incanted solemnly at sentence, but even then neither Bench nor counsel discuss it.

Why has the rehabilitative ideal depreciated so sharply? The answer must be traceable to ideas that drain belief in the notion of the mutability of human character and behavior. I will point to several of them.

The nineteenth century belief in the simplicity and perfectibility of human nature has been profoundly shaken by the Freudian revolution, to say nothing of the unprecedented savagery of the twentieth century. There is in America a continuing and almost apocalyptic increase in crime, notwithstanding that our average sentence is the longest in the western world. Inevitably, a sense of helplessness, a foreboding of a collapse of public order is present at every dinner table. As for confidence in the utility of traditional therapeutic means, it has all but vanished. Indeed, it is generally accepted that a rehabilitative technique of any kind is yet to be discovered. Belief in the power of the public educational system to perform its simplest objective has been lost, hence the claims of education are not received as once they were. There has been a profound depression in the structure and authority of the family, and with it a decline of those family virtues associated with rehabilitation. A pervasive pessimism, an almost open contempt, for government has seeped into the public mind. A new mentality has arisen, markedly anti-intellectual in orientation, disclosing in American culture a sense of dependency, a seeking out of comfort and self-awareness, a flight from pain and personal responsibility. Moral passion has not declined. It has disappeared. These social facts are fragments of deeper changes which strikingly distinguish the major political movements of the twentieth century from those of the nineteenth. As Isaiah Berlin has observed, two devastating elements, traceable to Freud or Marx, have united in the political movements of the twentieth century. One is the idea of unconscious and irrational influences that outweigh reason in explaining human conduct. The other is the idea that answers to problems exist not in rational solutions but in the extinguishing of the problems by means other than thought. So it is that the rehabilitative ideal, congenial to the essentially intellectual age of reform of the early 1800's, has depreciated with the twentieth century's devaluation of the intellect and the will. Looking back over the past two centuries, we see that science, as a new way of knowing, not only promised to augment man's power but dramatically delivered on that promise. The power it delivered, however, proved to be over nature only. It did not increase our power over ourselves to become better people. It has left man unchanged, sitting, as it were, in the evening of his life in a warehouse filled with his technology.

Prisons Are for Punishment

We are thus living at a critical point in the shaping of an American penal policy. We could increase penal sanctions by matching brutality for brutality, but ethics and utility argue against it. In any case, a political consensus fortunately does not support what is essentially a regressive, primitive gesture. Equally

20

without a political consensus are programs for social reforms directed at what some think to be causes of crime—unemployment, racial discrimination, poor housing. Whether such conditions cause crime is disputed and, in any case, a penal policy is too narrow a platform upon which a plan of social reform can be based.

Feel No Guilt About Punishing Criminals

We must understand that basic moral principles lie at the heart of our criminal justice system, and that our system of law acts as the collective moral voice of society. There is nothing wrong with these values. Nor should we be hesitant or feel guilty about punishing those who violate the elementary rules of civilized existence. In the end, the war on crime will be won only when an attitude of mind and a change of heart takes place in America, when certain truths take hold again. Truths like right and wrong matter, and individuals are responsible for their actions. Retribution should be swift and sure for those who prey on the innocent.

Ronald Reagan, presidential address, 1981.

In my opinion, the most desirable penal policy is that of just punishment, the swift punishing of blameworthy behavior to the degree of the offender's culpability. By such a policy we reaffirm the reality of moral values. Thus we answer those who challenge the conception of man's moral responsibility. Thus we create hope in a future based upon ancient moral truths from which so many have drifted into a night of philosophical neutrality.

Prisons, Rehabilitation Don't Mix

The idea of just punishment has a wide consensus. It is a statement of a natural, moral intuition. It declares the moral autonomy of man without which all value systems are bound to be anarchic. It recaptures the lost community of moral and legal elements which once characterized crime and punishment, and without which a society loses its stability. As for the rehabilitative ideal, it should be stripped of its pretentiousness, if not of its very name. It is a hope of changing behavior, and nothing more. It is a goal, not a reality. In prison it should be directed at objectives that can be realized, particularly the avoidance of the deformative influences of prison life. Efforts at rehabilitation might well be concentrated at the offender outside of the prison setting, the one place where rehabilitation might have a fair chance of accomplishment. Surely rehabilitation is unlikely in prisons in which minimum standards of personal safety, health, and humane treatment are often violated. Indeed one cannot

21

leave the literature of penology without the conviction that, if he were required to design a place in which the behavior of a man could never be improved, he would draw the walled, maximum security prison, very much like those into which men were led for rehabilitation in the early 1800's and are kept until this very day.

This time in which we live need not be an age of cynicism and despair. There is no principle that compels us to accept the philosophical debris of history. This time can, if we would but will it, be an age in which the fixed human values of Western civilization are brought back into their natural ascendancy. They who believe that man is not truly free, and hence not truly responsible, who market man as a rational animal without free will, who recognize neither good nor evil but only what is personally useful or harmful, who find the rule of right and wrong only in the current opinion of men, all these are strangers in the West. The values of Western civilization are ultimately the standards of men who hold themselves accountable for their moral acts. Upon that accountability all social institutions rise and fall.

"*Prison institutions which limit the pain of imprisonment to deprivation of liberty . . . would seem to be a sufficient punishment.*"

Prisons Should Not Punish

J. Roger Lee and Laurin A. Wollan Jr.

J. Roger Lee is an associate professor of philosophy at California State University at Los Angeles, and Laurin A. Wollan Jr. is an associate professor in the school of criminology at Florida State University in Tallahassee. In the following viewpoint, the authors argue that imprisonment, which deprives prisoners of both liberty and privacy, is punishment enough. Prisoners should endure no further punishment, they contend. Lee and Wollan advocate the 'libertarian prison', a free society behind prison walls, in which inmates can enjoy autonomy, rehabilitation, and personal safety.

As you read, consider the following questions:

1. How do the authors support their argument that imprisonment is sufficient punishment?
2. What are the potential advantages of the libertarian prison, according to Lee and Wollan?
3. Why do the authors believe that increased surveillance of prisoners will be necessary in the libertarian prison?

J. Roger Lee and Laurin A. Wollan Jr., "The Libertarian Prison: Principles of Laissez-Faire Incarceration," *The Prison Journal*, vol. 65 (1985). Reprinted with permission of the Pennsylvania Prison Society.

The growing interest in libertarian principles within the field of corrections—private construction and operation of prisons being only the most recent and stunning development—suggests that it might be interesting (and perhaps important) to take a look at the concept of a libertarian prison. By that we mean not a prison built and run by a business corporation, but one which is itself based, in its workings, on such principles as freedom from coercion, maximization of autonomy, and individual enterprise. In other words, what would happen if a prison somewhere were shifted to the same operating premises that should, and to an extent do, obtain elsewhere in the free or "outside" world?

Our Proposal

Thus, our proposal: inmates are free to do as they please, to come and to go as they please inside the prison, to enter into relationships on a basis of voluntary exchange, all of this subject only to the rules of the criminal code and other legal constraints applicable to citizens on the outside—plus the distinctive restrictions of imprisonment, which we suggest should be limited to intensive surveillance and the inability to move beyond the prison walls. Our much more mobile population of inmates, it must be remembered, is made up of hardened, many of them violent, criminals who have been imprisoned to segregate them from society and to keep them from committing more crimes either against the outside world or against each other.

We fully expect that a prison operated on the basis of permission rather than prohibition would rather early and fully develop into a flourishing economy. This is in part what we expect from what we know of human nature under such circumstances. But it is also an expectation based on what is found in prison anyway: an informal, virtually covert, economy based for the most part on voluntary exchanges, using tokens or barter if currency is unavailable, so that a remarkable variety of goods and services are provided. This occurs even in prisoner-of-war camps where conditions are much more oppressive than they are in civilian prisons. Thus, the foundation of our vision of a laissez-faire prison is only partly based on principle; it is partly based on practice, the seemingly inevitable realization of market economies operating under and in spite of (and even defiance of) the most handicapping conditions.

The Principles of Punishment

At the outset, it is necessary to say something about the concept and purposes of punishment. Punishment, all agree, must be painful. But, we argue, the "pains of imprisonment" (in Gresham Sykes' phrase) need not include all or even much of the deprivation which he identifies. In addition to deprivation of liberty, to

24

which we would add the compromise of privacy, both of which we endorse, he includes the deprivations of goods and services, heterosexual relationships, security, and autonomy, none of which deprivations we endorse.

The Immorality of Punishment

Punishment is immoral. It is weak. It is useless. It is productive of evil. It engenders bitterness in those punished, hardness and self-complacency in those who impose it. To justify punishment, we develop false standards of good and bad. We caricature and distort both our victims and ourselves. . . .

The penal department—the department set aside for punishment— must be eliminated from our state organization.

Frank Tannenbaum, *Wall Shadows—A Study in American Prisons*, 1922.

There is no reason why, as we approach the 21st century with sensibilities far more humane than 200 years ago, we cannot be content primarily with the one pain that was sufficient in the penology of the classical or Beccarian school: prison institutions which limit the pain of imprisonment to deprivation of liberty. That would seem to be a sufficient punishment for ordinary crimes, even violent ones, without loading onto it the variety of pains experienced even now in the typical maximum security institution. The pain of lost liberty, especially in a free society, should never be underestimated.

The Principles of Liberty

Surely it is one of the crimes of our penal system that we forbid prisoners to do what is natural, even necessary, for adult human beings, that is to engage in activity—sometimes playful, more often workful, and in any case active, as active as the inmate wishes to be.

We argue that one of the most important features of a prison might become the freedom to engage in activity, productive or otherwise, according to one's lights, as long as it does not violate the rights of others. This is fundamental to the realization of any substantial degree of one's humanity. And the humanity of the inmate is the one quality we insist must not be damaged, let alone destroyed, by degradations piled upon deprivations. Inmates whose lives are closely monitored in a prison, and who are deprived of the liberty to come and go beyond the walls, are deprived sufficiently for punitive purposes. They need be deprived no further of the autonomy that goes with the dignity of human life.

The freedom of the individual in the libertarian prison would be extensive enough to enable that individual to choose whether or not to work at all and for whom to work, if work is chosen. The principal difference between prison industries of the past and industries of the libertarian prison is the freedom of the inmate to be an entrepreneur, that is to say, to be the boss, one's own boss, and the boss of willing others. Further, to the extent that the inmate accumulates capital to invest in the means of production, that inmate would be free to produce and sell products to consumers either inside or outside the prison, employing other inmates in many cases, thus making jobs in the libertarian prison through private industry, not public works.

Another related principle of the libertarian prison is its abandonment of the notion that central planning of anything is necessary. Instead, a spirit of laissez-faire would permeate the prison. Everyone within the prison, from warden down to the lowest "fish" who has just entered prison, must understand that there is no direction of anyone's activities except by the requirements of observation, the criminal law, and other regulations to which outsiders are similarly subjected.

Of what utility is such a prison?

Maximize the Liberty of Prisoners

We insist that the libertarian principle needs no utilitarian defense: It is intrinsically right for men and women, even behind bars for crimes committed against the liberty, property, or security of others, to have their right to liberty diminished only to the extent we have described. They would be deprived of their physical liberty to leave the premises of the prison. Within those confines, liberty should be maximized for its own sake; even convicts deserve no less.

Having declared that principle, however, we hasten to note that there are abundant payoffs to freedom which make it worthwhile. First it would work as free economies work, to meet the demands of consumers of goods and services as variously and efficiently as possible. Only in a free economy are those wants and needs even revealed, let alone met; in a controlled economy, they are dimly discerned. Many of these needs are unmet in the typical prison today; certainly wants are unsatisfied, often for no good reason. Most of them, both needs and wants, are legitimate, deserving of satisfaction, and no threat to control or any other purpose or requirement of the institution, including the overriding punitive character of the experience.

Realizing Potential

Freedom permits the inmate to realize his or her potential for human excellence, whatever it may be, in whatever direction the inmate chooses for its development. No institution, not even

26

a prison, should be allowed to stifle that. No inmate need languish on a cot or while away the hours watching television or playing cards or doing or planning mischief. Inmates who are free to choose activity of suitable kinds will be better for it, more fulfilled by it, more content with their lot, and more agreeable if not more tractable from a managerial point of view.

Less Violence

Freedom—coupled as it must be with elimination of interaction based on force by anyone except in the administration of the law—will put a premium on wit and creativity and on a spirit of cooperation, rather than on force and cunning and undesirable alliances. Inmates are now vulnerable to the brutes in prison; their only protection, unless they are extraordinarily shrewd or lucky, is a relationship with a stronger inmate, whose protection is usually purchased for a price, frequently forced sex. This occurs in male social groups which equate forced sexual submission with emasculation.

A flourishing economy would enable the enterprising inmates to earn, save, and invest their income—in bodyguards, if necessary. We would expect, however, that an economy such as we envision would require less and less of that, as it shifted the tone of the prison society from one of forcefulness and intimidation to one of businesslike arrangements. The brutes would come to be controlled informally by the businessmen within the prison.

Private security forces and productive purpose keep most firms in the outside world relatively peaceful places, with the police called on to intervene only in unusual cases. Private security, but chiefly social pressures, keep much of the peace. In our entrepreneurial prison, the social forces and the privatization of some security functions, observed by the prison police, would combine to make the normal operation of the prison more peaceful than now. The occasional violence which would persist inside the prison should be punished by increased time to be served and by increased reparations to victims because such violence violates the criminal law. . . .

Improved Management

The management and control of the institution would be markedly less difficult. More prisoners for more of their time would be constructively engaged and they themselves, as noted, would have a lower level of tolerance than now for the brutal style. The prison bureaucracy would thus be able to attend to details it now lacks time and energy to deal with. And some of its imperfectly performed functions will have been privatized as an immediate result of our envisioned reform and operated by inmate firms themselves. Some rehabilitative services would be performed by the firms in job training programs. Other rehabilitative services will be offered by educators and psychologists who find themselves to be inmates.

Engagement in such activities, even if no fundamental change occurred in the character and personality of the inmate, would better prepare the inmate for successful engagement of life on the outside. These activities inside the prison would be more like those of the conventional, noncriminal world outside. Thus, there would be a better prospect for success, or at least for avoidance of further criminal activities.

The Importance of Walls

Deprivation of liberty as the sole punishment for crime puts an especially heavy emphasis on the walls of the prison. They are not only functional, but symbolic. Permeability of the outer perimeter of the prison can now be made almost impossible, thanks to new technologies. The libertarian prison requires impermeability in only one direction and of one sort; by the inmate physically and toward the outside. That permits others to come through from the outside and the inmate to communicate with the outside world by mail, telegram, telephone, radio, carrier pigeon, or any other means imaginable—for all of which, however, the inmate must pay as part of the cost of doing business (or pleasure) from within the prison, precisely as outsiders must bear the costs of their communications.

The Reality of Prison

Nothing is accomplished towards rehabilitation, with respect to preparing an inmate for his return to society, with oppression, punishment and harassment as the rule instead of the exception. Punishment should be the exception with rehabilitation and preparation for an inmate's return to society as the rule.

William H. Timas, *The Prison Mirror*, February 26, 1988.

But who would come into the prison? Few would, but those closest to the inmate would—and do—and might under appropriate circumstances come in on a more or less permanent basis. There is nothing in principle objectionable from a libertarian point of view to conjugal visits of an extended, even residential sort. Indeed, there are prisons in the world in which entire families reside with inmates. This would be something the inmate and his or her family could work to earn, inasmuch as they would have to pay the rent for the facilities in which they would live. . . .

In principle, there is no reason why an inmate should not be permitted to set up housekeeping within the prison with family, friend, or lover. If as a society we have come to tolerate "live-in" arrangements as generously as we have when it comes to our friends and children, there is little reason to be intolerant when it comes to an inmate. And the mere fact that the inmate has committed a crime is no justification for denying the spouses, children, or lovers of that inmate the contact they desire, as long as they are willing to travel to the prison to secure it. At one time, we made the mistake of confiscating the wordly goods of the families of convicts. That was wrong, because the family has not been proven to have done wrong. We still make the mistake of punishing them by denying them access to the imprisoned loved-one.

Developing Skills

The permeability of the prison perimeter by communication of various kinds short of the inmate's departure from the premises would make possible the prisoner's engagement of the outside world in a virtually unlimited variety of ways, commercial and otherwise, but mainly commercial, enabling the inmate to perform services for businesses on the outside with skills brought into or developed in prison. Inmate firms would compete, under certain handicaps of special costs of doing business . . . as well as handicaps of limited mobility and space, but the incentive to produce income to better one's circumstances would seem to be sufficient to induce the inmate to engage as energetically as possible in such activities. These firms would also have the beneficial effect of enabling the inmate to gain experience in certain styles and manners of verbal (oral as well as written) communication, which are valued in the outside world. Moreover, if the inmate would have to do business under the handicap of limited physical meetings, due to reasons of inaccessibility and security, it would cause further development of those skills in other modes of communication which are no less important in the outside world.

A Note on Privacy

There is one other pain the inmate would have to endure that would go beyond the pain experience in some typical prisons: surveillance, because inmates enjoying greater freedom to move about would need to be watched more closely. In addition, surveillance would extend to communication with the outside world.

The business enterprise especially, in the libertarian prison, would be subjected to intensive surveillance, by electronic and other means. This would include the monitoring of communication between members of the firm within the prison and those outside of the prison with whom it would deal. The costs of this supervision would be borne by the prison enterprise itself as one of the additional costs of doing business.

"Without new rehabilitation programs, it is unrealistic to expect the offenders we do have incarcerated to change."

Prisons Should Rehabilitate

Thomas W. White

Thomas W. White is the chief of psychology services at the United States Penitentiary in Leavenworth, Kansas. In the following viewpoint, White argues that the American correctional system has emphasized keeping offenders locked up at the expense of rehabilitation. Unless American prisons begin to provide meaningful rehabilitation programs for incarcerated offenders, he contends, crime rates and the size of the prison population will continue to increase.

As you read, consider the following questions:

1. What does the author mean by the "medical model" of rehabilitation?
2. What two events ushered in the era of the "balanced approach" to corrections, according to White?
3. What scenario does the author foresee if rehabilitation continues to be neglected?

Thomas W. White, "Corrections: Out of Balance," *Federal Probation*, December 1989. Public domain.

Historically, corrections has been asked very distinct and generally conflicting missions—retribution, deterrence, and rehabilitation. The relative influence of these objectives on the actual practice of corrections has shifted periodically as society struggled to find solutions for a steadily growing crime problem.

Initially, the desire for retribution characterized society's response to criminal behavior. The imposition of mutilation, torture, or even death was universally accepted as appropriate punishment for a wide range of social transgressions. The roots of this philosophy were inextricably entwined in our Judeo-Christian tradition and reinforced by years of biblical teaching which stressed the notion of an eye for an eye and a tooth for a tooth. However, by the beginning of the 18th century the more humane practice of imprisonment slowly began to replace branding, corporal punishment, and execution as the preferred method of dealing with lawbreakers. Under this new doctrine punishment actually served two purposes: to exact society's retribution and to deter the offender as well as others who may consider committing future crimes. Finally, the early 19th century saw the forerunner of the modern day prison system with the development of the Walnut Street Jail, a uniquely American creation designed to not only punish and deter, but to rehabilitate offenders by making them penitent (the penitentiary) for their actions by forced solitude and biblical reflection.

A Combination of Goals

From the early 19th century until well into the 20th century prisons attempted to combine the generally incompatible goals of punishment and deterrence with rehabilitation. The fact that prisons were able to reconcile these basically contradictory objectives at all can be attributed, in part, to the fact that little emphasis was actually placed on rehabilitation, at least as we define it today. Most correctional facilities were still long on work and short on education, training, or humane treatment. The prevailing attitude in society, despite its rhetoric, was still weighted heavily toward punishment, although it was commonly agreed that prisons should, in addition to providing punishment, be places where change could take place.

It was not until society discovered the value of the social sciences in the 1940's and 1950's that corrections began to implement an actual philosophy of rehabilitation. The model borrowed heavily from the newly emerging field of psychiatry which had gained considerable recognition during and after World War II. Essentially, this model, ultimately referred to as the medical model, viewed criminality as a "sickness" which could be treated and the offender as a person who, once treated, could be returned to the community cured of his social disease.

Armed with this new belief, legions of behavioral scientists invaded our prisons with a renewed conviction that crime could at last be brought under control like the great epidemics of the past. They tested, diagnosed, prescribed, and made release from prison contingent upon the successful completion of their treatment programs. Society, with its naive faith in the power of science, had unanimously endorsed the medical model, significantly shifting the emphasis of corrections away from punishment toward rehabilitation.

No Evidence of Success

Given their new social mandate, behavioral scientists tirelessly labored to therapize their patients into becoming law-abiding citizens. However, despite two decades of intensive therapeutic treatment, they saw crime rates increase, prisons become overcrowded, and correctional administrators begin to question the validity of their model. Then, two events occurred which marked a turning point in modern day corrections. The first of these events occurred in 1971 when the state prison at Attica, New York, erupted, culminating in one of the bloodiest uprisings in contemporary penal history. In the aftermath of the death and destruction the public outcry was overwhelming. Surprisingly though, the outcry was not for retribution, but for complete prison reform with a strengthened commitment to rehabilitation programs that would ensure a tragedy such as Attica would never be repeated. The renewed public demand for rehabilitation intensified research efforts studying the effectiveness of various programs. As an outgrowth of this search the second, and most important, historical event occurred.

In the Spring of 1974 Robert Martinson reviewed the findings of 231 experimental studies on the treatment of offenders between the years of 1945 and 1967. He found, with a few exceptions, these programs "had no appreciable effect on recidivism." As one might predict, Martinson's work hit the correctional establishment with the impact of a nuclear explosion. The conservatives who had never accepted the rehabilitation model as anything other than coddling prisoners used the results to press for more punitive, restrictive prison conditions. On the other hand, proponents of rehabilitation criticized Martinson's work for being superficial, being based upon outmoded rehabilitation programs, and ignoring the fact that prisons had never been able to implement meaningful programs due to inadequate funding and support from prison officials.

Martinson's findings, regardless of their scientific merits, were instrumental in initiating a national debate within the correctional community over the value of rehabilitation, and, more specifically, compulsory rehabilitation. His results made it painfully obvious to those who would look that rehabilitation, and particularly the medical model, had been conceptually flawed and fundamentally ineffective in changing offenders. Much like the fairy tale about the king's new clothes, Martinson had looked critically at the medical model's cloak of rehabilitative success and found the king naked, or at best in his underwear. Nevertheless, these results, while comforting to those with a less liberal view, did not give license to return to the days of inhumane treatment and corporal punishment, for society, despite its growing disillusionment with rehabilitation, still demanded that correctional institutions be operated humanely and do more than simply warehouse inmates.

Rehabilitation Reduces Recidivism

The most recent Justice Department study of recidivism shows that 62 percent of state prisoners are rearrested within three years of release from prison. With prisons seriously overcrowded and state budgets constrained across the country, inmates in most prison systems have fewer opportunities to gain an education or marketable skills than they did a decade ago. Further, more than half of all prisoners with a drug history are not enrolled in drug treatment programs. For those offenders who are sentenced to prison, it is in society's interest to attempt to reduce recidivism by providing a broad range of counseling, educational and vocational services appropriate to prisoners' needs.

Marc Mauer, *Americans Behind Bars: A Comparison of International Rates of Incarceration*, 1991.

The public's steadfast refusal to abandon the goal of rehabilitation placed correctional policymakers in a difficult position. On the one hand they were being told to implement innovative new rehabilitation programs, while on the other, they were acutely aware that they had no new programs to implement. Moreover, Martinson's review, which for the most part confirmed their personal experience, told them that, at best, the programs they did have were minimally effective. Clearly, they were in a no win situation. Thus, over the next several years, whether by design or necessity, the correctional establishment began to openly challenge the efficacy of rehabilitation, particularly compulsory rehabilitation. In the forefront of this assault was an emphasis on a more voluntary approach. Authorities advocated creating a new system in which rehabilitation would represent only one part of a total, integrated correctional package. This initiative stressed the need for a "balanced" approach with equal emphasis being given to retribution, deterrence, and rehabilitation. In this context, reliance on the medical model, the primary vehicle by which past programs were delivered, was denounced as the major cause of the failed rehabilitative efforts. It was argued, and probably correctly, that inmates could not be coerced into treatment and that criminality was not a sickness to be cured by psychotherapy. From this perspective, inmates would change only if they wanted to change, and therefore, inmates seeking change should be provided programs, but only on a voluntary basis. Although subtle, this philosophy set a new and very significant course in corrections. For the first time in almost 200 years it was the offender and not the system that was primarily responsible for the success or failure of rehabilitation. Now, it was the offender who must seek out and utilize available programs. The prevailing assumption was that programs having anything to offer would be utilized, while those not utilized would be terminated and the resources redirected. In this way effective programs would eventually emerge to be expanded and replicated.

A Balanced Approach

This bold new balanced approach introduced a unique concept to correctional rehabilitation, namely, the free market system. Much like the economic law of supply and demand, rehabilitative resources would now be supplied based upon inmate demand or participation—in short, no participation, no need for the program. Now, without an endless supply of inmates, social scientists had to provide services that were viewed as helpful and attractive by offenders or face reductions in staff and funding. By wholeheartedly embracing this perspective the professional correctional administrator was no longer saddled with the responsibility of changing recalcitrant offenders. If the social scientists could not develop successful programs, they were at fault. On the other hand, if inmates did not avail themselves of programs, they were at fault. Administrators, now freed from public accountability for ensuring rehabilitative success, focused their efforts on providing a more "balanced" approach to the correctional process and left rehabilitation in the hands of the social scientists.

Now that we have had more than a decade to evaluate the efficacy of the balanced, free market approach to correctional programming, what have we learned? To begin, it is undeniably clear that it has been no more effective at stemming the rising crime rate than the discredited medical model. While the available data are subject to considerable variation regarding specifics, the general trends are inescapable. Statistics available for 1979 through 1985 show a clear and consistent increase (19 percent) in arrest rates for violent crime, a more than 60 percent increase in rates of incarceration, and additional expenditures of more than 34 percent for state and local corrections, with no indication of an abatement in the years to come. Although the statistical evidence provides empirical validation for our subjective experience, most Americans do not need statistics to tell them that violent crime on our city streets has made citizens virtual prisoners in their own homes, that massive increases in drug interdiction rates have not decreased the supply of drugs in our communities, and that harsh sentencing laws have not reduced the number of crack houses or the incidences of gang violence in our major cities. In light of these facts, can we honestly say that the balanced, free market system has been more successful at deterring crime than past philosophies? I think the unfortunate answer is no.

What About Punishment?

One might ask if the free market system does not deter, has it at least been successful at punishing offenders? Again, the evidence seems to say no. The data on recidivism, although again subject to considerable debate and permutation, will vary from 60 percent to 80 percent depending upon your criteria. Regardless of the numbers you choose, it is obvious that punishment, if that is what incarceration actually is, does not persuade offenders to return to society and become law-abiding citizens. Although simplistic in its logic, the high rates of recidivism make a very compelling argument that imprisonment is not perceived as punishment by most experienced lawbreakers. If it were, they would not be willing to return to prison in such large numbers. This is a difficult concept for most Americans to accept, particularly those who have never had any direct contact with the criminal justice system, for they view imprisonment not only as punishment but as a deterrent for them. Therefore, they assume that if it deters them, it should deter others. Regrettably, this logic, while understandable, is not true and becomes pivotal to understanding the abysmal failure of our correctional process to either deter or punish offenders. Today we have created a correctional system in which a man has little or no obligation to provide restitution to his victim, to the state, or to the community for his transgressions. Moreover, he can enter prison with no education, no job skills, no motivation to change, and suffer no adverse consequences for remaining that way. As a result, many offenders leave prison no more prepared to cope with the demands of free society than the day they were incarcerated and, upon release, readily choose to resume their criminal life-styles.

At an average cost of $15,000 per inmate per year we must ask if we want or can afford to perpetuate this system any longer. Furthermore, does it really make sense to leave the choice of rehabilitation programs in the hands of inmates who have repeatedly demonstrated their inability to make responsible life decisions? Do we really feel that the majority of offenders who never become involved in any programs while incarcerated will leave prison with more pro-social attitudes than when they arrived? Do we really feel that inmates will voluntarily choose programs that will force them to confront their self-defeating life-style without some incentive to do so? Finally, do we really feel that prison make-work jobs teach either the skills or responsibilities necessary to compete in the community? I am afraid the logical answer to all these questions is no. Until correctional policymakers admit and the public accepts the fact that prison, although undesirable, is not aversive to the vast majority of offenders, we will continue to squander our resources building more and more prisons to house more and more offenders without having any appreciable effect on the crime rate. In light of these facts we must ask why the balanced correctional approach has been so unsuccessful.

Neglecting Rehabilitation Hurts Society

The rehabilitation ethic requires that society as a whole look beyond the desire to secure "just desserts" and recognize that the solution to deviance or criminality is a social issue that requires a critical assessment of the causes of crime, recidivism, and disorder. A failure to address social problems that place citizens at risk for becoming criminal, or abandoning institutional efforts at rehabilitation because "nothing works," does not bode well for society in the long run.

T. Paul Louis and Jerry R. Sparger, *Are Prisons Any Better? Twenty Years of Correctional Reform*, 1990.

Without appearing overly simplistic, it can be argued that the system's lack of success stems from the ungarnished fact that, despite its rhetoric, it has never actually provided a balanced approach. Over the years, rather than provided balance, the free market approach has done little more than steadily erode the number and variety of meaningful rehabilitative programs which could have introduced an element of aversion or psychological change into the offender's time in prison. Although unintended, the seeds of the present imbalance were sown by correctional decision makers in the mid-1970's when they replaced compulsory programs with a totally voluntary emphasis, while knowing they had no new voluntary programs to offer. As a result, they turned a basically neglectful eye to the whole concept of rehabilitation, hoping that something constructive would emerge from the supply and demand approach to programming. Regrettably, this environment did not favor increased program efforts. Inmates did not see the need for rehabilitative programs, and administrators, basically skeptical of existing rehabilitation models, did not support them because they feared repeating the painful mistakes of the past. In essence, the inmates and the administrators had, for their own purposes, collaborated unwittingly to create an environment in which an emphasis on rehabilitation had become unpopular. Consequently, as program participation dwindled, staff members were redistributed to other areas. This first took its toll on the quantity and then later on the quality of available programs, making it very difficult to provide basic program needs, not to mention experimenting with innovative new treatment approaches.

The Correctional System

With rehabilitation programs in disfavor but a clear and firmly established social mandate against harsh punishment, the correctional system had little choice but to focus its efforts on the one function at which it had become overwhelmingly successful, incapacitation. Clearly, if nothing else, the balanced approach has done a very good job of keeping people locked up. A review of any criminal justice statistics reveals the incontrovertible fact that prisons are locking away increasing numbers of offenders, and, for the most part, these offenders do not escape custody. However, while we are incarcerating more offenders for longer periods, our decreased level of programming is reducing our ability to have an impact on the basic attitudes and values that put offenders in prison in the first place. Even more disquieting is the realization that without new rehabilitation programs, it is unrealistic to expect the offenders we do have incarcerated to change, even if they are sentenced for longer periods of confinement. From a very practical standpoint, it is pure fantasy to believe that the present prison environment will return an offender to society to live crime free. In fact, most prison environments can be viewed as a subculture with a shared value system that actually reinforces criminal thinking. It is as if we gave up, admitting that since we could not "cure" crime we simply became content to warehouse criminals in clean, comfortable environments hoping they would change. Today, faced with that very prospect, we are building more prisons and keeping offenders for longer periods of time, still hoping they will change. Unfortunately, until we concentrate our efforts on changing offenders rather than simply confining them, we will continue to rely on incapacitation as our primary correctional tool.

"There is solid reason for saying that throughout its history, the prison has actually never rehabilitated people in practice."

Prisons Cannot Rehabilitate

Thomas Mathiesen

Thomas Mathiesen, professor of sociology of law at the University of Oslo in Oslo, Norway, was one of the founders of the Norwegian Association for Penal Reform. In the following viewpoint, Mathiesen examines the considerable research undertaken on prison rehabilitation programs. This research, he contends, demonstrates not only that prisons do not rehabilitate, but also actually increase criminal tendencies among prisoners.

As you read, consider the following questions:

1. How does the author interpret the findings of Robert Martinson?
2. What, according to Mathiesen, is meant by prisonization?
3. What does the author mean when he argues that prisoners reject their rejectors?

Thomas Mathiesen, *Prison on Trial*, pp. 20, 40-43, 45-47, © 1990 by Thomas Mathiesen. Reprinted by permission of Sage Publications Ltd.

The word 'rehabilitation' is frequently used in the context of prisons. Time in prison is supposed to rehabilitate, we say. . . .

[However] . . . there is solid reason for saying that throughout its history, the prison has actually never rehabilitated people in practice. It has never led to people's 'return to competence'. . . . The fact that today's prison does not rehabilitate, has a very solid social-scientific basis. It comes from three sources.

Treatment Results

First, it comes from studies of treatment results. . . . A long string of empirical studies has been produced showing that regardless of type of treatment, and even where very intensive treatment programmes are concerned, the results remain pretty much the same, and generally poor. I am thinking primarily of studies measuring 'results' in terms of recidivism. . . . Even treatment experiments with very careful built-in controls show this depressing lack of difference; this type or that type of treatment—the results are to a large extent the same. . . . The number of studies reviewed has been very large. More optimistic evaluations have appeared, but the optimism has been effectively countered. In some cases, those who have studied the programmes may have discarded sensible and well-designed programmes because they have not satisfied every scientific methodological demand, and certain variations do exist in the sense that certain types of institutional arrangements seem to suit certain types of offenders better than others. But the overall tendency in the reviews of the programmes is entirely clear.

The overall tendency has been summarized in bald terms by Robert Martinson in his now classic 1974 review of the literature. The review covered methodologically acceptable studies in the English language from 1945 through 1967 of attempts at rehabilitation in the USA and other countries. In the report, Martinson dealt with those studies which measured results in terms of recidivism. After having pointed to the methodological complications inherent in the reporting, he concluded:

> With these caveats, it is possible to give a rather bald summary of our findings: *With few and isolated exceptions, the rehabilitative efforts that have been reported so far have had no appreciable effect on recidivism.* Studies that have been done since our survey was completed do not present any major grounds for altering that original conclusion.

The critique which had come after such a statement has been effectively refuted. Martinson's summary still stands as representative.

Secondly, the social-scientific basis comes from our knowledge of the actual organization of most prisons, nationally as well as internationally. . . . As a blunt matter of fact, the actual realities

39

in almost all prisons are extremely far from anything which may be called 'treatment' in a qualified sense. . . . Prisons are often overcrowded, run-down, and more or less dangerous places to those who inhabit them. And as a rule they are large, authoritarian and bureaucratic machines. This is the everyday life of the prison—very far from any 'treatment situation'.

"ARE YOU ENJOYING YOUR REHABILITATION?"

Reprinted with permission of Morrie Turner and Catholic Charities.

Thirdly, the basis comes from sociological studies of the prison as an organization and of the prisoners' community. The very first large prison study in modern times, carried out in the US before World War II, clearly indicated that rehabilitation is not promoted by imprisonment. The author, Donald Clemmer, was a sociologist employed in the prison where the study was undertaken. Through intensive interviews, questionnaires and observation, he studied the prisoners' attitudes to the law-abiding society. His data supported the hypothesis that the prisoners were 'prisonized', as he called it, during the prison term. By 'prisonization' he meant the taking on of the folkways, mores, customs and general culture of the penitentiary. This culture made the prisoner more or less immune to attempts from the prison in the direction of readjustment. In more popular terms, according to Clemmer's study the prison in a cultural sense first of all functioned as a 'crime school'.

Every prisoner, Clemmer maintained, was subject to certain universal factors of prisonization. No one could fully escape it. To be sure, there were variations. He hypothesized that the shorter the sentence, the greater the adequacy of positive relationships during pre-penal life, the greater the number of positive relations on the outside, the greater the personal independence in relation to primary groups inside, the greater the personal ability to refuse the prisoner code, the greater the physical distance inside from inmate leaders, and the greater the personal tendency to refrain from certain types of activity which were introductory to the prisoner code, the *smaller* the tendency towards prisonization. The greatest degree of prisonization followed from the opposite ranking on these criteria. Yet not only were many prisoners exposed to a large number of the factors likely to promote a high degree of prisonization: also, the fact that no one could avoid it entirely, constituted a main point. Clemmer did not conclude that a high degree of correlation necessarily existed between extreme prisonization and later criminal behaviour, but he did suggest the likelihood of a correlation, and he certainly argued that prisonization did not aid rehabilitation.

Clemmer's comprehensive study attracted considerable attention in professional circles, but World War II put a temporary end to research activity. However, after the war the sociological study of the prison gained renewed importance, and around 1960 a series of important studies appeared which in various ways supported Clemmer's initial findings.

Further Research

The American sociologist Stanton Wheeler carried out a refined questionnaire study [in 1961] in which he tested Clemmer's findings concerning prisonization. Clemmer was primarily concerned with the early phases of prisonization, that is, with the prisoners' entrance into the inmate culture. His proposition about an association between prisonization and later adjustment was based on the assumption that the processes observed during the early and middle phases of incarceration continue until the inmate is paroled. Wheeler investigated this assumption by dividing the prisoners in a large American prison into three groups: those who were early, mid-way and late in their prison term. By dividing the prison population in this way, he was able to infer (the study was cross-sectional rather than longitudinal) that prisonization—measured by the prisoners' responses to a series of hypothetical conflict situations in the prison—increased significantly towards the middle phase of their stay, and decreased again when release approached. In other words, prisonization appeared 'U-shaped': the prisoners seemed to 'prepare' for release by to some extent abandoning the inmate norms and values characteristic of the earlier phases. But it is important to note that the 'U-shape' was not perfect: though a reorientation could be inferred towards the final part of the stay, the reorientation was not complete. And since many prisoners are incarcerated several times, it may therefore be inferred that prisonization is a kind of spiral, through which the individual becomes continually more involved in the inmate subculture.

Prison Life Destroys Lives

When persons are arrested and held in jail, their ties and arrangements with people outside very often disintegrate. They ·lose their jobs. Families abandon them. Friends forget them. Whatever property they had is frequently lost or stolen from them in their absence. Their cars are impounded and accumulate huge storage bills. They are profoundly disoriented by the arrest, booking and jail experiences. The jail experience destabilizes them and shatters, among other things, their skills at taking care of business, which requires that persons "be together."

The process of being arrested and held in jail embitters and damages their commitment to society. Finally, the jail experience prepares them for living among the rabble. In a sense, rabble life is concentrated in the jail. Persons learn to tolerate and live among rabble types and to make out in unconventional and illegal ways. They also acquire a set of contacts in rabble worlds, which will aid them in rabble walks of life.

In effect, persons who are arrested and thrown in jail experience a sudden blow that hurls them outside society. This blow unravels their social ties and stuns them and reduces their capacity and resolve to make the journey back into society. One or two blows will not permanently exile most people, but several blows will.

John Irwin, *California Prisoner*, September 1986.

Also around 1960, several studies appeared which not only suggested a process of prisonization on the part of the prisoners, but which, most importantly, tried to explain why such a prisoner culture appears in the first place. The authors discussed the various pains of imprisonment which the incarcerated prisoner experiences. The basic deprivation of liberty itself, the deprivation of goods and services, the deprivation of heterosexual relations, the deprivation of autonomy, and the deprivation of security in relation to other inmates, are so painful that they create a need for a defence. That defensive need is met through the establishment of the prisoners' community with its particular norms and values. Life in the prisoners' community does not remove the pain, but at least it alleviates or moderates it. A common culture protects against the pressures from the environment. This way, the prisoner culture becomes an understandable reaction. . . .

Rejecting the Rejectors

These are some of the prison studies which have been undertaken. There are also others, and though there are variations, they give the same general dismal picture. . . . Whether prisonization in Clemmer's classical sense is found or not, is perhaps partly dependent on the method used. Regardless of whether the mechanism is prisonization or not, the studies almost unanimously and clearly suggest or show that the goal of rehabilitation, attached to the prison, is not attained.

This general conclusion was in fact anticipated as early as at the beginning of the 1950s, in an important article by two American sociologists who were also prison administrators: Lloyd W. McCorkle, who was warden of the New Jersey State Prison in Trenton . . . and Richard R. Korn, who was director of education and counselling in the same prison. They created a key concept which summarized the core point in a large bulk of later prison research: police, courts, and especially prisons, argued McCorkle and Korn, imply a *rejection* of the prisoners as members of society. The prisoners' reply to the rejection is to reject those who have rejected them, *reject their rejectors*. McCorkle and Korn put it this way:

> In many ways, the inmate social system may be viewed as providing a way of life which enables the inmate to avoid the devastating psychological effects of internalizing and converting social rejection into self-rejection. In effect, it permits the inmate to reject his rejectors rather than himself.

Under these conditions, they argued, anything resembling 'treatment' becomes impossible. Even rehabilitation 'based on easing the harshness of prison life' becomes unproductive from a rehabilitative point of view (however important it might be from a humanitarian point of view), because the rejection which the prisoners react to is overarching or immanent in the system, so that new demands and new rounds of hostility are created. A long series of later studies have proved that McCorkle and Korn were right.

One can probably go further, by saying that not only does the goal of rehabilitation remain unrealized in the prison; also, the chances of rehabilitation are in fact reduced, on a long-term basis, among the inmates who enter the 'rejection syndrome' described above. . . .

The overall reply to the main question . . . 'does prison have a defence in rehabilitation?', may be put very briefly: an overwhelming amount of material, historical as well as sociological, leads to a clear and unequivocal *no* to the question. . . .

This conclusion receives extremely broad support in the extensive treatment research literature, and in a long string of in-depth studies of a sociological kind of the prison as a social system.

Not only can we most certainly say that the prison does not rehabilitate. Most likely we can also say that it in fact *de*habilitates. Actually, today this is often also granted by responsible authorities. . . .

It is only reasonable to demand that the authorities now take this correct understanding seriously in practice.

"We made comparisons of costs to society of crime versus the cost of a prison cell. When weighed against the price of crime . . . confinement is indeed a bargain."

Prisons Reduce Crime

Richard B. Abell

Richard B. Abell is a former assistant attorney general of the United States and is a member of the board of directors of the Federal Prison Industries Corporation. In the following viewpoint, Abell argues that the safety of the public is the most important goal of the criminal justice system. Because studies clearly demonstrate, he contends, that crime rates increase as incarceration rates decrease, the solution to the crime epidemic of the nineties is to build more prisons and incarcerate more offenders.

As you read, consider the following questions:

1. What does Abell mean when he states that the 1990s will be the Decade of Corrections?
2. According to the author, what was the result of coddling criminals during the 1960s and 1970s?
3. What does the author mean when he argues that certain offenders must be habilitated before they can be rehabilitated?

Excerpted from Richard B. Abell, "The 1990s: The Decade of Corrections and Winning the War on Drugs," speech delivered to the American Correctional Association, January 15, 1990. Public domain.

In accordance with this ancient principle, the establishment of justice is the highest duty of any government. Fairness and predictability are preeminent goals for a society such as ours that adheres to the rule of law. The goal of our criminal justice system must be the safety of the public. In order to secure this intrinsic social priority, we must, inter alia, restore equilibrium to our criminal justice system by building more jails and prisons.

The paramount issue facing our criminal justice system today is the need for jail and prison space to house those whose actions have shown that they cannot remain free members of society. All across this country, corrections officials at every level of government—federal, state, and local—are confronted with prisons and jails filled beyond capacity. In Philadelphia, Pennsylvania, there is no room in the local jails. Three thousand miles away, in Southern California, jail capacity problems are so severe that arrests are made only for the commission of a felony.

The time has come for this nation to make advancements in addressing corrections problems. Corrections has often in the past been regarded as the "step-child" of our criminal justice system. This neglected sibling is beginning to blossom. The *1990s* will be the *"Decade of Corrections."*

President Bush led the way with the introduction of his comprehensive crime package. . . . In presenting his crime bill, the President said that, "A common sense approach to crime means that if we are going to affect people's behavior, we must have a criminal justice system in which there is an expectation that:

"If you commit a crime, you will be caught.

"And if caught, you will be prosecuted.

"And if convicted, *you will do time.*"

Remove Criminals from Communities

No one disagrees that the breakdown of family and community structures makes it extremely difficult to pass down the moral values that enable individuals to be self-governing and thereby law-abiding. What we must reject is the idea that leaving criminals in the community will help. It hurts! It creates a terrible burden on already taxed communities. Crime, especially drug abuse, without the consequence of swift, consistent justice, discourages communities and families. We must not ignore the most basic of our Judeo-Christian values—that we each possess the God-given free will to make our own decisions about right or wrong, and that, in turn, each of us is responsible and accountable for our actions.

As Thomas Sowell explained, "People commit crimes because they are people—because they put their own interests or egos above the interests, feelings, or lives of others."

We saw the disastrous result of coddling criminals during the

1960s and 70s, when it somehow became unfashionable to sentence criminals who were convicted of serious crimes to lengthy prison terms. During those years, while the incarceration rates went down, the crime rate skyrocketed, increasing 332 percent!

Prisons Are Worth the Cost

Some [criminal] huggers might argue that it's too costly to build jails, pointing out that it costs $20,000 a year per inmate. I say it's more costly not to build jails. The average criminal costs us at least $100,000 a year in losses from burglaries, arson, robbery and grand theft auto. And that doesn't include intangible costs, such as personal trauma from rape, assault and the loss of loved ones. Neither does it include the cost of protection, including security services, locks, bars and the inconveniences we suffer such as fear and needing exact change. Considering these costs, the $20,000 to keep a criminal behind bars is quite a bargain.

Walter Williams, *The Washington Times*, October 29, 1990.

In 1960, according to FBI [Federal Bureau of Investigation] statistics, there were 1,900 serious crimes per 100,000 residents. By 1970, the rate had more than doubled—to nearly 4,000 serious crimes per 100,000 residents. It peaked in 1980 at approximately 5,900 per 100,000 residents.

At the same time, the prison population plunged. The number of prisoners serving time in federal and state institutions dropped from 119 per 100,000 population in 1960 to only 97 in 1970. Persons arrested, even for serious crimes, were not incarcerated. In 1980, only 25 of every 1,000 persons arrested for serious crimes, including murder, manslaughter, and rape, were sent to prison.

Fortunately, since 1981, we have made a sharp about-face back to tough sentences for hardened criminals. As a result, in 1989, the nation's federal and state prison population reached a record high of more than 673,000 inmates. This record growth more than doubled the demand for new prison beds—from the need for 800 additional beds a week to almost 1,800 additional beds a week. That's 1,800 more beds every week in the year, in addition to the 673,000 beds that we had as of June 30, 1989.

Tougher sentencing since 1981 is one reason for this tremendous increase. Even so, the average sentence for homicide is about 18 years, and the average prison sentence for aggravated assault is 5$1/2$ years. For most inmates, however, even these sentences are much longer than the actual time they will serve. The median time served in the U.S. is currently 5 years, 9 months for murder. The average is 4 years for aggravated rape, 3 years for manslaughter, and 2 years for assault.

Can America really afford to keep murderers in prison for only 5 years, 9 months? Is 5 years, 9 months long enough for a drug abuser who has taken the life of another human being? Twice-convicted murderer-rapist Willie Horton demonstrated how well he has been *"rehabilitated"* by his experience in our correctional system in an interview. "True," he said, "it's sad when someone is murdered. But, at the same time, the victim's family should not wallow in self-pity."

Habilitation, Rehabilitation

The infamous Willie Horton incident, and scores of other such tragedies, reveal the futility of attempting to rehabilitate violent offenders. Before any type of rehabilitation effort can have an impact, a person must first be *habilitated* into a common value system. There must be *habilitation*, otherwise, it is impossible to *rehabilitate*. Many of those in need of incarceration have never been habilitated. They lack the basic mores and socialization necessary to maintain law-abiding behavior.

I believe it is time that anti-incarcerationists face the fact that there are some criminals who can never be habilitated, whose crimes are so heinous that they disqualify themselves from free help at the taxpayers'—especially the taxpaying victim's—expense. There must be reparation to society.

In the words Cicero spoke almost 2,000 years ago: *Noxiae poena par esto*—"Let the punishment fit the crime." We must restore the death penalty for these unredeemable reprobates. Our latest scientific studies show amazingly low recidivism rates for those subject to the "ultimate penalty!"

Americans have seen enough "Willie Hortons" to realize the fallacy of "putting someone away for life." With too few prison cells, we are playing a dangerous game that all too often puts the criminal on the wrong side of the wall. Once legitimate alternatives to incarceration for offenders who posed little threat to the community and who showed a likelihood for rehabilitation—such as probation, parole, and "good time credits"—are now being routinely granted to dangerous felons as escape valves for crowded prisons. We must not allow prison capacity problems to drive judgments about who should be incarcerated.

Avertable Recidivism

A study by the Office of Justice Programs' Bureau of Justice Statistics of prison entrants in 1979 found that, at the time of their admission, 28 percent would still have been in prison on an earlier conviction if they had served their maximum prior sentence. The study found that these "avertable recidivists" accounted for approximately 20 percent of all violent crimes committed by all those sent to prison that year, as well as 28 percent of the burglaries and auto thefts, and 31 percent of the stolen property offenses.

Avertable recidivism has almost certainly risen in recent years, as probation, parole, and early release have been used increasingly to relieve bulging prisons, even when it means returning dangerous felons to the streets. A study by OJP's National Institute of Justice shows that giving convicted felons probation instead of a prison sentence is a tragic mistake. The study tracked 1,672 felons placed on probation in California's Los Angeles and Alameda Counties in 1983. Over a 40-month period, 65 percent of the probationers were rearrested, and 53 percent had official charges filed against them. Of the charges, according to the principal researcher, 75 percent "involved burglary, theft, robbery, or other violent crimes—the crimes most threatening to public safety." Fifty-one percent of the sample were reconvicted—18 percent for homicide, rape, weapons offenses, assault, or robbery; and 34 percent eventually were returned to prison.

Society Pays Eventually

While the public is certainly the victim of such unsound prison release policies, it is frequently an accomplice as well. At the same time citizens call for tougher and longer sentences, they often are reluctant to pay for prison construction to house convicted criminals.

Higher Imprisonment, Less Crime

Recent American history suggests that reductions in the certainty of imprisonment will lead to higher crime rates. In 1960, the chance that an offender would receive a prison sentence was 6.2 percent. By 1983, the chance was exactly half that. The low point in offender likelihood of incarceration was in 1974 when the chances fell to 2.1 percent. When chances of imprisonment were high (1960), crime rates were low. When chances of imprisonment were low (1974), crime rates were high.

Richard B. Abell, *Policy Review*, Winter 1989.

Ultimately, society will pay one way or the other, either by accepting the need to expend capital on prison and jail construction, or by continuing to incur the financial and physical cost of thuggery. A civilized and responsible society, however, cannot, in good conscience, fail to protect its citizens. We must never sacrifice the public safety to satisfy the public coffers. It is a hollow oblation.

49

Department of Justice research has found that prisoners, when they were on the streets, committed many more crimes per year than the one or two offenses for which they were sentenced. Victim losses and law enforcement, incarceration, and private security costs resulting from these undiscovered crimes are much greater than those associated with the offenses for which a criminal is sentenced.

We made comparisons of costs to society of crime versus the cost of a prison cell. When weighed against the price of crime—both in terms of financial losses and human suffering—that could be prevented by keeping serious, repeat offenders incarcerated, confinement is indeed a bargain. . . .

Nevertheless, a somnolent public has been slow to awaken to the pressing need to construct correctional facilities. Recent development of a number of alternatives to traditional construction techniques, however, show promise for making prison construction more palatable to a cost-conscious citizenry.

For example, steel-skin modules are appearing in prison construction, as entrepreneurs try to build a better facility for less money. One state reduced traditional construction costs by using convict labor to build a new prison, pairing frugality with vocational training!

Other jurisdictions are experimenting with the use of existing structures—such as barges and surplus property—for prison space. Prison privatization is another promising option for increasing prison capacity.

Another alternative to traditional correctional facilities that has been attracting considerable attention is shock incarceration, perhaps better known as "boot camps." Eleven states now have shock incarceration programs, and another 11 are developing them. Early findings from several studies underway with support from OJP's National Institute of Justice indicate that these programs are having a positive effect toward offenders' behavioral modification. One key lesson from boot camps is the role of discipline and work. There is no reason why all prisoners should not work to defray cost, support families, and pay restitution to victims.

Most Offenders Should Be Imprisoned

These nontraditional correctional alternatives, however, are only appropriate for those relatively few offenders who can, without risk to society, be handled in a less secure correctional environment. It behooves anti-incarcerationists to remember that 95 percent of those in state prisons are recidivists or are there for the commission of violent crimes. In addition, even offenders convicted on a first offense of drug abuse should receive a sentence of incarceration to assure adherence to the policy of user accountability. This country must have more jails and prisons to house the offender population.

Our foremost responsibility is to secure the public safety. If this necessitates, in the short term, so-called "warehousing" of offenders, so be it. It is a forfeit offenders must pay in retribution to the society they have victimized. As Theodore Roosevelt said in 1903, "No man is above the law and no man below it. . . . Obedience to the law is demanded as a right; not asked as a favor."

Our corrections system will face many challenges in the next decade, but we already possess both the tools and the knowledge necessary to shape the solutions.

*"A crime-prevention policy based primarily on
increased imprisonment is at best inadequate."*

Prisons Alone Cannot Reduce Crime

Joseph W. Rogers

Joseph W. Rogers is a professor in the department of sociology
and anthropology at New Mexico State University in Las Cruces.
In the following viewpoint, Rogers argues that a crime-prevention policy centered wholly on imprisonment will never be sufficient to protect citizens from crime. For one thing, he contends, most crimes are never reported and most offenders are
never caught, much less imprisoned. In addition he continues,
while the vast majority of criminals will eventually be returned
to the community, they will not have been "rehabilitated" into
becoming law-abiding citizens. The only really effective way to
reduce crime, he concludes, is to resolve the underlying social
and economic problems which produce crime.

As you read, consider the following questions:

1. What are the six myths of the imprisonment solution identified
   by the author?
2. What are the major by-products of America's prison-centered
   strategy, according to the author?
3. What two proposals does Rogers suggest for reducing the
   crisis in American corrections policy?

Joseph W. Rogers, "The Greatest Correctional Myth: Winning the War on Crime Through
Incarceration," *Federal Probation*, September 1989. Public domain.

Since . . . 1977, this country's prison population has more than doubled from 265,000 to a historic high exceeding 600,000. . . . In 1989 (with turnover), over one million persons were incarcerated, . . . 1 in 240 Americans, triple the total just two decades ago. To gain some idea of pace, we need go no further than a governmental report which shows a 1985 imprisonment growth rate of 8.7 percent. Were we to continue at this annual growth, the prison population would double in less than 9 years! The implications of such acceleration simply cannot be ignored.

Unfortunately, the 1988 presidential campaign provided little relief from either party or candidate. So many volleys were fired, we can hardly expect any serious attempt to win the "war on crime" by means other than through more concrete, mortar, and metal of additional penal institutions. Indeed, our political leadership seems second to none in seeking "room at the inn" of imprisonment for the Nation's criminal offenders. On the one hand we have long-standing belief in the powers of imprisonment, no matter how futile; on the other, we have the public's escalating fear of victimization, which seems to turn alternative approaches into perceptions of unforgivable "softness" on offenders. While we could hope this approach will succeed, honesty requires expression of doubt.

A Wave of Punitiveness

The contemporary *wave* of punitiveness is traceable to the mid-sixties. When Garrett Heyns wrote in 1967 that "the 'treat-em-rough' boys are here again," little did he realize they would continue to dominate our justice system for more than two decades. What this former Michigan warden and Washington State director of corrections saw was only the tip of an iceberg. It has since merged as a punishment glacier, composed of the hard ice of fear, hardened further in the cold atmosphere of deterrence and vengeance.

We must not make light of such fear, or the public's motives, for that matter. We have every right to want and seek security in our person and our property. Nor is it useful to advocate "tearing down the walls" or the abolition of maximum-security institutions. The position here concerns the narrowing focus and dependency on imprisonment to the neglect of a larger front in our battle against criminal victimization. Frankly, I am concerned lest the overwhelming success of the Willie Horton campaign waged against presidential candidate, Massachusetts Governor Michael Dukakis, makes cowards of us all. Differences in viewpoint notwithstanding, be assured all of us are in this thing together.

From the outset we must realize the fundamental weaknesses

in an extreme incarceration approach, which must take into account at least several basic factors.

First, 99 percent of those entering prison eventually return to society to become our neighbors in the communities where we live and work. Among the half-million inmates housed in state and Federal prisons in 1985 (not including another quarter million in jails), there were only 1,175 recorded deaths (1,148 males, 27 females). Of these, 731 were attributed to natural causes; 112 to suicides; 33 to accidents; 18 to executions; 105 to another person; and 176 to unspecified reasons. These deaths represented less than three-tenths of 1 percent of the population, not taking into account either turnover or length of stay. With few exceptions we can count on those persons entering prison to come out again better or worse for their experience.

Institutional Failure

The failure of major institutions to reduce crime is incontestable. . . . Institutions do succeed in punishing, but they do not deter. . . . They change the committed offender, but the change is more likely to be negative than positive. It is no surprise that institutions have not been more successful in reducing crime. The mystery is that they have not contributed even more to increasing crime.

National Advisory Commission on Criminal Justice Standards and Goals, *Corrections*, 1973.

Second, the median stay in prison varies from state to state within a range of 15 to 30 months. Actual time served (including jail and prison time) is generally much less than the maximum sentence length. For example, while the 1983 admissions reveal a median sentence length of 36 months, the median time served by releases that year was 19 months.

Third, there is a yearly turnover involving approximately a half-million prisoners. While 234,496 individuals were exiting state or Federal jurisdictions in 1985, even more, 275,366 were taking their places.

More Myths: Committing Crime, Getting Caught

Fourth, as striking as these data are, a crime-prevention policy based primarily on increased imprisonment is at best inadequate; at worst, a clogged pipe of human beings. The problems for criminal justice personnel exist at several junctures in the system, of course; but here our "trouble shooting" must be directed back to the community where the flow begins. Upon so doing, we discover an estimated 40 million victimizations for

1983 alone. In 1982, an estimated 3.2 percent of the Nation's population were victims of rape, robbery, or assault—the equivalent of about 6 million persons. Viewed somewhat differently, according to the respected National Crime Survey (NCS), more than 22 million *households* were victimized during 1985 by *at least* one crime of violence or theft. Their estimated total of 35 million individual victimizations is staggering when one considers the possibility of underreporting.

Fifth, the bulk of offenders are never caught, much less convicted or imprisoned. During the period 1973-1985 only about one-third of all crimes were reported to the police. Further, a review of Uniform Crime Reports covering the same time period will reveal an index crime clearance rate approximating 21 percent. In a compelling 1978 reanalysis of the President's Crime Commission Task Force Data, Charles Silberman provides a reasonable guide beyond this point. Of some 467,000 adults arrested (using rounded figures), 322,000 were punished in some way, with 63,000—about 14 percent—going to prison.

The Final Myth: Prisons Don't Rehabilitate

Sixth, prisons can hardly claim any great success when it comes to restoring criminals to law-abiding citizens. Assessments vary from about one-third to two-thirds for recidivism rates of released inmates. In his classic 1964 study, Daniel Glaser considers the latter figure as mythical, the former as more on target. While I agree with Glaser's cogent analysis, there can be little joy over even this positive claim. For example, in 1987 Steven Schlesinger, Director, Bureau of Justice Statistics, asserted their studies indicate about half of those released from prisons will return. He also points out that more than two-thirds of the burglars, auto thieves, forgers, defrauders, and embezzlers going to prison have been there before. Half of all the recidivists studied have been out of prison less than 23 months.

Consider, then, the implications of these six propositions which show that while we keep 600,000 adults locked up, some 35 to 40 million crimes are being committed annually. While all those incarcerated men and women were unable to engage in crime, who were these other people preying upon the public? Many were repeaters, and the Uniform Crime Report Program has been trying to learn more about them and about careers in crime. Doubtless, some were under some alternative form of correctional supervision. For example, in 1985, 254,000 were in jail; 1,870,000 were on probation; and 277,438 were on parole. Some were juveniles, of whom almost 50,000 were in some sort of custodial facility on February 1,1985.

The above statistics, fragile though they are, underscore the importance of the "war on crime" being waged outside of institutions, not in them. But to the extent we believe in prisons as our justice centerpiece, we must recognize the crucial importance of what we do with (or to) persons during whatever time period they are in custody. Simply put, postrelease failure rates are not acceptable.

By-products of Contemporary Prison Policy

American prisons have come to resemble bloated sponges. As extra sponges are added, they too become glutted. There are over 700 state and Federal prisons. The Federal Government, almost all of the states, and many countries have embarked upon prison and jail construction programs that will remain a legacy of dubious merit from the 1980's. As James Jacobs sees it, "While this expansion will permit incarceration of more people, it is unclear whether the additional facilities will succeed in relieving crowding; there seems to be almost limitless demand for prison beds."

Imprisonment Won't Solve Crime Problems

The primary argument offered in support of the high incarcerated population is that although costly, it is an effective method of crime control. There is little empirical evidence for such a conclusion. . . .

A 1978 report by the National Institute of Sciences documented the futility of trying to achieve significant increases in crime control through incarceration. The Institute estimated that in order to achieve a 10 percent reduction in crime, California would have to increase its prison population by 157 percent, New York by 263 percent, and Massachusetts by 310 percent.

Marc Mauer, *Business and Society Review*, Summer 1988.

One clear indicator is the population density of state prisons which are struggling to keep abreast of national standards. Both the American Correctional Association and the U.S. Department of Justice call for 60 square feet per single cell, provided inmates spend no more than 10 hours per day there; at least 80 square feet when cell confinement exceeds 10 hours daily. As of June 30, 1984, an assessment of 694 prisons revealed an average of 57.3 square feet per inmate; an average of 11.3 hours per day in unit confinement; and 66.5 percent of the inmates in multiple occupancy. This census also disclosed that 33.4 percent were in maximum security; that 11.8 percent of the facilities were over 100 years old, another 22.7 percent 50 to 99 years old; and that 50.8 percent of the institutions held more than 1,000 prisoners.

Some jurisdictions are desperate. New York City, for example, is now housing 400 inmates on a five-story barge anchored in the Hudson river. Reminiscent of 18th century England, authorities are planning to add two more barges, one with berths for 800 convicts. Their sense of urgency is conveyed by one official, who says bluntly: "We don't have the luxury of waiting five years to build from the ground up."

Cost of Imprisonment

Criminal justice is big business, as indicated by its "top 10" status among all government expenditures. Federal, state, and local spending for all such activities in fiscal 1983 was $39.7 billion—almost 3 percent of all government spending in this country. Approximately $23 billion was spent at the local level, $12 billion by the states, and $5 billion by the Federal Government. Police protection accounted for the highest amount spent, 52 percent, followed by corrections with 26 percent, and judicial/legal services with 22 percent.

Among types of justice spending, corrections increased the most—by 15.1 percent from 1982 to 1983; by 50.9 percent from 1980 to 1983. And although estimates vary widely, prison construction costs typically range from $50,000 to $100,000 per cell. The "capital investments," are supplemented by a yearly operating/maintenance expenditure ranging from $10,000 to $25,000 per inmate. The Criminal Justice Institute counts 130 prisons for some 53,000 inmates now being constructed at a cost of $2.5 billion, with still another 75,000 convict beds in the planning stage.

In short, we are talking big bucks here in an era of budget deficits, and fears of tax increases. . . . The money being poured into incarceration makes probation, parole, and college education look like great buys, at least on a cost-per-person basis. You can send your son or daughter to your choice of some of the finest private universities in the land—Cornell, Harvard, Stanford —for less! And if you are not too choosy, their entire 4 years of college tuition will cost less at a good state university than will housing a single inmate for 1 year in a typical state prison! And make no mistake, public education must compete for these dollars, just as do public welfare, housing, environment, hospitals, health, highways, and others. Given the recent concern with the quality of our public school system, where do you think an extra one billion dollars a year might be well spent to fight crime?

Corrections in Crisis

Stephen D. Gottfredson and Sean McConville have recently described this state of affairs as "America's Correctional Crisis," where far-reaching decisions are made with uncertainty and compromise. Instead, they hope, "for more informed and bal-

57

anced debate and for the encouragement of productive and acceptable solutions to problems that can be neglected only at some considerable risk to our nation's future." We should be listening to such counsel which, if anything, seems understated, requiring added emphasis and urgency.

Broad Proposals

Accordingly, two broad proposals are offered.

First, it is time to convene another President's Commission on Law Enforcement and Administration of Justice. President Lyndon B. Johnson established his Commission on July 23,1965, a quarter century ago. President Bush could initiate the largest scale "brain trust" this Nation has ever known to plan the most comprehensive strategy for crime prevention, treatment, and control in history. So doing is no panacea, of course, for many difficulties are attached to such task forces.

But somehow, a concerted collective effort must be made to bring together the vast reservoir of knowledge and ideas accumulating in various disparate forms and places, both here and abroad, during the past three decades.

It would be presumptuous to suggest an agenda here, but no issue should be sacrosanct or beyond debate. From the start it must be recognized that corrections is a component of an interdependent but uncoordinated system of justice which must be understood in relation to the wider structures of social control in American society. This means we must examine criminality in a multilayered fashion—from inception and process to change; from societal ills and malfunctioning to social reform; from community roots to community return. Criminality and delinquency are not unrelated to conditions and problems of other social institutions—family (e.g., domestic violence, runaways); economy (e.g., poverty, unemployment, homelessness); education (e.g., dropouts, drugs); and government (e.g., mismanagement, inadequate funding). . . .

Second, it would be appropriate to seriously consider William G. Nagel's advocacy of a moratorium on prison construction. Imagine such a joint state and Federal policy effective from, say, 1991 through 1995. The 5-year "savings" could be well invested in the Commission's work; to improving existing prisons; to upgrading community-based corrections; and to fundamental programs involving the health, education, and welfare of the Nation's youth.

This last point is particularly important in light of Lamar Empey's fear that a war on crime could be waged against our country's youth, with a severe loss to basic humanitarian values. Indeed, we must take exception to a social control policy based primarily on measures of exclusion (e.g., isolation, segregation) rather than inclusion (e.g., resocialization, integration). Neal Shover and Werner J. Einstadter, have stated well the implications:

> . . . precisely those conditions which prevent persons from becoming productive, socially conscious members of society, conditions which exclude and cast them out, are the conditions which create the dangerous crime potential we wish to prevent.
> The current direction corrections is taking is exclusionary. Whether the cycle will change in the near future remains an open question, but our ultimate well-being as a democratic society depends on the answer.

There are no easy answers to complex problems. But perhaps we could discover some profound responses through starting the final decade of this millennium with a high-level Commission with the authority, organization, talent, time, and incentives to develop imaginative, innovative, comprehensive policies on behalf of the Nation's citizenry.

"Americans are willing to pay the price to lock up criminals for as long as is necessary. By building more prisons we can . . . enjoy safe streets and homes again. "

Prisons Protect Society

Eugene H. Methvin

Eugene H. Methvin, a senior editor of *Reader's Digest* magazine, argues in the following viewpoint that America needs more prisons to protect itself from dangerously violent criminals. Citing several examples of criminals who terrorized innocent citizens after being released early from overcrowded prisons, Methvin contends that these offenders should be locked away for as long as they are a danger to society. Society must be prepared to pay the considerable financial costs of prison expansion if it wishes to be safe from dangerous felons, he concludes.

As you read, consider the following questions:

1. How convincing is the evidence provided by the author to support his argument that violent criminals are a continuing danger to society?
2. What five suggestions does Methvin make for resolving America's prison crisis?

Sprung from the Florida state penitentiary after serving only eight years of a 15-year sentence for attempted murder, Charlie Street promptly shot and killed two Miami policemen. Like tens of thousands of other felons, Street had been freed under an early-release program prompted by a federal judge's ruling against prison crowding. Of nearly 3966 convicts released in six central-Florida counties, nearly a third were later rearrested, the Orlando *Sentinel* found. Incredibly, 20 percent of *those* were released early a second time and rearrested *again* for crimes ranging from robbery to attempted murder.

In Atlanta, officials freed 263 prisoners to comply with a federal judge's order to reduce the cramped Fulton County jail population by almost 15 percent. Among them was Ronnie Fisher, who had been arrested on auto-theft charges. Barely 35 minutes out of jail, according to police accounts, Fisher accosted a man near a bus stop, demanded money, pinned him against a wall and began going through his pockets. An observant cop promptly nabbed the young thug. (Charges were later dropped when the victim failed to appear in court.)

Each year America's cops arrest about 625,000 people for violent crimes and 2.3 million more for serious property crimes. By January 1990, our prisons housed 703,687 inmates—an all-time high. By 1994, projects the National Council on Crime and Delinquency, the prison population will grow to 1.1 million.

America simply does not have enough prisons to cope with all its criminals. The reasons range from federal judges who insist upon costly reforms, to legislators who prescribe severe sentences but quail at voting money to build more prisons, to bureaucrats who mismanage prisons we do have.

Michigan's Experience

Consider Michigan's experience. In 1978 voters in a "get tough" mood abolished good-behavior sentence reductions for dozens of serious crimes. Two years later the same voters defeated a referendum to raise income taxes to build new prisons. Result: chaos. Faced with a court order against overcrowding, the governor invoked emergency powers to free 10,000 inmates in a four-year period—some more than two years early.

Predictably, the criminals had a field day. The Detroit *Free Press* analyzed the records of 5762 parolees and found more than 80 percent had been released before serving their minimum sentences. A third were rearrested within three years; 12 committed murders.

One burglar, released early, committed 500 burglaries in seven months. A rapist, freed four years before his ten-year minimum, sexually assaulted and murdered a woman. A paroled killer broke into two homes and killed three people.

61

Bowing to public outrage, Michigan legislators finally launched a $900-million program to build 28 new prisons by 1992. The state's inmate population went from 14,392 to 33,062. But the payoff is impressive: Since 1984, serious-crime rates have declined nine percent, robbery and burglary rates more than 25 percent.

© Dobbins/Rothco. Reprinted with permission.

Research has shown that incarcerating serious offenders reduces crime and is cost-effective. By one estimate, 5000 additional imprisonments in 1985 would have prevented 104,000 serious crimes.

As costly as prisons are, letting hardened criminals roam the streets is far more costly. National Institute of Justice economist Edwin Zedlewski, in a study of 2190 criminals, estimated that each cost the public $430,000 a year in victim and insurance losses, private security measures and law-enforcement expenditures. Yet building more prison space can cost $25,000 or less per inmate.

To pen every serious offender will cost billions, but it's money well spent. According to a Justice Department study, 95 percent of the prison population is either violent or habitual. Nearly half are three-time losers or worse.

Moreover, you don't have to be very promising to get out. A Justice Department study of 108,580 prisoners released in 1983 found that almost two-thirds committed new crimes within three years. To solve our prison crisis we must:

Rein in Federal Judges

Until 1965 the federal judiciary had not intervened in state-prison management. Then federal-appeals judges, confronted with horrors from the Arkansas state prison, held that the Eighth Amendment's prohibition of "cruel and unusual punishments" applied to prisoner complaints. Soon federal judges seized control of jails and prisons, even entire state-prison systems. While the original case involved prisoner floggings, eventually a federal judge compelled a Georgia county jail to install air conditioning and TV or be ruled "unconstitutional." By 1987 prisoners, often aided by the American Civil Liberties Union, filed 37,000 federal court petitions asking for improved conditions. The "reforms" have cost taxpayers billions.

In the past decade thousands of Americans have been murdered, raped, robbed and assaulted by convicted criminals freed by federal judges interpreting nonexistent standards of "prison capacity." Some judges have approved keeping prisoners in space as small as 22 square feet, while others have required cells as large as 75 square feet. In Massachusetts, Suffolk County sheriff Robert Rufo, forbidden to bunk two prisoners in his 88-square-foot cells, must spend $1 million a year busing inmates to distant counties with no such judicial orders. There they end up two to a 48-square-foot cell. . . .

Manage Prisons Better

Maximum-security prisons cost up to ten times as much to build and twice as much to operate as medium- and minimum-security prisons. Only about 15 percent of prisoners need be kept in them, since experience shows that many dangerous offenders may be held at little risk in less secure custody. Yet the latest Justice Department census showed 35 percent of inmates assigned to maximum-security facilities. More careful classification could cut that number by half or more, saving billions at no cost to public safety.

Georgia has experimented with a military-style "boot camp"

for young offenders. Its veterans get rearrested at about the same rate as ex-cons released from prison. "But we get the same payoff with only 90 days' incarceration compared to an average of 14 months, so the cost is much lower," says Samuel Austin, executive deputy commissioner of the Georgia Department of Corrections. At least 14 states are emulating the Georgia program.

Prisons Promote Safety and Security

Should we be building more prisons? Is society better off with serious repeat offenders behind bars? You bet! An extraordinary study done in 1987 for the National Institute of Justice found that habitual criminals can be one-person crime waves, and their trips through the revolving door of justice are incredibly costly to society.

The study revealed that these career criminals average between 187 and 287 crimes per year—not counting drug deals. The study showed that "these crimes represent about $430 million in social costs." Some costs, of course, cannot even be estimated. What is the value of human life taken by a murderer? But one thing is absolutely certain: The costs of keeping hardened criminals in jail is only a tiny fraction of letting them walk free. Building more prisons is among the best investments we can make in our safety and security.

Ed Meese, *Human Events*, December 31, 1988.

Many governors and legislators impose incredible costs on taxpayers by treating prison maintenance and construction as patronage for unions and contractors. Outside the South, for instance, most states forbid inmate labor on major prison maintenance and construction projects. Thus, Michigan soaks taxpayers $70,000 apiece to build the same bed that Florida builds for $14,000 in half the time using skilled inmates.

In South Carolina, long-termers learn construction methods and do other skilled work at less than half the cost of outside contractors. "Not once have we had a serious incident," says Harry Oberlies, the program director. "We're giving a guy a chance to learn a skill that will pay $10 an hour on the outside."

"Idleness is the most serious problem in virtually every penal institution," says Norman Carlson, former director of the Federal Bureau of Prisons. At least half the nation's prisoners are idle every working day. This situation exists largely because Congress, prodded by unions and businessmen in the Depression year of 1935, prohibited the sale of prisoner-made goods in interstate commerce. In 1982 it added a prohibition against using prisoner-made materials on federally aided highways, thus idling inmates who made road signs.

"It's a travesty and a scandal," says American Correctional Association executive director Anthony Travisono. "We're creating a new leisure class who expect free room, board and medical care at tremendous cost to taxpayers." Prisoners should be required to earn support for their families, restitution for their victims and contributions to their own upkeep. To this end, Congress should repeal the bars to prison labor.

Get Serious Offenders Younger

Since prison space is costly, it must be used efficiently. Says Jacksonville prosecutor Ed Austin, "If Florida has only 50,000 beds, let's at least have the right 50,000 people filling them."

A study by criminologist Marvin Wolfgang followed males born in 1945 and 1958 and raised in Philadelphia from ages ten to 18. Wolfgang found an astonishingly small number of offenders committed most crime in the group. A mere seven percent collected five or more arrests by age 18 and were responsible for two-thirds of all the violent crime committed by the group, three-fourths of the rapes and robberies and virtually all the murders. Moreover, if not locked up, these "dirty seven percenters" went on committing felonies, and got away with a dozen crimes for every arrest.

A Justice Department program begun in 1983 shows we can curb crime sharply by getting such offenders off the street at an early age. Twenty cities were persuaded to install Serious Habitual Offender (SHO) programs that focus on youngsters who are habitual offenders before their 18th birthday. Such offenders get priority attention from probation authorities, and if they are arrested anew, prosecutors seek to put them away.

After a concentrated effort to get SHOs off the street in Oxnard, Calif., violent crimes plummeted 38 percent in 1987. In 1989 Oxnard had 30 SHOs behind bars, and its 133,000 citizens experienced the lowest crime rate in a decade. Murders were down 65 percent, robberies 41 percent, burglaries 29 percent.

Improve Parole Supervision

Probation officers now must often oversee caseloads of 200, with the average probationer getting a mere phone call a month. Yet these programs are important both as an incentive to better prison behavior and to make more room for the truly dangerous.

Georgia has pioneered an intensive supervision program in which a probation officer, aided by a surveillance officer, oversees no more than 25 releasees. Over three years, 2322 carefully screened convicts went through the program, which includes mandatory employment and community service, at least five face-to-face contacts weekly, nightly curfews and unannounced alcohol and drug tests. These convicts had lower recidivism rates than either prison releasees or regular probationers, at a taxpayer savings over imprisonment of $13 million.

To work, alternative sentencing and parole programs must be tough, well monitored and perceived as punishment. Only 326 of 1807 convicts so sentenced have had their probation revoked for new offenses.

Build More Prisons

States where convicts face a higher probability of imprisonment enjoy lower crime rates. Research has shown that in Utah a person convicted of homicide is almost 90-percent certain to go to prison, about four times as certain as in South Carolina, where the homicide rate is much higher.

Prof. Isaac Ehrlich's classic study on deterrence calculated how the probability of imprisonment affected the known rates of seven major crimes in 1940, 1950 and 1960. He found that the higher the likelihood of imprisonment for convicted offenders, the lower the crime rate. This led him to conclude that the certainty of punishment is a deterrent to crime.

A Lou Harris poll in 1989 found Americans willing by nearly three-to-one to pay for a sharp increase in prisons to lock up convicted drug pushers. And the people are right. America's huge investment in prisons has paid off: we are safer, and crime has fallen steadily since the prison population began to climb.

The Justice Department's surveys of victimization document a steady 15-year decline of 21 percent in the robbery rate and an overall nine-percent decline in crimes of violence. Rape and burglary rates are down by a third. The total crime-rate reduction since 1975 means that an estimated 7.6 million American households will be spared victimization by violence or theft. Americans are willing to pay the price to lock up criminals for as long as is necessary. By building more prisons we can further improve on this record and enjoy safe streets and homes again.

"Across our nation we are promised that get-tough sentences and more prisons will make our streets safe. But that has simply not happened."

Prisons Cannot Protect Society

Charles Colson and Daniel Van Ness

Charles Colson directs Prison Fellowship, a Christian ministry organization. Daniel Van Ness is the president of Justice Fellowship, a division of Prison Fellowship, which is dedicated to reforming the criminal justice system. In the following viewpoint, Colson and Van Ness argue that America's prisons cannot protect society from crime. Indeed, as the resources devoted to prison expansion have soared, so too, they argue, has crime. Prisons, they continue, are "graduate schools of crime" which reinforce criminal tendencies in incarcerated offenders.

As you read, consider the following questions:

1. Do you agree with the authors' premise that America's prisons are graduate schools of crime?
2. According to the authors, what are the two main elements in today's law-and-order approach to criminal justice?
3. Why do Colson and Van Ness believe that harsh penalties, including long prison terms, will not deter criminals from committing crimes?

In recent years the "get tough on crime" mentality has resulted in enormous prison population growth. There were 604,824 prisoners in America in mid-1988-83 percent more than in 1980. Prison construction has not kept pace. Federal prisons are as much as 73 percent over capacity, while state prisons operate between 105 and 120 percent of capacity.

As of mid-1988, thirty-seven states were under full or partial court order because of overcrowded, inhumane, unconstitutional prison conditions. One California judge noted that prisoners were being held in less space than state law required kennels to give dogs and cats!

Prison Costs

In this decade of soaring budget deficits, governments are spending enormous sums of money to build and operate prisons. It costs an average of $15,900 to keep an inmate in prison for one year—about the same as sending a student to Harvard University. Because of the overcrowding problem, state and federal governments are rapidly building more and more prisons—to the tune of almost $5 billion in one fiscal year alone. And when all that money is spent, American prisons will still be over capacity.

A sobering case in point is the California state prison system. By 1990 California added thirty thousand new prison beds to its facilities, at a cost of $2 billion. The continuing prison population explosion, however, has forced the California Department of Corrections to ask for an additional $1.5 to $2 billion. It turns out they need 17,500 more beds. Imagine the shock to California taxpayers when they were told that even after adding space for nearly fifty thousand inmates, by 1995 their prison system will still be thirty thousand beds short!

As a result, the tax burden grows heavier. . . . The cost of operating California's prison system has risen to a staggering $1.3 billion per year—and it's headed up.

The forecast is similarly bleak across the rest of the nation. The National Council on Crime and Delinquency forecasts that prison populations will increase by 50 percent in the next ten years. Are taxpayers and communities ready for what that will mean?

Skyrocketing Crime

One out of every four households in the U.S. is touched by crime each year. More than six million Americans are the victims of violent crime annually. Nearly 75 percent of all inmates released from prison are rearrested within four years of their release. A study by the respected Rand Corporation found that ex-prisoners are actually *more* likely to commit new crimes than similar offenders who were placed on probation. Crime is an epidemic in America—and the current system doesn't seem to have an antidote.

Forgotten Victims

Crime victims suffer emotional trauma, physical injury, and material losses (nationally, more than $13 billion a year). Too often excluded from any meaningful participation in the criminal justice process, they typically receive no payment for their losses and have no say in the plea bargaining, prosecution, or sentencing of those who have victimized them. In most cases, they serve only as witnesses in the state's case.

ROTHCO

VADILLO - SIEMPRE, MEXICO

© Vadillo/Rothco. Reprinted with permission.

Any crime wreaks emotional havoc on its victim, and many leave physical and financial wounds as well. Yet victims are forgotten parties in our nation's criminal justice system.

So who benefits from the current system of justice and punishment? . . . Victims certainly do not. They may as well be invisible. Their suffering is deemed irrelevant. Their losses are not repaid.

Nor do nonviolent criminals. . . . They are stuffed into prisons that are little more than overcrowded warehouses. These "graduate schools of crime" take nonviolent offenders and make them live by violence. They take the violent and harden them further. Of course, prisons are essential for violent and dangerous offenders. But let's not kid ourselves. They do not rehabilitate.

Communities don't benefit either. Across our nation we are promised that get-tough sentences and more prisons will make our streets safe. But that has simply not happened. Overflowing with ever-increasing numbers of inmates, prisons can't be built fast enough. And even as we build more prisons, crime rates continue to rise. . . .

Aside from kissing babies and getting re-elected, talking tough on crime is the most popular of political pastimes. But one point is often forgotten in the midst of all the heated rhetoric. A policy is tough only if it actually works. The so-called law-and-order approach of more prisons and longer sentences surely works as a political strategy. But does it work in the real world of victims, offenders, and communities?

The answer, quite simply, is no.

It isn't as if we haven't tried. The nation's prison population has doubled in the last decade. The inmate population is actually increasing at ten times the rate of the general population. . . . America's pack-em-in prison experiment is unprecedented in history; we spend billions of tax dollars each year on more prisons, more courts, more police. If stiffer sentences stopped crime, we shouldn't have any crime at all.

But we do. In fact, we have one of the highest crime rates in the entire world.

Baffling? At first glance, yes. But the problem is understandable when you take a closer look at it. As we just noted, tough policies are tough only if they work. The "get tough" approach is defended on two grounds: it discourages potential offenders from committing crimes (deterrence), and it gets dangerous offenders off the streets (incapacitation). Both deterrence and incapacitation could be—should be—important weapons in our war on crime. But ironically, "get tough" policies hamper our ability to use those weapons effectively.

Most Criminals Not Caught

Criminologists agree that harsh penalties won't deter criminals who believe they won't get caught. Most offenders today are convinced they won't get caught. And the following evidence, compiled from federal reports, shows they are right.

Only one out of three crimes is reported to the police. Of that one in three, police make an arrest only 20 percent of the time. This means there are only seven arrests for every one hundred crimes.

But the bad news doesn't stop there.

Nearly half of the people arrested have their charges thrown out by the prosecutor. Eighty to 90 percent of the rest are convicted. Of those found guilty, half are put on probation, 25 percent are sent to jail, and 25 percent go to prison.

In other words, *one* person goes to prison and *one* person goes to jail for every one hundred crimes that are committed.

No matter how tough politicians talk about long prison terms, it simply doesn't mean much to a criminal who knows the odds. This is especially true when the rewards of crime are high.

A young New Yorker named Nick offers a good example. Nick had been involved in organized crime since childhood, and then had made a career of dealing drugs. On its face, drug retail seemed an illogical choice in a state which then had a law imposing a mandatory life sentence for convicted narcotics dealers.

The Myth of Societal Protection

Prisons have pacified the public with the image of "safety," symbolized by walls and cages located in remote areas. But prisons are a massive deception: seeming to "protect," they engender hostility and rage among all who are locked into the system, both prisoner and keeper. Society is victimized by the exploitation of its fear of crime.

Indeed, rather than protecting society from the harmful, prisons are in themselves harmful. It is likely that persons who are caged will become locked into a cycle of crime and fear, returning to prison again and again.

Prison Research Education Action Project, *Instead of Prisons: A Handbook for Abolitionists*, 1983.

But before Nick started selling drugs, he had worked as a rod carrier on the eightieth floor of the World Trade Center. One slip up there, he figured, and he was dead. For his salary of $18 an hour, he risked his life.

Then he found he could make $300,000 a week selling heroin. If he got caught (which he thought was unlikely), it would only mean life imprisonment. The rewards were great, the possibility of capture was small, and Nick decided the choice was easy. The trade-off was worth it.

Of course, most crimes are not premeditated, carefully weighed choices at all. Crime is usually impulsive. By some estimates as many as eight out of ten crimes are committed through a haze of drugs or alcohol. Crimes done under the influence of passion, impulse, or chemicals are undeterrable, since the offender is not likely to pause and soberly reflect on the consequences of his act.

Convincing evidence refutes the notion that harsher prison sentences will deter crime. Over a twenty-year period (from 1955 to 1975), crime actually increased more in fifteen states where prison capacity grew by 56 percent than in fifteen other states where prison capacity increased only 4 percent.

It wasn't any different in earlier times. In eighteenth-century England, for example, government officials set out to get tough on crime by hanging pickpockets. To reinforce their point and intimidate potential offenders, they conducted the executions in public, before large crowds. But there was a problem. The hangings drew droves of pickpockets, who had a field day stealing the wallets of those gathered to watch the executions of pickpockets.

Dangerous Felons Let Loose

But even though harsh sentences fail to deter, don't they at least incapacitate: ensure that dangerous offenders are kept off the street? Unfortunately, they may do just the opposite. . . .

Longer and harsher sentences can actually mean that serious offenders serve shorter prison terms. This is because most "get tough" bills are so broadly written that they sweep up many offenders who pose little danger to society. These nondangerous offenders then use up scarce prison space, forcing early release of the dangerous.

The federal government reports that just under half (46 percent) of all state prisoners were sent to prison for nonviolent crimes. And 35 percent of all prisoners have *never* been convicted of a violent crime in their lives! In Florida, where half the state's prisoners committed nonviolent property crimes, 85 percent are classified minimum security. One in eight have never even been on probation. . . .

Some nonviolent offenders may need to be locked up because they are professional or career criminals. But it makes sense that most nonviolent offenders should be sentenced to punishments other than prison. This would free up prison beds for dangerous offenders who *should* be kept away from society.

In short, prisons are filled with people they failed to deter. Ironic, isn't it? The "get tough" policy on crime fails on the two very counts on which it is defended—deterrence and incapacitation.

a critical thinking activity

Understanding Words
in Context

Readers occasionally come across words they do not recognize.
And frequently, because they do not know a word or words, they
will not fully understand the passage being read. Obviously, the
reader can look up an unfamiliar word in a dictionary. By carefully examining the word in the context in which it is used, however, the word's meaning can often be determined. A careful
reader may find clues to the meaning of the word in surrounding
words, ideas, and attitudes.

Below are excerpts from the viewpoints in this chapter. In each
excerpt, one of the words is printed in italics. Try to determine
the meaning of each word by reading the excerpt. Under each excerpt you will find four definitions for the italicized word. Choose
the one that is closest to your understanding of the word.

Finally, use a dictionary to see how well you have understood
the words in context. It will be helpful to discuss with others
the clues that helped you decide on each word's meaning.

1. Most Americans do not support a return to the punishments of old, such as mutilations, floggings, and torture. Indeed, they are appalled at such *REGRESSIVE* measures.

   REGRESSIVE means:

   a) caring
   b) uncomfortable
   c) modern
   d) backward

2. If it is found, beyond a reasonable doubt, that the accused person actually committed the crime, the law should punish that person based on the extent of his or her *CULPABILITY.*

   CULPABILITY means:

   a) guilt
   b) health
   c) attractiveness
   d) legal representation

3. Most citizens view criminals in a completely unrealistic manner. They exaggerate their dangerousness and *CARICA-TURE* them as evil, violent monsters.

   CARICATURE means:

   a) love
   b) support
   c) execute
   d) misrepresent

4. People who support the punishment of prisoners think that they themselves are perfect and never do anything wrong. They are *COMPLACENT.*

   COMPLACENT means:

   a) fat
   b) self-satisfied
   c) caring
   d) modest

5. In a libertarian prison, prisoners could be busy setting up and managing their own businesses and becoming *EN-TREPRENEURS.*

   ENTREPRENEURS means:

   a) slaves
   b) trainees
   c) businesspersons
   d) stressed

6. Because criminals cause their victims to suffer pain and financial loss, criminals should be forced to pay *REPARA-TIONS* to victims.

   REPARATIONS means:

   a) damages
   b) repairs
   c) visits
   d) attention

7. Criminals need rehabilitation and treatment in prison. Unfortunately, while a wide variety of programs are provided, many prisoners are *RECALCITRANT* and refuse to participate in the programs or take them seriously.

RECALCITRANT means:

a) cured
b) resistant
c) dead
d) aggressive

8. Contrary to popular opinion, Robert Martinson did not believe that "nothing works" in the rehabilitation of offenders. Unfortunately, despite the many *CAVEATS* Martinson put in his work, his findings were still badly misinterpreted.

CAVEATS means:

a) mistakes
b) cautionary statements
c) confusing statements
d) jokes

9. Some criminals are so bad that nothing but the death penalty will cure them. There are many such *REPROBATES* in America's prisons today.

REPROBATES means:

a) nonviolent offenders
b) drunks
c) evil people
d) poor people

10. Before becoming a drug dealer, Nick thought about drug dealing for a long time and carefully weighed all the pros and cons involved. When he was eventually caught, however, he was punished severely because his crime was *PREMEDITATED*.

PREMEDITATED means:

a) unplanned
b) violent
c) planned
d) victimless

Periodical Bibliography

The following articles have been selected to supplement the diverse views presented in this chapter.

Richard B. Abell — "Beyond Willie Horton: The Battle of the Prison Bulge," *Policy Review*, Winter 1989.

Robert and Delorys Blume — "The Crime of Punishment," *The Humanist*, November/December 1989.

Stanley C. Brubaker — "In Praise of Punishment," *The Public Interest*, Fall 1989.

John J. DiIulio Jr. — "Getting Prisons Straight," *The American Prospect*, Fall 1990.

Ernest L. Fortin — "In the Shadow of the Gallows," *The World & I*, March 1990.

Paul Gendreau and Robert R. Ross — "Revivification of Rehabilitation: Evidence from the 1980s," *Justice Quarterly*, September 1987.

Ira Glasser — "Why We're Losing the War on Crime," *USA Today*, November 1990.

Mark Olson — "No More Prisons, No Not One," *The Other Side*, May/June 1989.

Kent W. Perry — "Cops: We're Losing the War," *Newsweek*, March 13, 1989.

Jim Pickford — "How to Reduce Crime and Cut the Budget Deficit: Longer Prison Sentences and Low Cost Prisons," *Conservative Review*, October 1990.

Alexander E. Rawls — "Of Rawls, Responsibility, and Retribution," *The Public Interest*, Spring 1990.

Denny Smith — "How to Keep the Criminals in Jail," *Conservative Digest*, July 1988.

William H. Timas — "Is This Corrections?" *The Prison Mirror*, February 26, 1988. Available from PO Box 55, Stillwater, MN 55082-0055.

Woody West — "Bars Bent Out of Shape? Skewed Penal Priorities," *The Washington Times*, November 30, 1988.

How Do Prisons Affect Criminals?

Chapter Preface

The effect of prisons on criminals is the subject of considerable debate. While many people argue that imprisonment destroys the psychological well-being of criminals and reinforces their criminal tendencies, others disagree with this view. This disagreement has an effect on public policy in that if prisons indeed harm criminals, as critics of prisons argue, society should reduce reliance on incarceration in favor of alternative punishments.

Much of the evidence for prison's destructive effects on the criminal comes from the testimonies of prisoners themselves. For instance, consider the following statement made by Larry Maier, a prisoner at Lompoc, California in 1974, "I became a little smarter. I learned how to be 'slick,' how to 'con' real good, how to really hate, how to gang-fight and how to kill. I learned how to be real 'tough' and not get weak by showing my emotions." That Maier's experience of prison life is representative is supported by evidence from both investigative journalists and academics. Researcher Robert Martinson argued in *Depopulating the Prison* that the shock of incarceration deals criminals a blow from which they can never recover. "All you can do is destroy him [the criminal] if you put him in the pressure cooker of prison," he says. "Prison is a damaging institution, this damage is a long-term process, and the cost to society of its continuation is enormous."

However, in an essay entitled "Reexamining the Cruel and Unusual Punishment of Prison Life," published in the journal *Law and Human Behavior*, James Bonta and Paul Gendreau evaluated the accumulated evidence concerning the destructive effects of prison and found it to be inconclusive. According to the authors, "The facts are that long-term imprisonment and specific conditions of confinement such as solitary, under limiting and humane conditions, fail to show any sort of profound detrimental effects." Furthermore, on some measures, including physical health, the authors found inmates to be more healthy than their counterparts in the community. According to Bonta and Gendreau, individual prisoners appear to respond and adapt differently to different conditions, so that critiques that suggest prisons have a wholly negative effect on all prisoners are inaccurate. The authors conclude that their findings can be used to identify those prisoners who have the most difficulty adapting to prison. Once they have been identified, prison-based treatment programs can be focused on these inmates, thus increasing the prison's role as a humane institution of penalty and rehabilitation.

The authors in the following chapter debate the effects of prisons on criminals in theory and practice.

"No one has ever come out of prison a better man."

Prisons Create a Criminal Personality

Jack Henry Abbott

In prison since his early teens, Jack Henry Abbott has spent his lifetime in jail. With the publication of his book *In the Belly of the Beast*, from which this viewpoint is taken, he became a literary sensation. Norman Mailer, a prominent novelist and biographer, wrote a long and laudatory article for *The New York Times* about Abbott, in which he argued that it was a tragedy that such a talented writer should be wasting away in jail. Mailer continued to campaign for his early release, and in June 1981 his hopes were realized. Abbott's newfound freedom lasted scarcely a month. In July 1981 Abbott murdered a twenty-two-year-old bartender in a barroom dispute. Although these events cast doubts on the idea of rehabilitating prisoners, Abbott's letters remain a poignant and powerful testimony to life in prison. In the following viewpoint, Abbott describes how prison's dehumanizing effects actually create a criminal personality, leaving the prisoner's emotional state forever mangled by hate, distrust, and fear.

As you read, consider the following questions:

1. What evidence does Abbott cite so the reader will believe that he does not "belong in prison"?
2. How is rehabilitation practiced in prison, according to the author?

Can you imagine how I feel—to be treated as a little boy and not as a man? And when I was a little boy, I was treated as a man—and can you imagine what that does to a boy? (I keep waiting for the years to give me a sense of humor, but so far that has evaded me completely.)

So. A guard frowns at me and says: "Why are you not at work?" Or: "Tuck in your shirttail!" Do this and do that. The way a little boy is spoken to. This is something I have had to deal with not for a year or two—nor even ten years—but for, so far, eighteen years. And when I explode, then I have burnt myself by behaving like a contrite and unruly little boy. So I have, in order to avoid that deeper humiliation, developed a method of reversing the whole situation—and I become the man chastising the little boy. (Poor kid!) It has cost me dearly, and not just in terms of years in prison or in the hole.

I cannot adjust to daily life in prison. For almost twenty years this has been true. I have never gone a month in prison without incurring disciplinary action for violating "rules." Not in all these years.

Does this mean I must die in prison? Does this mean I cannot "adjust" to society outside prison?

The government answers *yes*—but I *remember* society, and it is not like prison. I feel that if I ever did *adjust to prison*, I could by that alone never adjust to society. I would be back in prison within months.

Now, I care about myself and I cannot let it happen that I cannot adjust to freedom. Even if it means spending my life in prison—because to me prison is nothing but mutiny and revolt.

. . . A round peg will not fit into a square slot. I don't think they'll ever let me out of prison so long as my release depends upon my "good adjustment to prison."

I Don't Belong in Prison

In the beginning the walls of my cell were made of boiler-plate steel, and I would kick them all day every day, hollering, screaming—for no apparent reason. I was so chocked with rage in those days (about sixteen or seventeen years ago), I could hardly talk, even when I was calm: I *stuttered* badly. I used to throw my tray as casually as you would toss a balled-up scrap of paper in a trash can—but would do it with a tray full of food at the face of a guard.

That is what I mean by a response to the prison experience by a man who does not belong there.

Hell, if I never went to prison, who knows what "evil" I would have committed. I'm not at all saying that because I don't *belong* in prison that I should not have been sent there. Theoretically, *no one*, should *belong* in prison! I was sent there for punishment—and I happen to have gotten it. I do not think it is like that with most men who are sent to prison. Everyone hurts in prison, but not like that. . . .

I have never accepted that I did this to myself. I have never been successfully indoctrinated with that belief. That is the only reason I have been in prison this long.

Indoctrination begins the moment someone is arrested. It becomes more thorough every step of the way, from the moment of arrest to incarceration. In prison, it finds its most profound expression.

Prison's Psychological Effects

Citizens who have (admittedly) committed grievous mistakes are so damaged by their experience behind bars that the majority never successfully live in society again. We are in here for antisocial behavior in the first place. But instead of effecting change for the good, our prisons condition a man to be hard, to isolate himself, to reject his need for others, to further his antisocial adaptation. In short, to become a "con."

Alec Spencer, *Mennonite Central Committee, U.S. Office of Criminal Justice Network Newsletter,* July/December, 1987.

Every minute for years you are forced to believe that your suffering is a result of your "ill behavior," that it is self-inflicted. You are indoctrinated to blindly accept *anything* done to you. But if a guard knocks me to the floor, only by indoctrination can I be brought to believe I did it to myself. If I am thrown in the prison hole for having violated a prison rule—for having, for example, shown insolence to a pig—I can only believe I brought this upon myself through *indoctrination.* . . .

Responsibility? I am not responsible for what the government —its system of justice, its prison—has done to me. I did not do this to myself.

That is not easy to say; it is not a *point of view* to hold. Why? Because it has cost me, so far, almost two decades of imprisonment. This I hold is the *greater* responsibility: I did not do this to myself.

I do not share in the sins of this guilty country; we are not "all in this together"! Who in America today would *dare* take the responsibility for himself and others that I and countless other prisoners like me have taken? . . .

Cowards Are the Norm

. . . The law has never punished anyone for hurting me. If I want justice to punish a wrong done me, it is entirely up to me.

Just picture yourself in that position right there in New York.

81

You can't call a cop or the law when your house is burgled, when you are mugged downtown. The police walk into your home, slap you around (to put it mildly) and help themselves to whatever they want. Your wife and kids even. Anyone there in New York can accuse you of anything and you are punished without even knowing who your accuser is. You have absolutely no rights to legal protection by prosecution. The most you can do is file a civil complaint against the city. Hands are "slapped," but nothing is done. The "slapping of hands" is merely this. The judge says: "Now, Mayor (Warden), I hope this doesn't happen again." That's it. The mayor doesn't even bother to respond to the "admonition." He stands up, stretches, yawns and ambles away. All the faces around you, even the judge's, are covered with smirks. That's it. That's how I have had to live all my life.

What would you do? I assure you, you'd become a deranged coward or the exact opposite. If you become the former, everyone is happy and they'll give you little rewards. If you become the latter, they'll destroy you at every opportunity they get. They'll say you are "crazy," a psycho, etc. The "norm" is the coward in this situation.

Prison and Rehabilitation

To become *rehabilitated* means to accept and live by the values of your society. It requires not just faith in the laws and customs of your society, but faith in the people of your society—and to *extend* those values, and *reproduce* that faith, in your transactions with others in social intercourse.

To rehabilitate someone is a process of teaching. It is a process of *learning* by experience for the man in need of rehabilitation. He requires to know the benefits of the values of his society; he requires a firm understanding of the proper uses of the laws and customs of his society.

Only a man who is a social anomaly can fail to pursue his best interest, especially when the pathway becomes clear to him, for a social anomaly *knows* the values of his society and its laws and customs.

The system of justice in America teaches these lessons to men as if they were social anomalies *already*—as if they had *knowledge* of the values and customs and laws of this society. This reflects the American maxim: *Ignorance does not acquit.*

So rehabilitation is presumed and American justice seeks to *punish* men who *(theoretically)* know better.

And what does *punishment* that aims at *rehabilitation* entail? It does not aim at winning men over by reason—it is *presumed* a prisoner cannot be won over by reason. It is the application of force.

. . . A system of justice that does not instruct by *reason,* that does not rationally demonstrate to a man the error of his ways,

82

accomplishes the opposite ends of justice: oppression.

No one in any prison in this country has ever been shown the errors of his ways by the law. It is an annoyance no one involved in the administration of justice wants to be bothered with. So it is relegated to the prison regimes.

Who Belongs in Prison?

Everyone in prison has committed crimes, could be called a criminal. But that does not mean everyone in prison *belongs* there. I would like to suggest that there are men who are justly in prison but do not belong there. And there are men justly in prison who *do belong* there. Perhaps the great majority of prisoners belong there. They keep returning. I've seen at least one entire prison turn over in population. Almost every one of them (in fact, *everyone* I've seen) feels relieved to be back. They need shaves and showers; they are gaunt, starved-looking when they come in from outside. *Within a week* they are rosy-cheeked, starched-and-pressed, talking to everyone. Laughing a lot (hail-fellow-well-met). They fit in in prison. This is where they belong. Or, to be more charitable—because if men pursue their best interests, no one really "belongs" in prison—let me say that there are less uncertainties in life in a prison than on the outside. It is not a matter so simple as that they have become institutionalized out of *habit*. That is not it. Prison is much more than a habit with men who belong here.

The point is: there are those—and they are not many, but they are men for whom prison does punish and punishes every day—who do not belong here in prison. . . .

Society and not prison prevents their rehabilitation. For rehabilitation is something we *all* stand in need of; the rehabilitation of society itself has not been accomplished. This is reflected *also* in the fact that so many men in prison are not rehabilitated there (there in prison).

If society is so intolerable that a man can only feel himself to be a man in prison, it is the "fault" of society.

And I suggest that a few men are constantly rehabilitated in prison: they belong in society or they belong to the dead. But not in prison.

. . . No one has ever come out of prison a better man. I'm not talking about places like Allenwood and Maxwell Field—the places they send government informers and that frail species of individual who falls from the graces of the government or the Republican party or the Stock Exchange.

I'm speaking of the *penitentiary*. There is at least one in every state. Some states—like New York, Texas, California, Michigan, Illinois—have at least a half-dozen of them. The federal government itself has over forty prisons but only about a half-dozen penitentiaries. . . .

For almost twenty years I have seen prisoners come and go. There is not *one* of them who comes to prison for the first time who is *capable* of the vast repertoire of crimes he is capable of when he finally gets out of prison. I'm not talking about the fine technicalities of, say, safe-cracking or the mechanics of murder. I'm not talking about methodologies.

No one learns those things in prison, contrary to the government's claims: prisoners do not learn how to commit crimes from other prisoners. . . .

What is forced down their throats in spite of themselves is *the will* to commit crimes. It is the *capability* I am speaking of.

Michael Keefe for the *Denver Post*. Reprinted with permission.

It used to be a pastime of mine to watch the change in men, to observe the blackening of their hearts. It takes place before your eyes. They enter prison more bewildered than afraid. Every step after that, the fear creeps into them. They are experiencing men and the administration of things no novels or the cinema—nor even the worst rumors about prison—can teach. No one is prepared for it. Even the pigs, when they first start to work in prison, are not prepared for it.

Everyone is afraid. It is not an emotional, psychological fear. It is a practical matter. If you do not threaten someone—at the very least—someone will threaten you. When you walk across the yard or down the tier to your cell, you stand out like a sore thumb if you do not appear callously unconcerned or cold and ready to kill.

Many times you have to "prey" on someone, or you will be "preyed" on yourself. After so many years, *you are not bluffing.* No one is.

For want of a better expression, this is a *cynical experience* of life so *dangerous*, it changes you so that you don't even notice the change in yourself. In five or ten years, it's a way of life. You see pigs commit murder, and everyone from the warden on down are *active* accomplices. That is putting it mildly. The most well-known politicians and judges *actively* suppress evidence of such crimes. They are *rife*. You see it so often, it is routine. . . .

By the time you get out—*if* you get out—you are capable of *anything*, any crime at all.

Have you ever seen a man *despair* because he cannot bring himself to murder? I am not talking about murder in the heat of combat—that very seldom occurs in prison—I am speaking of cold-blooded premeditated murder. The only prisoners I have ever seen who do not suffer from that despair of being incapable of murder are those who *are* capable of it (not a few).

The Capability to Murder

Most of them find—somewhere down the line—that they *are* capable of it. To discover that there was no basis for your anxieties about murder is a feeling similar to that of a young man who has doubts about being capable of consummating his first sexual encounter with a woman—and when the time comes, if he did not perform magnificently, at least he got the job done. You feel stronger.

If you can kill like that, you can do anything. All of the elements of every crime come into play. There is the deception; the ability to hold a secret; the calculation; the nerve—and the activity of well-planned and executed *violence*.

Most important, you learn never to trust a man, even if he seems honest and sincere. You learn how men deceive themselves and how impossible it is to help them without injuring yourself.

You know all of this and more in a conscious way before you get out of prison.

Why do you *steal* when you get out? Why do you commit crimes you never dreamed of being able to commit before you entered prison? You have changed so that you are not even aware there was a time you were incapable of such things. If you meditate on it, you tell yourself that you steal because you are no longer afraid of going to prison. This is because you do not remember you were not afraid originally.

"One major [criticism] that is inaccurate and misleading is branding correctional institutions as schools for crime."

The Criminal Personality Exists Before Prison

Stanton E. Samenow

Stanton E. Samenow, a clinical psychologist, is in private practice in Alexandria, Virginia. He is a consultant and speaker on criminal behavior and was a member of President Reagan's Task Force on Victims of Crime. During his eight years as a research psychologist at Saint Elizabeth's Hospital in Washington, DC, he co-authored, with the late Dr. Samuel Yochelson, the much-heralded three-volume study *The Criminal Personality*. In the following viewpoint, Samenow states that it is not prison that is the corrupting influence in the lives of criminals, but the opposite: criminals corrupt the prison system. A criminal's personality does not stop being criminal in prison. He or she just continues to exhibit the same mind-set once in prison.

As you read, consider the following questions:

1. Does Samenow believe that criminals are imprisoned unjustly? Why or why not?
2. How does a criminal employ "psychological warfare," according to Samenow?
3. Does the author believe that criminals can "outgrow" crime? Why or why not?

From *Inside the Criminal Mind* by Stanton E. Samenow. Copyright © 1984 by Stanton E. Samenow. Reprinted by permission of Times Books, a division of Random House, Inc.

Over the last two decades, the prison reform movement has gathered strength, and much of the criticism leveled at correctional facilities has been constructive. However, one major thrust that is inaccurate and misleading is branding correctional institutions as schools for crime with the implication that people are turned into something that they weren't before.

Prison is a breeding ground for crime only insofar as a criminal expands his associations and finds support for antisocial patterns of thought and behavior. He hears new ideas for crime in prison, but *he* is the one who accepts or rejects those ideas. No one forces him to continue a life of crime either within the institution or when he returns to society. He is not a hapless victim who is corrupted by fellow inmates. He has made choices in the past and continues to make choices.

Criminals Remain the Same

Criminals exhibit the same behavior patterns inside prison as on the streets. Being locked up does not alter a criminal's perception that he is top dog. Once he adjusts to his surroundings, he becomes determined to establish himself, his stance being, "If you serve time, let time serve you." And so he continues his manipulations and power plays. Some inmates abide by the rules, but not because of any inner personality transformation. Rather, they are building themselves up as model inmates in order to gain special status or privileges. Then there are the inmates who find incarceration to be truly unsettling, if not a major crisis in their lives. They make genuine efforts to change, even seeking the help of institutional counselors, but the counseling that they receive usually turns out to be inadequate.

Wherever he is sent, the criminal believes that confinement is the final injustice in a string of injustices that began with his arrest. In the past, laws and others' rights meant little to him, but now that he is confined, he becomes highly legalistic about asserting his own rights. One inmate who was serving a sentence for a string of burglaries acknowledged, "You break a law to get what you want and treasure the law when it gets you what you want." The criminal looks for a way to beat a charge, and even long after he has begun serving his sentence, he seeks a means to overturn a verdict or reduce his sentence. Some spend hours poring over law books in the prison library and weeks laboring over writs. Among them are men who make a career in prison as jailhouse lawyers, conducting legal research and preparing documents for themselves and other inmates, collecting, in the latter case, money, property, and personal favors. . . .

Despite being behind bars, the criminal still expects to do as he pleases. This is not surprising because it is a lifelong attitude. However, inmates have different methods of getting what they want in prison just as they did outside. Some wage open warfare with staff members, flouting authority and brazenly defying regulations. One teenager bragged about his defiance in a state institution: "I tore up my room. I loved hearing glass break." At another juvenile facility, several ringleaders assembled all the kids of one unit, barricaded the staff out of the lounge, and demolished the place. Some prisoners prefer to be locked in their cells or banished to "the hole" rather than capitulate to anyone. Even in their cells they can create a commotion by setting bedding afire or cause floods by stuffing up toilets. Said one inmate, "I am going to play my cards the way I want to and when I want to. Go straight—hell! I would rather remain a hoodlum than let anyone walk over me. No one is going to stop me unless they kill me."

© Beutel/Rothco. Reprinted with permission.

In a struggle for status among fellow cons, the physically aggressive inmate is quick to lash out with a stream of profanity or throw a punch whenever he feels infringed upon. A prisoner who calls him a string of names may wind up with a fork jammed in his gut. A melee may erupt when someone switches the channel on the television. An unaware staff member may suffer a fractured skull from a flying chair after denying an inmate's request. One irascible inmate, displeased with the vegetable soup served at lunch, stared into his bowl, glowered at the man serving him, and complained that he had received the "dregs of the pot." He declared the "slop" unfit to eat and demanded another portion. When the worker ignored him, he threw the soup in his face. . . .

Whether he locks horns with the staff or cons his way into their good graces, the criminal wages psychological warfare. With his customary finesse, he preys upon human insecurity, weakness, greed, and prejudice. Knowing how staff members feel about him and other inmates may be of considerable advantage. If he can touch a sensitive nerve, he may provoke a staff member into losing control. It is a triumph to divert attention from himself and put the other person or even the whole institution on the defensive. . . .

Don't Snitch

In prison, just as on the street, the dilemma of whom to trust hangs heavily in the air. Criminals don't know what trust is. If they use the word, it usually means that a person won't betray them. "Don't snitch" is a code among inmates. The price of squealing on another con may be a beating or even death. Even so, the inmate realizes that every man is out for himself and that even his best buddy may turn informant to save his own skin or to acquire privileges. Although convicts share an understanding of "no snitching," the dominant ethos in prison is, as it was outside, "[Damn] everybody else but me." Writing in *Corrections Magazine*, Stephen Gettinger reports, "Some prison observers say that the inmate code's prohibitions against informing are more honored in the breach than in the observance. The trading of information is as common, and as necessary, to the daily life of any prison as taking the count.". . .

A criminal's absorption with crime does not necessarily diminish just because he is locked up. Despite the restrictive environment, he schemes, talks about, and continues to engage in illicit activities. Any external stimulus, such as a television cop show, a detective movie, or a lurid crime story in the paper feeds an already busy mind, as do his daily conversations with other inmates about crime. Through letters and visitors, the criminal hangs on to old ties in addition to establishing new ones in prison. To some, confinement means that the challenge to engage in illicit activities is greater than ever. Theft is rampant in prisons. Anything that a man wants to hold on to must be kept on his person or surrendered to a trustworthy staff member. An inmate may be robbed when he sleeps (if he shares a cell or dormitory), while he takes a shower, or at any other moment when he relaxes his guard. Inmates not only steal from one another but also pilfer personal belongings from the staff and food and other supplies from the institution. . . .

All the above is intended to underscore the point that criminals are criminals, no matter where they are. In prison, their personality remains as it was. What may vary is the degree of risk they will take and therefore the method by which they operate. Those abstaining from crime still miss it, but they content themselves with fantasy and conversation about crime. Said a 22-year-old burglar, "I'm still not afraid while I sit here in prison. The only thing I think about is stealing when I'm out of here in a few years and not the consequences. They don't mean anything."

The Criminal's Contempt for Society

Unless criminals are serving terms of life without parole, which very few do, they will be free eventually to prey upon us all. There is still a job for corrections to do in the institution and the community—that is to correct. But rehabilitation as it has been practiced cannot possibly be effective because it is based on a total misconception. To rehabilitate is to restore to a former constructive capacity or condition. *There is nothing to which to rehabilitate a criminal.* There is no earlier condition of being responsible to which to restore him. He never learned the ways of getting along in this world that most of us learned as children. Just as rehabilitation is a misconception, so too is the notion of "reintegrating the criminal into the community." It is absurd to speak of reintegrating him when he was never integrated in the first place. The criminal has long stood apart from the community, contemptuous of people who lived responsibly.

Stanton E. Samenow, *Inside the Criminal Mind*, 1984.

No criminal wants to return to prison, and no criminal expects to. Some offenders serve time, and that in itself is a powerful deterrent to further criminal activity. They do not repeat. But these are not the people who have made crime a way of life. There are no studies of these people and no figures as to how numerous they are.

Contrary to what some people believe, most criminals do learn from experience, but it is not what society wants to teach them. In prison, such a person has ample time and opportunity to learn how to be a better criminal. Some decide that upon release they will lie low, limit themselves to smaller crimes, and forgo the big-time ventures. Or perhaps they will mastermind a crime but stay behind the scenes rather than participate directly in the action. Such intentions are short-lived. Once they leave prison behind, their appetites become voracious for the high excitement of the old life. Some in fact do become more success-ful criminals, immersing themselves heavily in crime but being slick enough to avoid apprehension. Others avoid arrest for a long time but eventually land back in the slammer. Then there are the big losers. Hardly has the prison disgorged them into so-ciety than they slip up, get caught, and are charged with a new offense.

It is widely believed that criminals outgrow crime, but this is based on the fact that some never return to prison. Rand Corpo-ration researchers observe that some criminologists have hy-pothesized that the criminal reaches a "burnout stage." Dr. Richard Schwartz states, "By the time a man reaches age 40 his criminal career is essentially over." The burnout theory may be based on the fact that some older criminals cease to get arrested for street crimes. It is true that as the street criminal ages, he is not as agile and literally cannot run as fast as he used to. He has mellowed only in that he takes fewer big risks and his offenses may be less serious. But his criminal personality remains un-changed, and people still suffer at his hands.

"Most convicts are now stacked up in prison warehouses where they do their time in physical and social isolation. . . . [They live with] deprivation, fear, and distress."

Prisons Are Violent and Dehumanizing

John Irwin and Michael Snedeker

John Irwin and Michael Snedeker are members of the board of directors of the Prisoner's Rights Union. This California-based organization includes convicts, ex-convicts, and others interested in improving the conditions of those incarcerated in California's prisons. In the following viewpoint, Irwin and Snedeker argue that conditions in America's prisons have deteriorated badly since the late 1970s. The causes of this deterioration, they contend, are an enormous increase in prison populations, and a declining faith in rehabilitation. America's prisons, now desperate places of stagnation, alienation, and violence, are a national disgrace, Irwin and Snedeker conclude.

As you read, consider the following questions:

1. What were America's prisons like in the 1970s, according to Irwin and Snedeker?
2. In what ways have prisons changed over the last two decades, according to the authors?
3. How do Irwin and Snedeker describe the psychological effects on prisoners of today's prisons?

John Irwin and Michael Snedeker, "Warehouse Prisons: Life Inside in the Modern Age," *The California Prisoner*, August 1989. Reprinted with permission.

Prison populations are skyrocketing. Overcrowding, together with the shift from a rehabilitative to a punitive penal philosophy, has meant that most services in prison have diminished or disappeared. In the face of increased turmoil and violence among prisoners, prison administrators segregate and lock up more and more prisoners. Prisons are becoming human warehouses where prisoners are stored.

Prisons in the Past

People have been referring to prisons as warehouses for decades, but the analogy was inaccurate. Instead, prisons were slow paced, monosexual, enclosed little communities where the convicts lived a monotonous, but complete social life. First of all, convicts performed all the tasks required to keep the community alive. They cooked and served the meals, washed the clothing, fixed the plumbing and electrical wiring and appliances, painted the buildings, tended the boiler, landscaped the grounds, delivered most of the medical services and kept all the records. They worked in prison industries, making "jute," clothes, furniture, license plates or other commodities consumed by the State. Prison staff oversaw all these activities and kept track of the convicts, but convicts supplied all the labor.

In addition to all these "instrumental" tasks, convicts collectively engaged in wide varieties of leisure activities, some of them unique and creative. They played all the sports possible within limits imposed by the physical plant: baseball, football, basketball (when there was a court), handball (there was always a wall for this), and even marbles. They carried on the favorite convict pastime, shucking and jiving that is, telling stories about theirs and others' exploits, mostly in crime, drugs and sex. They wheeled and dealed. They smuggled food from the kitchen and ran sandwiches and other food businesses. They made the prison brew: pruno, which required sugar, yeast, fruit and some place to stash it during fermentation (which was not easy to locate, because it was such smelly stuff). They bought or sold any contraband they could steal, smuggle in or manufacture: Food, coffee, stingers (to heat water with), special clothing items, radios, phonographs, typewriters, paper, illegal drugs, even nutmeg (which gives one a cheap high when several spoonfuls are swallowed.) Some of them participated in the special prison sexual life with its punks, queens and jockers.

Most of them were members of vast friendship networks, "tips," based on their particular deviant identity (e.g., dope fiends, thieves, hustlers, etc.), the town or neighborhood where they were raised ("homeboys"), and prison interests. These networks supplied them with companions for expressive activities and connections for acquiring commodities and privileges.

Many tenaciously struggled to improve themselves for life after prison. They attended the prison schools, learned trades, read hundreds of books, studied languages, completed correspondence courses, learned to play a musical instrument and took special care of their health.

Chuck Asay, by permission of the *Colorado Springs Gazette-Telegraph.*

All together, they composed a small society, with a pronounced stratification system, a strong convict value system, a unique set of behavior patterns (such as patterns of speech and bodily gestures), and an array of social roles—right guys, politicians, crazies, regulars, punks, queens, stool pigeons and hoosiers. Importantly, their participation in this world with its powerful value system, the convict code, gave them a sense of pride and dignity.

The administration tolerated, even promoted most of the convict activities and the society, because their existence promoted a high degree of order within the prison. In fact, it was infrequent that the administration had to intervene to exercise their mechanisms of control. The convicts ran the prison and kept the peace.

Now, however, the warehouse analogy is becoming more and more accurate. Most prisoners have retreated from the prison society. The only prominent public figures in many prisons are the Administrators in their attempts to cope with the new problems of social control, mainly the racial violence and the gangs.

They have greatly increased the separation of prisoners by breaking prisons into smaller and smaller units and segregating a larger portion of the prison population in special units. Also they have encouraged informing, which has greatly demoralized and divided prisoners into bitterly divided groups: rats and those who are ratted on. The televisions in every cell further isolate each "plugged-in" viewer from the people in cells around them. So in a sense, most convicts are now stacked up in prison warehouses where they do their time in physical and social isolation. This and their elevated level of deprivation, fear, and distress are having a profound detrimental effect upon them.

Probably the most pernicious consequence of the modern warehouse prison is that so many prisoners now "stagnate." That is, for the duration of their prison terms, they make no progress toward being better equipped to live a non-criminal life on the outside; in fact, they become less equipped. This is particularly regrettable because most prisoners are relatively poorly educated, vocationally unskilled and some have serious physical and psychological problems when they go to prison. In addition, most express some desire to better themselves during their prison sentence.

After Prison

One of the authors interviewed 152 prisoners randomly picked from the states of Washington, Illinois and Nevada. Most in the sample interviewed, for example, stated that they wanted to improve their education and job skills: "I want to go to school and get a trade. Then when I get out I want to be married, have my kids with me, have a good job so I can support them. I have to get the drugs out of my life. Prison has really scared the hell out of me." Or "I'm going to school, get a job and stay away from gangs. I'm going to get into electronics. I want a job I don't get laid off on. As long as I have a job I don't get into trouble. It's when I get laid off I get into trouble."

Also, many prisoners indicated they intended to take care of serious health problems, participate in drug or alcohol programs to deal with their addictions, and in general take advantage of whatever resources exist to better themselves.

In preceding decades, particularly during the rehabilitative era (1950 to 1965), prison administrators encouraged these betterment activities and they supplied the resources and programs for accomplishing them. For example, educational opportunities expanded during this period, and by the early 1970s, prisoners could receive a high school education in most prisons and some college credit in many. Most prisons offered a wide variety of vocational training programs. Also, many forms of counselling were available.

Currently, the general shift in the society toward fiscal conservatism and punitive penology and the dramatic expansion of prison populations have greatly decreased the betterment programs. Even where there has been no reduction in money for rehabilitative programs, caring for the expanding prison populations has depleted the funds, resources and space formerly allotted to rehabilitation.

Also, the greater restrictions on prisoners' mobility and the segregation of many prisoners have greatly diminished their access to schools, the library, shops and counselling programs. Now, instead of busily going about seeking help, as many prisoners did in the "correctional institutions," more and more prisoners stagnate within the warehouse prison.

Alienation

In earlier eras, prisoner solidarity, which was underpinned by a special world view and code of ethics, not only promoted peace, it bolstered the prisoners' self-esteem. Though they were society's outcasts, "losers," they took pride in being "right guys," "regulars," or "real convicts." They endured the deprivation of imprisonment, which was itself a matter for pride, and responded to their degradation by terming the conventional people, "squares," as petty, corrupt, weak and hypocritical.

Prisons Are the End of Hope

Prisons hurt, maim, and kill. Prisons demoralize and feed the self-hatred generated by failed human potential. To be a person caged, shackled, and bound is a humiliation which makes one feel subhuman. The slow and methodical rape of the spirit continues day after day: men and women inside our prisons are convinced that they have no worth, no purpose, no hope, no rights, no chance. For too many, that terrible lie becomes truth, a prophecy fulfilled in a thousand ways each day and night.

Philip Brasfield, *The Other Side*, May/June 1990.

They particularly felt contempt for society's representatives who they were the closest to, the guards and prison administrators. Most convicts sincerely believed that they were more honorable than squares. Now, they not only shy away from, but distrust and feel contempt for other prisoners. A former politically active prisoner who was about to be released after serving 20 years, addressed a pre-release class: "If I catch any convict coming around my neighborhood after I'm released, I'm calling the cops, because I know he's up to no good."

Also, prisoners are acutely aware the general society's contempt for them has increased sharply in the last 15 years. The news media usually plays up the ex-convict status of any person

96

in the news in a negative way. Politicians harp on the criminal acts committed by released prisoners. Legislators and policy makers, usually with a dramatic public display, have passed laws or established policies against hiring ex-convicts for this or that job. Consequently, most prisoners are presently understanding that they are society's leading pariahs.

An "Outlaw" Identity

Partly as a reaction to their negative image, some prisoners have taken on the extreme "outlaw" identity. These are mainly persons who present themselves as "convicts" in the prison and participate in the rapacious, violent activities of gangs. The outlaw scorns the disapproval of society, reveals no mercy or compassion for others and remains ready to use violence to protect himself or achieve his ends. An archetypical outlaw, Jack Abbott, describes the types: "The model we emulate is a fanatically defiant and alienated individual who cannot imagine what forgiveness is, or mercy or tolerance, because he has no experience of such values. His emotions do not know what such values are, but imagines them as so many 'weaknesses' precisely because the unprincipled offender appears to escape punishment through such 'weaknesses' on the part of society."

However, most prisoners, as they have withdrawn from most prison public activities, attempt to disassociate themselves from the convict identity. But their experience of being held in contempt and having no supporting counter value is destructive. Mainly, it completes their full alienation.

The concept of alienation, which has been so central in the analysis of modern society, has been recognized to have several separate components: a sense of powerlessness—the expectation one's behavior will not succeed in bringing about the outcomes he/she seeks; meaninglessness—lack of a sense of what one ought to do or believe; detachment—the disassociation from the central beliefs and values of the society; and self-estrangement—the experience of oneself as alien and illworthy. All these aspects of alienation are cultivated in the contemporary prison milieu.

Fully alienated persons are incapable of anything close to normal participation in conventional rounds. They float unattached around the edges of society (like the homeless), violently lash out at others, escape into drug addiction or succumb to psychosis or suicide.

Prisoners Less Able to Cope Outside

In addition, prisoners' withdrawal and stagnation are exacerbating some of the usual detrimental processes of serving time. Being held away from the general society and subjected to the highly routinized prison regime tends to orient persons to the role of prisoners. Upon release, they experience unique difficulties in coping with the outside world with its faster pace and very different and more complex routines. It has been recognized that the re-entry experience produces confusion, depression and self-estrangement. Now that prisoners are subjected to greater social and physical isolation during their imprisonment they are becoming more socially and psychologically "maladjusted" for the outside world.

Despicable Pariahs

More prisoners are leaving our prisons socially crippled and profoundly alienated. Moreover, they understand that they will be returning to a society that views them as despicable pariahs. They are also aware that they will be having more difficulty finding employment than was the case before the onslaught of this latest punitive era. Consequently, their expectations are low.

The fiscal crunch caused by the binge of new construction means that money is seen as scarce even for essential, constitutionally required services like medical care. Physical and mental activity of any kind for convicts is outside the new warehouse model. Education, sports, etc. are viewed as "frivolities," or as something that would be nice but is not affordable. Prisons are now stagnant pools of humanity, breeding disease all across America.

"Going to prison should be like reaching a point of no return, like descending into Hell."

Prisons Should Be Dehumanizing

Graeme R. Newman

Graeme R. Newman has written extensively on crime and justice. His book, *The Punishment Response*, is considered the definitive history of punishment. He teaches criminology at the State University of New York, Albany. His book, *Just and Painful,* from which this viewpoint is excerpted, is a straightforward case for the use of corporal punishments such as electric shock and whipping. In the following viewpoint, Newman outlines what he believes prisons should be like: hellish workhouses in which criminals are taught the meaning of suffering.

As you read, consider the following questions:

1. What is the essential difference between those who commit crimes and those who don't, according to the author?
2. Under what conditions does the author believe that the pain and suffering of prison is justified?
3. What do you think of Newman's prison idea? Do you feel it would be justified for the types of criminals Newman believes should be incarcerated?

Acute corporal punishments are more justifiable than prison because they can be limited in their effects more easily to the offender, often only to his actions, leaving the offender's life generally untouched. Prison takes over the whole of the person's life, so that we must justify it only on the basis that the offender either (1) has committed a crime of such proportions that only a punishment that punishes the whole of the offender's life is adequate to fit the crime, or (2) the offender has committed so many crimes that we are justified in punishing him as a criminal rather than for his particular crimes.

In actual fact, both these justifications boil down to the same thing: we are saying that either because of the horror of his single criminal act or because of the terrible extent of his past record, the offender may be viewed as a person imbued with the aura of criminality—in other words that he is an evil person. Thus, it is only through a punishment of similar aura that we can hope to match him or his deeds.

There are red herrings that are thrown across the path of this argument by many social scientists. They claim that researchers have been unable to find any consistent differences between offenders (of any kind of crime) and non-offenders. The reply is:

1. The scientific evidence is inconclusive. Some studies find differences, others do not.

2. Their claims are, frankly, nonsensical, for they ignore the most obvious fact that those offenders they compare us with have in fact committed serious violent crimes, usually a lot of them, and it is this fact that sets them apart from the rest of us. While this point might be more difficult to defend if we were dealing with the whole range of crimes from least to most serious, since probably everyone has committed a little crime or two in the past, it certainly does not apply to the extreme end of the scale which is what we are concerned with.

Morality Is the Difference

Very few of those reading this would have committed murder, rape or serious assault or burglary. It is this fact that sets us apart from the criminals who deserve prison. We have little difficulty in judging such criminals as bad persons.

In sum, the difference, the essential difference, between those who have committed a lot of crimes, or just one very serious crime, and the rest of us is one of morality. The modern social scientists, because of their *amorality* have failed to attend to this difference—in fact they try to explain it away.

[I] suggest that only prison terms of 15 years or more should be allowed. While there are good retributive reasons for such a policy . . . there is another important reason: the goal is to make the gap between us and the truly horrible criminals even greater in practice than before. This is the opposite to the social scientists who keep trying to fudge over the line.

Indeed, going to prison should be like reaching a point of no return, like descending into Hell.

Making Prisons Retributive

To understand the true functions of prison, we must understand that, in contrast to acute corporal punishments, prisons work on a person's mind as well as his body. This fits in with a special kind of retribution which may be called religious retribution, and which takes a basic principle of retribution—that only the guilty should be punished—far more seriously than the old retributivists did. . . . They were more concerned with rule-breaking than with guilt. In fact it would be more accurate to describe the old retributivists as secular retributivists.

The religious retributivists naturally take the word "guilt" in its moral sense, which is to say that the offender has a guilty mind, and that only by a series of ritually purgative functions can this guilt be assuaged. Therefore, one must not only fit the punishment to the crime, but one must fit the punishment to the criminal's guilty mind, and the first step in the process is that the criminal must be contrite, or at least work towards contrition.

Criminals Must Recognize Guilt

The individual must be contrite: he must recognize the error of his ways. He must come to want to make amends, and the only way to effect such a transformation since the sins of evil people are so deeply entrenched, is through a long process of suffering. The originators of American prisons, the Quakers, almost understood this when they thought that solitary confinement and the Bible would be enough. But our prisons have long ago lost contact with their religious roots.

Graeme R. Newman, *Just and Painful*, 1983.

Thus, in answer to those murderers who hypocritically say that "they can't bring back murder victims, so what else can they do?" we say to them: they should suffer the long journey towards contrition. They should work off their guilt, and for some not even a lifetime will be long enough. Surely this is not too much to ask when one considers the innocent lives that they have ruined?

Unfortunately, penologists have lost sight of this important function of retribution, so that they have allowed punishments to destroy souls rather than save them.

One often hears prisons described as soul-destroying. The experience has been likened to Dante's Hell, and aptly so, for the famous inscription above the gates of Dante's Hell is often found scratched on prison walls:

ABANDON HOPE ALL YE WHO ENTER HERE . . .

In Purgatory, Dante, and the Christian religion generally, did not abandon hope, and looked toward the possibility of some kind of salvation, or today we would say cure: salvation is a better word though, since it does not side-step the process of contrition that is inherent in the logic of resolving a crime through its punishment. This is the *religious* as against the *secular* version of retribution.

It is the religious version of retribution that we must apply to the criminals we have locked up, because it is only they whom we have seen fit to imbue with the aura of evil. For those receiving acute corporal punishment and other alternatives, we do not make the leap of judgment to say they are truly evil because they have committed a crime or two of middling seriousness. We punish only their acts, we do not judge their persons. We do not want a Draconian system of criminal justice, and so we save our harshest judgments for only the very few.

Making moral judgments about the quality of the lives of people is an arrogant undertaking, one that should not be taken too lightly, or too often. But once we have made the judgment, we must have the courage to follow up our convictions.

The religious version of retribution requires basically two things: the crime must be resolved through its punishment, and the punishment must involve long term suffering.

The Judeo-Christian tradition has long recognized the importance of ritual suffering as a way of resolving or assuaging the terrible guilt that must fall upon someone who has committed a crime or crimes of unspeakable horror. Most religions do in fact have some equivalent system for dealing with guilt. The pagan religions of classical Greece and Rome were clear about this. The bloody cycle of retributive vengeance in the plays of Aeschylus (*The Orestian Trilogy*) could only be stopped by Orestes spending a long period of time suffering in an effort to assuage the guilt of having murdered his mother. The theme is deeply embedded in western thought. It is the only way that the cycle of vengeance can be stopped. It is the reason why the trappings of justice—the courts, procedures, dress, etc., have a ritual aura about them. . . .

Treatment in Wolf's Clothing?

The process just described begins to sound very much like a form of "treatment" and not punishment, if one translates it into modern day terminology. For example, instead of talking about the deeper or inner layers of sin that must be penetrated and brought out into the open, one would today talk about uncovering the unconscious, analyzing the offender's inner motives and conflicts.

If this is so, we are in trouble, because criminologists will tell us that it has been found time and time again that treatment does not work, that all manner of treatment programs have been tried out with offenders and none have been shown to produce results any better than chance. That is, criminals who were treated by some method or another who were released, were reconvicted of a subsequent crime in just about the same proportions as those who were released but were not treated.

"The Old Prison Discipline"

Custodial, punitive, and productive practices, sometimes called the "old prison discipline," have been outlined by Howard B. Gill. According to Gill, prison discipline stood for the following:

Hard Labor—Ranging from "making little ones out of big ones" and carrying cannon shot from one end of the prison yard to the other, to constructive prison industries.

Deprivation—Of everything except the requisites for a spartan existence and religious instruction.

Monotony—Essentially no variation in diet and daily routine.

Uniformity—Rigidly consistent treatment of prisoners.

Mass Movement—Individuality was squashed through mass living in cell blocks, mass eating, mass recreation, even mass bathing.

Degradation—To complete the loss of identity, prisoners were housed in monkey cages, dressed in shabby, nondescript clothing, and denied courteous contact with guards.

Subservience—To rules, rules, rules!

Corporal Punishment—Among the uses of force were the paddle, the whip, the sweat box, and the famous boot.

Noncommunication—Absolute silence or solitary confinement, without relief from letters, visits, or other contacts.

Recreation—At first none; later a daily hour in the yard.

No Responsibility—Prisoners were denied every social, civic, domestic, economic, and even personal responsibility.

Isolation—Often 16 hours a day, thereby increasing prisoners' egocentricity.

No "Fraternization" with the Guards—This rule prevented any attempts to solve problems through staff-inmate contacts.

Howard B. Gill, "A New Prison Discipline: Implementing the Declaration of Principles of 1870," *Federal Probation*, vol. 34, no. 2, June 1970.

But the difference between punishment as cure and the treatment model of penology is substantial. When one reads the punishments described by Dante for those in Purgatory, there is little doubt that they *are* punishments, designed primarily to teach a lesson in a painful way; to ensure that the offender suffers while he learns, through his punishment, the quality of his crime. The religious—and logical—assumption is that a crime is by definition a hurt (whether to others or to oneself), so it is only through hurt that any understanding of one's crime can be reached. In contrast, treatment does not require that the offender suffer any pain at all.

In sum, the proper punishment for a despicable criminal is one that allows for expiation, for a slow learning through a punishment that expresses his crime. It is essential that the basic sin or sins underlying the crime be played out through its opposite so that the individual will learn the evil of his way. For the terrible few, this can only be done through a process of pain and suffering. This is obviously a long and time consuming process, and it is why prison is a most appropriate medium for contrition. . . .

And although, strictly speaking, according to the old retributivists, one should only match the single crime with the single punishment, it is clear from the religious view of retribution that one must match the despicable criminal's *sins* with the punishments, not his *crimes* with the punishments. In other words, one must go beyond the particular offense to the soul of the offender. By this model, one is justified in matching the punishment to the criminal's entire person. Prison is most apt in this regard. It takes over each inmate's total life.

An Indeterminate Sentence?

Lest this be seen as another form of the indeterminate sentence, we should be clear that this cannot be so if we are to be faithful to Dante's Purgatory. There is hope in Purgatory and it is assumed that eventually all will go through to the top of the mount into Paradise. In fact, Dante even spoke of matching particular amounts of time in Purgatory to the amount of time spent as a sinner on earth. Without this limitation on punishment, it would be a punishment the same as Hell, with no hope. By placing finite limits on the duration of punishment, one recognizes that there is hope. Hope, indeed, is the central force underlying atonement. This is why the initial prison term for any criminal should be finite and of long duration—say 15 years.

Prison as Atonement

All of this is based, of course, upon the assumption that the offender undergoing atonement is convinced that what he has done requires atonement, that he is really guilty of an evil act, and in the most severe cases of having led an evil life. If he is not convinced of this, then he is no different from those relegated by Dante to Hell. For it is the unbelievers, pagans and heathens, and especially those blatantly so, for whom Hell is reserved. In the same way, the offender who does not believe in the evil of his act, or at least in the right of the judge to pronounce him convicted of a crime and deserving of punishment—for this offender there is no hope of redemption. His punishment will be eternal and it is for him that we say, "lock him up and throw away the key." . . .

Obviously, prisoners cannot be subjected to the same terrible tortures in prison as Dante dreamed up for Hell and Purgatory. But it is time that we took prison seriously as a punishment, and realized that these few criminals, these bad people, have been sent there for punishment and that is what they should get. The chronic punishment of prison must be made to have some meaning. That meaning must hinge on the criminal's recognition of his crimes. It must require acts of contrition, including acts that respond in a direct way to the sin of the crime.

For example, on the simplest level, it seems morally required that incarcerated murderers should devote their time to saving lives in whatever way possible, and that they should see it as quite deserving that they should risk their lives for others. Their use for risky medical research might well be justified on this basis.

We might also note in passing that the saving of one life to make up for one murder would not be sufficient. We do not try to match the injury to the victim in such a specific way, for this would be merely the reflection of the crime without any analogical or educative function to punishment. The criminal must devote himself to saving many lives, for it is the guilt of his own actions that must be assuaged, not the actual injury to the victim (though of course, it plays a part). In some cases there may simply not be enough time for the most evil of criminals to make up for the guilt of the sins underlying his crimes.

In Conclusion

If we were to develop a prison-intensive system based on the use of prisons in ways outlined, and on strictly limiting prison terms to 15 years or more, it can be seen that prisons would become very harsh places indeed. But at least there would be a clear purpose to their harshness, and we would have to take direct and clear responsibility for what happened in them. This is in contrast to today where we have all kinds of excuses for not taking responsibility for the violence and aimlessness of prison life. The prison-intensive system also means that the decision to incarcerate individuals is going to be very weighty indeed.

a critical thinking activity

Recognizing Stereotypes

"Which are you—a victim of society or a crook?"

Drawing by Ed Arno; © 1979 The New Yorker Magazine, Inc. Reprinted with permission.

A stereotype is an oversimplified or exaggerated description of people or things. Stereotyping can be favorable. Most stereotyping, however, tends to be highly uncomplimentary and, at times, degrading.

Stereotyping grows out of our prejudices. When we stereotype someone, we are prejudging him or her. Consider the above cartoon: the prisoner's question, while funny, also expresses two common stereotypes of the criminal.

The following statements relate to the subject matter in this chapter. Consider each statement carefully. *Mark S for any statement that is an example of stereotyping. Mark N if the statement is not an example of stereotyping. Mark U if you are undecided about any statement.*

S = *stereotype*
N = *not a stereotype*
U = *undecided*

Part I

1. Prisoners are animals and should be treated like animals.

2. A person becomes a criminal because of poor upbringing.

3. Prison guards are brutal pigs.

4. No one really knows the reason people commit crimes.

5. Prisons are schools of crime.

6. On average, more blacks than whites are imprisoned.

7. Most criminals are drug addicts.

8. Some criminals can outgrow crime.

9. Many prisoners have serious personal problems.

10. People are imprisoned for committing crimes.

11. Conditions in prisons are disgusting and violate prisoners' constitutional rights.

12. Criminals are clever and attractive to members of the opposite sex.

13. Prisons sometimes alter a criminal's personality.

14. Some criminals don't belong in prison.

15. Criminals are born, not made.

16. All criminals lack a conscience.

17. Most criminals can be rehabilitated.

18. All criminals are victims of social problems such as poverty and racism.

19. Criminals are like children who never grew up.

20. Criminals come from poor families.

Part II

Based on the insights you have gained from this activity, discuss these questions in class:

1. Why do people stereotype one another?

2. What are some examples of positive stereotypes?

3. What harm can stereotypes cause?

4. What stereotypes currently affect members of your class?

Periodical Bibliography

The following articles have been selected to supplement the diverse views presented in this chapter.

Kevin Acker	"Off with Their Overhead: More Prison Bars for the Buck," *Policy Review*, Fall 1989.
George M. Anderson	"Prison Violence: Victims Behind Bars," *America*, November 26, 1988.
Marc C. Austin	"Inmate Education: A Wise Use of Correctional Funds," *Corrections Today*, August 1987.
Donald H. Bouma	"The Pendulum Swings from Rehabilitation to Punishment," *USA Today*, July 1980.
Philip Brasfield	"No Tender Mercies," *The Other Side*, March 1988. Available from 300 W. Apsley St., Philadelphia, PA 19144.
John R. Coleman	"What I Learned Last Summer," *Psychology Today*, November 1980.
Murphy Davis	"Prison Slavery," *The Other Side*, May/June 1990.
Bernard Farbar	"My Life Inside," *Esquire*, September 1988.
J. Forbes Farmer	"A Case Study in Regaining Control of a Violent State Prison," *Federal Probation*, January 1988.
Mark S. Fleisher	"The Costly Business of Warehousing Violent Criminals," *USA Today*, March 1989.
Ted Gest	"Teaching Convicts Real Street Smarts," *U.S. News & World Report*, May 18, 1987.
Paul Glastris	"The Life of Riley on Murderer's Row," *U.S. News & World Report*, February 26, 1990.
Dan Goodgame	"Mayhem in the Cellblocks: Gangs Terrorize Folsom and Other Crowded Prisons," *Time*, August 12, 1985.
Alex Herbage	"World Behind Bars," *Friends Journal*, December 1989. Available from 1501 Cherry St., Philadelphia, PA 19102-1497.
Robert Hillegass	"Warehousing Violence," *Friends Journal*, March 1989.

Dirk Johnson

"More Prisons Using Iron Hand to Control Inmates," *The New York Times*, November 1, 1990.

Perry Johnson

"The Snitch System—How Informants Affect Prison Security," *Corrections Today*, July 1989.

Adrian Lomax

"Crushing the Code," *The Humanist*, January/February 1988.

Peter L. Nacci and
Thomas R. Kane

"The Incidence of Sex and Sexual Aggression in Federal Prisons," *Federal Probation*, December 1983.

Anne Farrer Scott

"The Workhouse Was Strangely Like My Grade School," *The New York Times*, November 22, 1984.

Bert Useem

"Disorganization and the New Mexico Prison Riot of 1980," *American Sociological Review*, October 1985.

How Can Prison Overcrowding Be Reduced?

AMERICA'S PRISONS

Chapter Preface

Prison overcrowding is one of the gravest problems facing the American criminal justice system today. While many people are unconcerned about the damaging effects of overcrowding on prisoners, the problem becomes important to them when overcrowding forces prisons to grant early release to violent criminals who all too often resume their brutal victimization of society.

For instance, according to an *Orlando Sentinel* report on Florida's early-release program, from February 1987 to March 1989, 25 percent of prisoners released early were rearrested. A total of 2,180 offenses were committed by these criminals, including eleven murders or attempted murders. The *Sentinel* stated, "[These] inmates don't need to work for [early release] or to perform heroic deeds. They get it simply because they are in a prison system that is forbidden by federal court order from crowding cells."

When one goes beyond the figures, however, to look at the victims of prison overcrowding, the seriousness of the problem becomes even more apparent. Consider the case of Wayne Lamarr Harvey, who was originally convicted in Michigan of two second-degree murders in 1975 and received a twenty- to forty-year prison sentence. When he entered prison, Harvey was automatically granted nine-and-a-half years of "good-time" credits, which he was allowed to keep despite several major infractions of the prison rules. He later received an additional two years off under Michigan's 1980 "Prison Overcrowding Emergency Powers Act." Harvey was paroled to a half-way house in July 1984 after serving only eight-and-a-half years in prison. In October of that same year, Harvey and an accomplice killed two people, a young woman and an East Lansing police officer who was the father of six children.

While Americans are outraged about crimes like these, they disagree vehemently over how to solve the problem of prison overcrowding. The response of many observers, including Dana C. Joel, a research associate at the Heritage Foundation, is to relieve prison overcrowding by building more prisons. On the other hand, commentators like Marc Mauer, the assistant director of the Sentencing Project, suggest that prison space be reserved exclusively for violent criminals like Wayne Harvey, and alternative punishments be developed for non-violent offenders.

The authors in the following chapter debate prison overcrowding and offer a variety of solutions to the problem.

"New construction is critical to meeting the overcrowding dilemma."

Building More Prisons Will Solve Prison Overcrowding

J. Michael Quinlan

J. Michael Quinlan is the director of the Federal Bureau of Prisons, established in 1930 to develop and oversee the federal prison system. The following viewpoint is taken from Quinlan's testimony before a U.S. House of Representatives subcommittee examining overcrowding in the federal prison system. Quinlan contends that the federal prison system must expand its capacity if it is to deal with increased overcrowding. While building new institutions is central to this expansion, Quinlan also advocates a number of additional related measures designed to reduce overcrowding.

As you read, consider the following questions:

1. What factors are responsible for the increased growth in the federal inmate population, according to Quinlan?
2. What other measures does Quinlan suggest for increasing the capacity of the federal prison system to house inmates?

J. Michael Quinlan, statement before the Subcommittee on Courts, Intellectual Property, and the Administration of Justice of the Committee on the Judiciary of the U.S. House of Representatives, July 27, 1989. Public domain.

These are challenging and difficult times for the Nation's criminal justice system and in particular America's prisons. As a whole, correctional institutions in the U.S. in 1989 held about twice as many inmates as they did in 1980, and that proportion of growth has been paralleled in the Federal Bureau of Prisons as well. The Bureau's population as of July 18, 1989, was 49,418 —an all-time high. With a design capacity of 31,091 beds in 58 locations, this equates to an overcrowding rate of 159% of capacity.

Prison overcrowding, if not properly managed, endangers internal institutional security, places staff and inmates in environmentally unsafe, potentially life-threatening conditions, and jeopardizes public safety. It also invites court intervention, and indeed many State correctional systems are under some type of court order or other intervention for overcrowding or conditions of confinement.

[The Federal Bureau of Prisons] projects that the Federal inmate population will increase by at least 70% between 1989 and 1995. The Bureau has in years past used conservative population projection models, in order to avoid over-building. However, the projected level of growth is virtually assured, spurred by new legislation, heightened enforcement and prosecution initiatives, and changes flowing from the implementation of the Sentencing Guidelines. Even if increased enforcement activity were not a factor, longer sentences and elimination of statutory good time and parole are important variables that clearly portend significantly increased average length of time served. . . .

New Construction Needed to Relieve Overcrowding

To meet these future needs, the Bureau of Prisons is aggressively pursuing all practical construction options to reduce overcrowding. In calendar year 1988, about 2,100 beds were brought on-line; six new facilities (including camps) were activated, as well as many other small construction or renovation projects which incrementally increased the capacity of existing Bureau facilities. The Bureau currently has 12,000 beds funded and under design or construction; 11 major facility construction projects are either underway or planned. These are part of a long-range expansion program that the Bureau has developed in response to continued, rapid inmate population growth. . . .

The Bureau of Prisons already confines offenders less expensively than the national average—$14,000 per year versus $16,000. But to further reduce new prison construction costs as well as future operating expenses, the Bureau is planning several prison design changes. For example, complexes of several correctional facilities of different security levels (e.g., a maximum security U.S. Penitentiary, a medium security Federal Correctional Institution, and a minimum security Federal Prison

Camp) will be constructed at one site. Core facilities of institutions now on the drawing board are larger, in order to accommodate higher base populations, and we are pursuing internal design changes that will increase institutional capacities. These include modestly increasing cell size and initially designing two-thirds of the prison's cells for two inmates each.

Increase Prison Space Now

It is time for Congress to acknowledge that a crime emergency exists—that there is a steadily rising crime rate coupled with an acute shortage of prison space at both the federal and state levels. Instead of passively allowing the courts to shift the burden from the prisons back to the streets, lawmakers need to take decisive action to provide more prison space as quickly and economically as possible.

Dana C. Joel, The Heritage Foundation *Backgrounder*, November 15, 1989.

Cost considerations are important in this era of legitimate budget concerns, and will be even more critical in the future as the Bureau seeks funding to support operational costs that our present construction program will be creating. Over the typical life cycle of an institution, construction costs are usually only 5-7% of the total expense. This means that from 15-20 times the construction costs will have to be budgeted over the life of each prison now being built, for its actual operation. This will be a significant factor in future budget planning. Therefore, in designing our facilities, we always emphasize the ability of the design to facilitate inmate supervision by staff in the most cost-effective manner. If not designed correctly, the extra personnel costs of a prison can be extremely high, far outweighing any initial advantage in construction costs that a more staff-intensive design might have. I might add that the Bureau's use of the "correctional worker" concept, where all staff are trained and have as their first priority the security of the institution, enables fewer overall staff to supervise a given inmate population. This philosophy and more efficient designs have resulted in a relatively low staffing cost in Federal prisons; the average inmate-to-officer ratio for all U.S. prisons is 5:1, but in contrast, that of the Bureau is 9:1. This is in large part due to the Bureau's reliance on all employees for performing important security functions that in many State systems are performed only by security staff.

Concerns about the dollar expenditures for today's prison construction are legitimate. However, the secondary use of prison facilities is an idea that can and should be discussed. Just as the

114

Federal Correctional Institution in Ray Brook, NY was built for dual service, first as an Olympic housing area and then as a prison, today's prisons can some day be used for non-prison purposes. Should demographic and crime trends abate in the future, then the institutions constructed today are fully capable of conversion to local community facilities, such as convalescent homes, vocational training schools or other civic purposes.

Other Ways to Increase Capacity

New construction is critical to meeting the overcrowding dilemma, but it is not the only answer. A multifaceted approach is going to be vital in meeting the Nation's correctional needs in coming years. Additional bedspace must be found through the use of suitable surplus military bases, deactivated colleges and hospitals, and other locations. The Bureau has recently converted former school properties in Yankton, SD; Bryan, TX; and a seminary in Loretto, PA.

Military base conversions are a particularly timely, appropriate, and cost-effective strategy for housing some low security inmates, and the Bureau is actively interested in any suitable land or facilities which may be available through the Base Closure and Realignment Act. In addition to screening suitable bases as they become available, we will continue to review the possibilities of locating additional minimum security prison camps on active military bases, such as those already in operation at Eglin AFB, FL; Maxwell AFB, AL; and others.

Other promising expansion strategies include lease options, continued use of private contractors for selected programs, and full-scale privatization of institutional operations for confining special populations. One such possibility is the full privatization of a convalesence facility. Overall, we believe the Bureau can provide as cost-effective an operation in traditional institutional settings, but our costs may exceed those of the private sector for small, specialized populations.

The Bureau has found over the years that community acceptance is a critical part of the process of locating new prison sites, whether on military bases, or when acquiring private or other public lands. For that reason, the Bureau has operated a well-developed site acquisition and public information program for a number of years, and we will be bringing additional resources to bear in this important area, so that we can locate and secure the additional sites needed in the 1990s.

While construction and other site acquisition activities are important in reducing the future impact of overcrowding, from an operational standpoint, employment, and particularly industrial jobs, is the key factor in combatting the adverse impact of overcrowding in prison. Federal Prison Industries is a wholly-owned Government corporation whose mission is to employ inmates and provide training opportunities for offenders. However, to avoid adverse impact on any single part of the private manufacturing sector, UNICOR [the trade name of Federal Prison Industries] provides an intentionally diversified range of products and services, all of which are manufactured under conditions which conform with OSHA [Occupational Safety and Health Administration] regulations; UNlCOR's products themselves thoroughly conform with industry quality standards. UNICOR presently employs about 40% of all qualified Federal inmates. This factor is considered to be one of the major, positive, distinguishing features between most State correctional systems and the Federal system, enabling us to successfully manage severe overcrowding.

Other Initiatives

Other important initiatives will be necessary if overcrowding is to be stemmed without even more construction. The Community Correctional Center concept is one which the Bureau is expanding. These are community institutions that provide more stringent sanctions and higher levels of supervision than found in ordinary community treatment facilities, but still short of the traditional prison setting.

Quick and Inexpensive Construction

If criminals are to receive swift and certain penalties, more prisons need to be built. And while state spending rose faster for prisons than for any other major program in the 1980s, construction has not kept pace with the influx of prisoners. . . .

Yet, there are quick, inexpensive ways to obtain badly needed prison space. For example, existing facilities, such as closed military bases and vacant dormitories, can be used to hold nonviolent offenders, thereby freeing prisons for inmates convicted of violent crimes. Many states, and to a lesser extent the federal government, are exploring ways to convert existing buildings to prison use and to use innovative short-term solutions.

Dana C. Joel, The Heritage Foundation *Backgrounder*, November 15, 1989.

Yet another is the home confinement and electronic monitoring programs, which are now coming into increasing use nationwide. These programs use computer technology to enable better supervision of suitable non-violent offenders at a far lower cost than traditional confinement or even halfway house programming. I envision the time will come when these programs will supplant a large proportion of our current reliance on community treatment centers.

The creative use of fines and other financial sanctions can also be considered a realistic option in some cases. Expansion of this sanction can even be tied in with the "day fine" concept, in which inmates pay fines that are linked to their actual earning power by some mathematical formula. But even the existing fine options which the courts have can be expanded, and the Bureau's Inmate Financial Responsibility Program is a model for collection of debts of this type. In the past, collection of fines from committed offenders was a relatively low priority activity because their assets were few and earning power relatively low. This program motivates inmates through institutional incentives to pay fines, court costs, and other obligations while incarcerated, using industrial earnings and outside monetary resources. It is managed in conjunction with the Executive Office of the U.S. Attorneys, began as a pilot in 1987, and at present is generating collections of about one million dollars a month from incarcerated inmates. There is no reason why it could not be adapted by other agencies, so that the courts can rely more on fine options, particularly for those offenders in Bureau custody. . . .

These are challenging times for America's criminal justice system and its correctional component. Overcrowding, a surge of serious drug offenders, and major changes in the demographics of our Nation make sound, professionally managed prisons more important than ever.

"Building new prisons will solve neither the crime problem nor the overcrowding problem."

Building More Prisons Will Not Solve Prison Overcrowding

Christopher Baird

Christopher Baird is a senior vice president of the National Council on Crime and Delinquency (NCCD), an organization of criminologists and others interested in crime prevention. Baird, like J. Michael Quinlan in the preceding viewpoint, testified before the U.S. House of Representatives subcommittee examining overcrowding in the federal prison system. However, Baird disagrees with Quinlan's argument that expanding prison capacity will solve prison overcrowding. Instead, Baird's solution for prison overcrowding is to punish nonviolent offenders using alternatives such as intensive probation, electronic monitoring, and community service.

As you read, consider the following questions:

1. According to the author, how do the problems faced by California and Michigan demonstrate the futility of building more prisons to reduce overcrowding in the federal prison system?
2. What are the advantages of Baird's solution to prison overcrowding?

Christopher Baird, statement before the Subcommittee on Courts, Intellectual Property, and the Administration of Justice of the Committee on the Judiciary of the U.S. House of Representatives, September 27, 1989. Public domain.

Throughout the nation, prison systems are experiencing a crisis of unprecedented proportions. The nation's rate of imprisonment is growing at an alarming rate having more than doubled between 1979 and 1989. As a result, expenditures on prison construction and operations are consuming an ever increasing share of state and federal revenues. Projections of future prison populations are even more ominous. Fueled by the War on Drugs and increasingly punitive legislation, many systems, including the Federal Bureau of Prisons, are facing growth rates that exceed the phenomenal expansion recorded over the last decade. In 1987, before the War on Drugs was even declared, the General Accounting Office (GAO) estimated that the number of federal inmates could quadruple by 2002.

Increased Incarceration Won't Reduce Crime

Yet this trend toward increased incarceration has had no perceivable impact on crime rates. Indeed, comparisons of very different incarceration policies among the 50 states indicates there is little relationship between crime and rates of imprisonment. *Clearly, increasing the use of incarceration has not and will not solve the crime problem.* Greater reliance on stringent community-based sanctions is a tough and smart response to street crime. We must disengage ourselves from policies that result in the mere warehousing of hundreds of thousands of individuals while failing to reduce the nation's crime rate.

Despite the necessity to implement viable alternatives to incarceration, many states have been willing to continue to pour more resources into prisons. A few jurisdictions, most notably California and Michigan, have adopted strategies comprised almost entirely of new prison construction and have clearly stated objectives calling for incarceration of more offenders for longer periods of time. Proponents claim that this is the best method for ensuring public safety as it incapacitates known criminals and serves as a deterrent to would-be offenders. However, this theory and reality are at odds. There now exist enough data to conclusively state that this approach is both inordinately expensive and ineffective. It is clear that judicious use of recent research findings coupled with advancements in technology could free corrections from its narrow range of options and result in a more effective and less expensive system of punishment and control.

A review of current correctional practices reveals that corrections is encumbered by misconceptions and the public's understandable frustration with career criminals and violent criminal activity. Facts regarding the relationship between crime and incarceration have little influence on practice. However, circumstances have now evolved to the point where correctional policy must change and change dramatically. To continue along the present course will result in the decimation of other social programs needed to educate children, care for the elderly, and conserve our natural resources. Adding to this tragedy is that despite enormous expenditures on prison construction and operations, prisons are likely to be as overcrowded and the public as vulnerable to crime in the year 2000 as it is today.

Chuck Asay, by permission of the *Colorado Springs Gazette-Telegraph.*

What is wrong with current practice; why are parole failure rates increasing at the same time that more offenders are going to prison and staying for longer periods of time? First, there is a clear need for additional structure in decision making. Many recent studies have all reached the same conclusion: criminal justice decisions are inconsistent, inappropriate, or both. Variance in sentences handed out cannot be explained by the offense committed, prior criminal record, employment, substance abuse or any other factor remotely relevant to sanctioning. As a result, offenders are frequently placed in the wrong programs; a fact that diminishes corrections' ability to optimize the use of resources, and fails to adequately protect the public. The problems noted in sentencing are equally evident in the parole and revocation decision processes as well.

The Federal System, to its credit, attempted to alleviate the problems of lack of consistency and equity with the development of sentencing guidelines. However, unlike the Minnesota experience, where guidelines have clearly limited the use of prison sanctions and controlled the growth of the prison system, the Federal Guidelines exacerbated the problem. They instituted a sentencing policy far more punitive than past sentencing practice, despite the fact that Congress directed the Commission to consider the capacity of the federal prison system and formulate guidelines that "minimize the likelihood that the Federal prison population will exceed the capacity of the Federal prisons..." Clearly, this did not occur.

Secondly, and most importantly, there is the widely held and mistaken perception that sending more offenders to prison enhances public safety. As a result, the average property offender committed to prison in the U.S. stays approximately 18 months in an overcrowded facility and is released to community supervision that requires, at best, two contacts with the parole agent per month. The typical *maximum* supervision case on probation or parole throughout the nation receives an average of less than three hours total supervision each month, even in the best parole systems in the country. Several states, such as Florida, offer no parole supervision following release from prison.

Nationwide, the vast majority of all offenders eventually return to the community, most within three years. They emerge from overcrowded prisons, often after receiving inadequate programming which does not improve vocational and academic skills or deal with serious substance abuse problems. Once released, they receive little or no supervision in the community. Present policies, if pursued, will pump billions of dollars into corrections only to enlarge the system rather than improve it.

Experience Shows Building New Prisons Is Futile

The fact is building new prisons will solve neither the crime problem nor the overcrowding problem. Consider the following data from two states that have attempted to "outbuild the problem", California and Michigan.

- In 1978 there were 21,325 inmates in California prisons; in 1988, more than 71,000. By 1993, 100,000 inmates are predicted. Only 10% of this growth is attributed to demographic factors.
- The Corrections' budget in California is growing twice as fast as the state budget and four times as fast as the prison population. It was $300 million in 1982; $1.3 billion in 1988.
- Since June of 1984, fifteen new institutions have been opened; 19,000 beds have been constructed and 12,000 are either under construction or authorized. The cost has been $2.6 billion. *Still, in May of 1988, prisons were operating at 157% of capacity.*
- A similar pattern emerges in Michigan, another jurisdiction with a stated policy to outbuild the crowding problem. Michigan

has added 9,691 cells since 1985 (with another 9,000 planned), yet the crime rate has remained relatively unchanged.

• Corrections now consumes 7% of total Michigan revenues, while corrections' spending has increased 321% over the last decade, social services received only 98% increase and education a 40% increase.

There are better answers. Public safety can be increased significantly, while the cost of corrections is reduced. What follows is a strategy for changing corrections in the United States. It is based on the premise that the primary function of corrections is to promote public safety. As such, it relies on the best corrections practices and is supported by results of innovative community-based programs from all over the country.

A Different Path

Before discussing how the nation can disengage itself from a policy of massive prison construction, it is necessary to present what has been learned in the recent years. Some jurisdictions have been in a state of crisis for over a decade. Forced to deal with huge increases in admissions coupled with longer sentences, often while under court-imposed prison capacity limits, these jurisdictions have initiated large scale programs to serve as alternatives to incarceration. These programs use levels of control never before attempted in the community. In many cases, daily case contacts are augmented by electronic surveillance, frequent drug testing, curfew, work and program requirements, community service and victim restitution payments. In some of the most promising approaches, offenders are not on probation or parole status, but simply inmates living under house arrest in the community. This provides corrections' officials with the power to return cases to prison immediately when even minor violations occur. Thus, staff can take action before misbehavior escalates into a new offense. The fact that violations have immediate and severe consequences brings accountability to a community corrections system often criticized for lacking "teeth". Intensive supervision and house arrest programs operate from Florida to New Jersey, Oklahoma to Oregon. Evaluations consistently show these programs produce positive results, often significantly reducing recidivism when compared to more traditional approaches.

These programs are expensive, but the costs pale beside those of prison construction and operation. Caseloads are kept small (nearly always 20 or under, sometimes as low as 10), and contact requirements are high. Electronic monitoring, urinalysis and other staff support requirements add to the overall costs of the program, but offer a degree of control that clearly enhances public safety. The highly publicized case of a pedophile on parole in my hometown of Madison, Wisconsin, provides the perfect illustration of the monitoring capabilities of intensive supervision. Devoting the necessary time to a single case, the high risk intensive supervision team was able to quickly ascertain when conditions of parole were violated (contact with children) and return the offender to prison before a new offense was committed. This case was not an isolated instance of success. A recent evaluation comparing outcomes of cases on intensive supervision with similar cases on regular supervision in Wisconsin concluded that intensively supervised cases committed fewer new offenses than the reference sample.

These programs offer punishment in the form of home confinement, fines and fees, victim restitution and community service while availing offenders of community-based substance abuse and vocational programs that are generally superior to those available in prison. And because offenders work to support themselves and their families, the public is relieved of the additional economic costs associated with incarceration.

In summary, these programs are producing positive results at a lower cost to taxpayers. Expanding their use in a systematic fashion, combining elements of punishment and rehabilitation, will save the U.S. citizens millions of dollars and produce a safer society.

The following strategy, if implemented in its entirety, would sharply reduce the nation's need for prison bed space. At the same time, it represents a real "get tough" approach to crime, stressing public protection, offender accountability and restitution to the community and to victims of crime. It will result in a less expensive, but more effective system of corrections.

Focus on the Nonviolent Offender

The focus of the plan is the non-assaultive offender—burglars, car thieves, check forgers, etc. In 1986, property offenders comprised 25% of all court commitments while drug offenders accounted for about 35% of new admissions to the Federal Bureau of Prisons. These offenders stayed in prison for over 18 months on average, yet prison has proven particularly ineffective for this group. After release they reoffend at higher rates than any other offender cohort. Simply put, keeping someone guilty of burglary, fraud or drug use offenses in prison for 18 months or more, and then releasing him to regular parole supervision has not produced the degree of community safety the public expects.

Consider the following alternative: non-assaultive offenders serve a significantly shorter time in prison; an average of six months—and then are placed in highly structured community-based house arrest programs, still under inmate status. During the prison stay, intensive programming is provided to break the cycle of substance abuse, lack of skills and unemployment. In the community, movement outside the home is restricted to necessary activities—basically employment and mandated program participation—and all activities are carefully monitored on a daily basis. Drug tests are administered on frequent randomly scheduled intervals. Restitution and community service are required of offenders. Violation of rules are not tolerated and a continuum of progressively restrictive sanctions (including return to prison) assures immediate consequences.

Construction Is Not a Panacea for Overcrowding

Expansion of prison capacity through construction is a common approach taken to alleviate prison crowding. . . .

Prison construction is not, however, a panacea to the crowding problem. . . . A prison normally takes several years to construct. It is nearly impossible for prison construction to keep pace with the growth in population. Although many states have undertaken massive construction programs, the gap between population and capacity is widening. From 1972 to 1977, over 23,000 beds were added nationwide, however population increased by 81,000. From 1978 to 1980, 7,000 beds were added, and population increased by 61,000 inmates. In 1981, 21,000 beds were added, and population grew by 39,000.

Sandra Evans Skovron, *Controversial Issues in Crime and Justice*, 1988.

Because the costs of this approach are well below that of prison, high quality programs could be purchased to help offenders overcome problems and deficits, further increasing their likelihood of successful reintegration into the community.

In sum, this approach offers the following advantages over current practice: 1) a level of community control not feasible when billions of dollars are devoted to prison construction and operation; 2) meaningful services to provide the opportunity for rehabilitation; 3) a greater emphasis on offender accountability and restitution to victims and the community; and 4) assurance that prison space is available for offenders convicted of assaultive offenses. . . .

In essence, greater reliance on stringent community-based sanctions allows us to get tough and smart at the same time. We must get out of the situation that results in the mere warehousing of hundreds of thousands of individuals while failing to reduce the nation's crime rate and the suffering it causes. As former Chief Justice Warren E. Burger noted in 1980, "To put people behind walls and bars and do nothing to change them is to win a battle but lose a war. It is wrong. It is expensive. It is stupid."

> *"Jails require extraordinary resources and services, but they are a necessity and worth the expenditure."*

Building More Jails Can Solve Jail Overcrowding

Robert L. Scharf

Jails differ from prisons in that they are usually run by local governments and hold people awaiting trial, serving relatively short sentences, or awaiting transfer to state prisons. Many prison-bound offenders are held in jails when prisons are overcrowded. In the following viewpoint, Robert L. Scharf argues that the solution to the problem of jail overcrowding is simply to build more jails. Scharf was a deputy city attorney in the Los Angeles City Attorney's Office for twelve years until his retirement in 1984. He served with the FBI (Federal Bureau of Investigation) for thirty-three years prior to his tenure at the city attorney's office.

As you read, consider the following questions:

1. According to Scharf, what was the solution to jail overcrowding in eighteenth and nineteenth century England?
2. How serious is the jail overcrowding problem in Los Angeles, according to the author?
3. Why does Scharf reject the development of alternatives to jail?

From "No Space for Prisoners," by Robert L. Scharf, *Los Angeles Lawyer*, September 1989. Reprinted by permission of the Los Angeles County Bar Association.

Jail congestion, a popular topic today, is not a new problem. It existed in eighteenth century England where about half the English jails were privately owned and operated by jailer-landlords who profited by extorting money from their prisoners. Wealthy inmates led a life of relative ease. Poor prisoners who could not afford food and drink were less fortunate. The prison taproom dispensing gin was a prime source of income for jailers.

However, even then there was insufficient jail space. Crime was rampant. It was estimated that in 1797 one of eight Londoners lived by criminal pursuits.

In an effort to solve jail overcrowding, an unusual practice was initiated. Prisoners were shipped to Australia, a far-off, desolate, uncrowded continent where there was lots of space—and little else.

On May 13, 1787, the "first fleet" departed from Portsmouth, England, carrying 736 convicts consisting of men, women and a few children. No murderers or rapists were in the group which was composed mainly of persons found guilty of thefts or robberies.

The fleet arrived in Australia 252 days later. Forty convicts failed to serve their terms; they died while en route.

Between May 1787 and the final shipment of prisoners in 1868, approximately 160,000 convicts were sent to Australia.

Jail overcrowding continues to plague society today in the United States. The problem can no longer be corrected by sending convicts to a sparsely populated continent as the English did many years ago. There are, of course, vast areas of unoccupied space on the moon which could be utilized—but that would be cruel and unusual punishment! Building new jails here is a much more acceptable solution.

Jail Overcrowding Getting Worse

U.S. Department of Justice statistics show that in mid-1987 local jails throughout the country held an estimated 295,873 persons, 8 percent more than the previous year. Jail occupancy was 98 percent of full capacity. The average daily jail population for one year ending June 30, 1987, had increased 28 percent since 1983.

The situation in Los Angeles County is particularly acute. The county has 10 jails, including two for women. By federal court order, no more than 22,000 prisoners can be kept in those 10 jails, which are operated by the Los Angeles County Sheriff's Department under Sheriff Sherman Block.

The 10 jails were originally built to hold 13,464 inmates, according to Assistant Sheriff Richard Foreman. They now hold 22,000, including 2,700 women.

To comply with the federal court's order, since May 24, 1988, convicted misdemeanants whose bail is set at less than $5,000 are not accepted for incarceration in Los Angeles County jails. Sentence-shortening procedures for other convicted misdemeanants are also in place to ameliorate the jail-overcrowding problem. The overall result of these efforts is that 110,000 persons convicted of non-violent misdemeanors have either not served any time in jail or at the most one day.

A Question of Will

The criminal huggers might ask, "Williams, our jails are overcrowded; where are we going to put the criminals?" Fly across our country and you'll see plenty of space. Besides, the United States has territorial possessions in the Pacific that can be made to alleviate our jail overcrowding. We lack the will, not the space.

Walter Williams, *The Washington Times*, October 29, 1990.

Currently, when a misdemeanant is sentenced to jail for a period of up to 37 days or, in the alternative, to pay a fine, the knowledgeable violator usually will select a jail term knowing that he or she will serve no more than one day.

One suggested solution to jail overcrowding is to place convicted misdemeanants under a type of house arrest where they are confined to their residences. Foreman said that under current law, misdemeanants who refuse to remain in their residences could not be charged with escape but would merely be sent to jail with no added punishment.

While these programs may be necessary in the short run, the real issue is public safety—and that means making sure that criminals are effectively separated from society. Alternatives to jail do not provide the protection that incarceration guarantees. Jails require extraordinary resources and services, but they are a necessity and worth the expenditure.

Foreman said that in 1995 space will be needed to hold an estimated 32,000 prisoners (including 4,000 women) in Los Angeles County jails. By the year 2000 space for 34,000 inmates will be needed.

Related Problems

The problem of an ever-increasing number of prisoners is exacerbated by the additional task of transporting them on round trips between jails and courts five days a week. More than 2,000 make that trip daily. While in the courthouses, they are kept in crowded lockups, often waiting 10 hours before making a brief court appearance.

While in jail the prisoners are visited by family members and friends. Gang members, whose street-wise know-how has temporarily kept them out of custody, visit fellow delinquents. Jail visitors have been arrested for possession of drugs and/or weapons. Custodial personnel must remain constantly alert for escape attempts or evidence of smoldering turbulence that can erupt into brawls. . . .

State Prisons Also Overburdened

State prisons are also affected by overcrowding as the following statistics indicate. Los Angeles County Criminal Courts Presiding Judge David Horowitz reported that in 1982-83 there were 37,975 felony complaints filed by the Los Angeles County District Attorney's Office. In 1987-88 that number rose to 60,558.

Judge Horowitz noted that 163,377 misdemeanor cases were filed by the district attorney's office in 1982-83, with that figure jumping to 227,676 in 1987-88. The Los Angeles City Attorney's Office filed 116,744 misdemeanor cases in 1981-82 and 130,782 in 1986-87.

Michael P. Judge, bureau chief of Central Court Operations in the Los Angeles County Public Defender's Office, states that his office handles about 450,000 felony and misdemeanor cases a year. About 40 percent of convicted felons go to state prisons. About 40 to 45 percent go to county jails. . . .

F. Bentley Mooney, Jr., president of the Lawyers' Club of Los Angeles County, speaks for many when he says that the safety of law-abiding citizens depends in large part on society's ability to keep in custody those whose activities might threaten any of us. His viewpoint is difficult to challenge.

"Building more jails is the most expensive and least effective way to eliminate overcrowded jails."

Building More Jails Cannot Solve Jail Overcrowding

Barbara Flicker

In the following viewpoint, Barbara Flicker argues that building more jails will not solve the problem of jail overcrowding, primarily because the nation's jails cannot possibly accommodate the flood of offenders arrested in the war on drugs. Instead, she contends, communities must begin to tackle the underlying causes of crime, develop alternative punishments to incarceration, and use existing jail space more efficiently. Flicker is the consulting director of the Institute of Judicial Administration at New York University and the chair of the Overcrowded Jails Committee of the American Bar Association Judicial Administration Division Lawyers Conference.

As you read, consider the following questions:

1. What examples does Flicker provide to demonstrate the severity of the jail overcrowding crisis?
2. According to the author, what was the experience of Jefferson Parish, Louisiana, after it abandoned its strategy of building more jails to relieve jail overcrowding?
3. How would Flicker relieve jail overcrowding?

From "To Jail or Not to Jail," by Barbara Flicker. Reprinted with permission from the February 1990 *ABA Journal*, The Lawyer's Magazine, published by the American Bar Association.

The premise underlying the public attitude toward criminal justice seems to be, "Better to lock up 100 innocent men than to let one guilty man go free." Governed by that standard, the benchmark for overcrowded jails and prisons rises yearly.

The Crisis of Jail Overcrowding

But by acting as if jailing suspects will solve the problem of crime in America—particularly drug-related crime—we have elevated the consequent jail problem to what amounts to crisis proportion nationwide.

Consider:

• William J. Bennett, former director of the Bush administration's National Drug Control Policy, announced in April 1989 an $80 million federal initiative to combat drug-related crimes in Washington, D.C. An expanded drug task force, using federal intelligence and forensic experts, would track down drug offenders, while two new federal facilities—a 500-bed jail and a 700-bed prison—would be built for the Washington-Baltimore area.

The plan also authorized the immediate transfer of 250 inmates from the District of Columbia jail to federal prisons, but D.C. officials later said they would need at least 1,500 additional beds. Less than a week later, the plan to build the 700-bed prison was dropped because of public resistance to the proposed site. . . .

• The New York City Commissioner of Corrections ordered his staff to prepare contingency plans for the early release of inmates from dangerously overcrowded city jails. Since some of the inmates targeted for early release are convicted drug offenders, the city will be releasing people convicted of crimes to make space available for people suspected of crimes.

• Los Angeles has responded to gang and drug violence with waves of arrests. In 1988 voters in California approved a state bond measure for $161.4 million for a new jail in Los Angeles County. A subsequent report by the county's chief administrative officer said the measure would not keep pace with inmate overcrowding and increasing court backlogs. . . .

Building and operating jails is expensive, with costs rising almost as rapidly as hospital care. According to an editorial in The New York Times on April 17, 1989, it costs $14,750 to detain a typical drug suspect from indictment to sentencing.

Today, widespread drug busts and the connection between drug abuse and other crime have produced an endless cycle: drug abuse, drug trafficking and other crimes, arrest, jail, and then, again, drug abuse. We need jail and prison cells for the overflow of violent and dangerous criminals.

Yet many believe, there are other, better ways to deal with the drug problem and to stop the cycle.

While community attitudes favor arrest and confinement, they contrast sharply with expert opinion that recommends developing other strategies for crime control. The threat of the collapse of the criminal justice system has inspired tough-minded public officials, judges and lawyers to explore innovative approaches to solving the problem of overcrowded jails.

Lack of Leadership in Controlling Jail Overcrowding

Unfortunately, criminal justice personnel who could provide the leadership to deal with the problem either ignore or do not realize that overcrowding can be controlled. City and county officials depend on jail administrators and sheriffs to present them with an accurate analysis of their needs regarding jail maintenance and construction. The common answer of the criminal justice personnel is to deal with overcrowding by expanding the available bed space. This myopic response has resulted in an incredible increase in the jail system.

Robert L. Marsh and Dana J. Marsh, *Journal of Contemporary Criminal Justice*, May 1990.

During the 1970s, to develop a more comprehensive approach to the jail problem, the Justice Department, through its Law Enforcement Assistance Administration (LEAA), established Criminal Justice Coordinating Councils (CJCCs). These were the local planning agencies. The LEAA Jail Overcrowding Programs required the creation of local jail-population management boards as a prerequisite to funding.

In "Alleviating Jail Crowding: A Systems Perspective," author Andy Hall of the Pretrial Services Resource Center cited the final report of the Jail Overcrowding Program in recommending collective planning to control jail population. This means that everyone connected with the jail must participate, from the sheriff to the director of the county data-processing service.

For example, in New York City a CJCC functioned as a city planning agency in the 1970s until it lost its funding when the Reagan administration dismantled LEAA. The city now has a criminal-justice coordinator appointed by the mayor to negotiate among the agencies involved in the justice system.

However, while borough CJCCs meet periodically, the results are negligible because the members have little clout (or discretionary funds) to implement their decisions.

The Jefferson Parish Experience

But jurisdictions that have empowered their CJCCs to deal with systemwide problems have found that they work—as in Jefferson Parish, La., a suburb of New Orleans, population

476,000. Its jail problems are a microcosm of the national phenomenon of the past two decades. According to the Bureau of Justice, Jefferson Parish is one of the 361 jurisdictions with at least 100 jail inmates, one of the 23 percent under court order to limit population, and one of the 27 percent ordered to improve one or more conditions of confinement.

Jefferson Parish followed the same path as other communities throughout the 1970s in trying to reduce overcrowding by building more jail space. In 1982, it formed a jail-overcrowding advisory committee and began an organized assault on its jail problems.

The linchpin of its system-oriented response is its CJCC director, John V. Baiamonte Jr. In "The Need for a Systemic Policy Approach to Jail Overcrowding: A Case Study of Jefferson Parish, Louisiana, 1971-1987," Baiamonte details his community's experience—which began with the filing of a lawsuit challenging the local jail system.

Battling Jail Overcrowding

Under a 1976 federal court order in *Holland v. Donelon*, the jail capacity and type of offenders subject to confinement were restricted. The parish responded predictably by building a new jail. Two months after the new facility was opened in 1978, the old parish jail had to be reopened because of overcrowding.

According to Baiamonte: "After battling with jail overcrowding since May 1971 in an uncoordinated manner . . . the local criminal justice officials . . . finally recognized in June 1982, that the only solution to this perennial problem was a systemic planning and policy development approach."

The original advisory committee was absorbed into an executive committee of the Jefferson Parish CJCC, which is composed of the district attorney, who is its chair as well as CJCC chair, the sheriff; the chief of police; the clerk of the court; the council chairman; the parish president; three judges; and a member of the Indigent Defender Board.

The CJCC 1988 annual report shows the results of abandoning the popular strategy of building more jails in favor of a formal planning process shared by the responsible criminal justice officials. Its executive committee maintained the average daily population at a bare 2.7 percent increase over 1987, producing an incidental saving of nearly $50,000 in reduced inmate-feeding costs.

The annual report states: "[T]he Committee has established a policy of giving the highest priority to 'jail cases' so that they may move quickly through the system. Additionally . . . focusing on those cases that could result in a probation sentence, thereby causing a case to exit from the Parish's correctional system into the State's probation system.

"Also, the Magistrate Court, related agencies and the CJCC staff have carefully conducted an early release of non-violent inmates who were near the end of their sentences.". . .

Overcrowding Reduction Strategies

Strategies to relieve jail overcrowding fall into four broad categories at the prearrest, post-arrest and post-conviction stages: 1) screening suspected and convicted criminals; 2) initiating delay-reduction measures; 3) developing alternative programs; and 4) expanding jail capacity.

The goal of screening mechanisms is to identify those who should be in jail and to release those who should not. . . .

The screening process operates at every stage. At intake, the most successful innovation has been the use of pretrial release services to collect pertinent information concerning the arrestees, evaluate their eligibility for conditional or unconditional release, and even to assist in arranging for bail, third-party bond, community custody or other prerequisite for release.

Screening by the prosecutor includes assessing the charges to decide whether the case should be pursued, the charges should be reduced or subject to plea bargaining, and the policies to apply to divert certain types of cases (DWI [driving while intoxicated,] misdemeanors, mentally disabled). Prosecutorial discretion is used to screen out people who do not belong in jail. . . .

These screening policies are most effective if they are part of a systematic process. Options to consider are:
• Unconditional release,
• Third-party custody,
• A treatment center,
• Bail,
• Intensive probation supervision,
• Electronic surveillance, or
• A work-release program. . . .

The next strategy used in reducing jail overcrowding is to reduce the time a person is held in jail. The systemwide approach coordinates the activities of the agencies at the various stages. Here, people record, monitor and report the time required to complete each stage and try to prevent undue delay caused by backlogs along the way.

Thus, a shortage of clerks, prosecutors, defenders, judges, pretrial release services or bondsmen, stenotypists, or probation officers can delay the case and compel longer jail time regardless of otherwise efficient actions and systems. . . .

Bricks and Mortar Are Not the Solution

The conventional wisdom now claims that building more jails is the most expensive and least effective way to eliminate overcrowded jails. In the 1970s correctional specialists recommended a moratorium on jail and prison construction to compel communities to develop other solutions.

There has been tentative movement toward privatization—delegating building and operating facilities to private industry—with the government paying the bills. As in most contracting-for-services arrangements between the public and private sectors, accountability, maintenance of standards, monitoring of compliance with the contract and relevant laws and regulations, coordination with criminal justice officials, and similar issues have arisen. While private construction of jails presents fewer problems than private operation, there are many obstacles, and several recent privatization experiments are being evaluated.

Use Alternatives to Reduce Jail Overcrowding

Jails usually hold two classes of inmates. Those sentenced to some form of county time and those awaiting trial. The inmate awaiting trial usually poses a high risk, and because of his pretrial status the administrator does not have any alternatives as far as quick releases go. Inmates doing county time are a different story, however. The overcrowding caused by these inmates is controllable to a degree by the presence of alternatives to incarceration programs. Electronic surveillance or home arrest, misdemeanor citation releases, video arraignments, work release programs, and some form of work alternative programs are examples.

Francis R. Ford, *American Jails*, Summer 1989.

Other experiments to expand jail space by converting barges, hospitals, schools, shelters for the homeless, boathouses, housing units, and shopping malls into cells have not been promising because of the difficulty in meeting minimum confinement standards.

Is society ready to pay the price for creating a class of millions of ex-inmates? The usual effect of institutionalization is exacerbated by often substandard living conditions in overcrowded jails. Some inmates are sleeping on stone floors and in gymnasiums and libraries.

Yet non-custodial arrangements for suspected criminals before conviction and for criminals convicted of less serious offenses are achievable. Community-based options cost far less and involve little risk with proper screening and monitoring.

We still have a choice. We can continue to fill our jails. Or we can begin to work as a community to find new approaches to the problems of drugs and crime and violence.

"If [legislators] want to incarcerate more offenders for longer periods of time, then they have to pay the cost of incarcerating more offenders for longer periods of time."

Responsible Lawmakers Can Reduce Prison Overcrowding

American Bar Association

In the following viewpoint, the American Bar Association (ABA) blames much of the problem of jail and prison overcrowding on state and federal legislators. The ABA argues that legislators have changed sentencing guidelines by increasing the lengths of most sentences and requiring a prison term for a wider range of crimes. The ABA contends that these changes have resulted in underfunded, crowded prisons. To alleviate these problems, the ABA insists that any sentencing reform that increases prison or jail populations should also be accompanied by legislation to increase funding or reduce prison populations. The ABA, one of the foremost legal organizations in the U.S., works to improve the civil and criminal justice systems and to increase public access to legal services.

As you read, consider the following questions:

1. According to the ABA, what problems arise when prisons and jails are overcrowded?
2. What does the ABA mean by a jail or prison impact statement?

"Report on Prison Overcrowding," submitted to the American Bar Association's House of Delegates by the ABA Criminal Justice Section, February 1990. Reprinted with permission.

In recent years, [according to the Federal Bureau of Prisons] the overcrowding in the nation's prisons and jails has been widely recognized as "the most critical problem in the field of corrections." By the end of 1988, 627,402 prisoners filled the federal and State prisons in this country, 90% more than were housed in those institutions in 1980. Thirty-two States, the District of Columbia, and the federal prison system were filled to or beyond their highest reported capacities. For example, at the end of 1988, the operating capacity of the federal prison system, which means the number of inmates that federal correctional facilities could handle based on the amount of staff, programs, and services available in the facilities, was 37,469 inmates. A total of 49,928 inmates were, however, actually housed in federal correctional institutions.

Many city and county jails were no less crowded. In 1987, 28% of 866 jurisdictions responding to a survey on jails reported having jails under court order to reduce overcrowding.

The Damage Caused by Overcrowding

The problems stemming from this overcrowding of our prisons and jails are innumerable. In 1989, thirty-five States, the District of Columbia, the Virgin Islands, and Puerto Rico were operating some or all of their prisons under court order because of unconstitutional conditions spawned largely by overcrowding. These problems include failure to attend to inmates' basic medical needs, grossly unsanitary living conditions, and pandemic violence.

One of the most consternating results of prison overcrowding is the attendant disruption of institutional work and educational programs. With too many inmates, too little space, and too few staff members, correctional officials have been unable to provide many inmates with the schooling and meaningful job training which might make it more likely that they would abandon a life of crime upon their release from prison.

Recreational opportunities for inmates have also been severely curtailed because of overcrowding. Gymnasiums and other rooms once used for recreation are now packed wall to wall with beds.

The idleness engendered by limited work, educational, and recreational opportunities has exacerbated the tension and frustration that attend institutional confinement. The end result has been rampant violence in the nation's prisons and jails with correctional staff as well as inmates being the victims of this violence. As evidenced by prison riots in recent years, overcrowding has made it increasingly difficult for correctional authorities to maintain even the semblance of control over their prisoners.

Responding to public pressures to "get tough with criminals," legislators have enacted laws which have contributed to the overcrowding problem. Mandatory sentencing laws, which require a period of incarceration as part of a criminal sanction, and laws extending the minimum and maximum jail or prison sentences that can be imposed as criminal penalties are examples of the types of laws being passed which are increasing the number of offenders entering the nation's penal institutions and the amount of time they will remain there.

Chuck Asay, by permission of the *Colorado Springs Gazette-Telegraph.*

Even assuming that these legislative measures are the appropriate way in which to respond to the problem of crime in this country, what is troublesome and alarming to most correctional authorities, is that the legislatures have frequently failed to appropriate the additional funds needed to implement these laws. Having passed laws to placate the public, the legislators have too often simply packed up their books, and their microphones, leaving to correctional authorities the intractable and dangerous job of caring for and supervising burgeoning numbers of prisoners without sufficient space, staff, or other resources.

The purpose of [the ABA] recommendations is to ensure that in the future, there is fiscal responsibility on the part of Congress and the State legislatures when enacting laws which will increase the size of prison or jail populations. Towards that end, the preparation of a prison or jail impact statement would be required whenever a legislature is considering proposed legislation which would increase the number of inmates housed in prisons or jails or the length of their confinement. The prison or jail impact statement would inform legislators of the costs which will be incurred if the proposed legislation is passed and no countervailing steps are taken to decrease the size of prison and jail populations. Having received this information, legislators could better determine whether enactment of the proposed legislation is advisable.

The recommendations go one step further towards ensuring fiscal accountability. Should Congress or a State legislature, after considering a prison or jail impact statement, decide in any event to pass legislation which would increase the number of inmates in the correctional system or the length of their terms of incarceration, Congress or the State legislatures would have to make sure that the resources are available to handle the larger prison or jail populations. If there is "fat" in the correctional department budget to pay for the extra space, staff, and other resources needed, there would be no problem. Otherwise, the legislature would have to either appropriate funds to cover the costs of the legislation or take counterbalancing steps to decrease the size of prison or jail populations. An example of such a step would be to decrease the minimum terms of incarceration for some types of nonviolent offenders if the legislature has decided to increase the minimum sentences of certain violent offenders.

Make Legislators Face Reality

Implementation of the proposed recommendations will at a minimum force legislators to recognize the elementary proposition that if they want to incarcerate more offenders for longer periods of time, then they have to pay the costs of incarcerating more offenders for longer periods of time. Perhaps in the long run, implementation of these recommendations will yield even greater benefits. Demanding fiscal accountability from legislators may help to forestall reflexive reactions to the serious crime problem in this country, and perhaps induce legislators to find more innovative and effective means of combatting crime and punishing criminal offenders.

6

VIEWPOINT

"[We must] oblige judges themselves to control the prison population level."

Increasing Judicial Responsibility Can Reduce Prison Overcrowding

Bruce L. Benson and Laurin A. Wollan Jr.

Bruce L. Benson is a professor of economics at Florida State University in Tallahassee, and Laurin A. Wollan Jr. is an associate professor in Florida State University's school of criminology. In the following viewpoint, Benson and Wollan argue that the solution to prison overcrowding is to assign each judge a certain amount of prison space. According to the authors, judges would have to carefully evaluate whether each defendant's crime actually merits a prison sentence. In effect, the authors conclude, judges would have to reserve prison space for dangerous criminals and find alternative punishments for nonviolent offenders.

As you read, consider the following questions:

1. Why do Benson and Wollan believe that building more prisons cannot solve America's overcrowding crisis?
2. How does the concept of the "commons" explain prison overcrowding, according to the authors?

Bruce L. Benson and Laurin A. Wollan Jr., "Prison Overcrowding and Judicial Incentives," *Madison Paper* no. 3, 1989, of the James Madison Institute for Public Policy Studies. Reprinted with permission.

The nation's jails and prisons are overcrowded. Nearly everyone has reacted by asking, "How can we build more prisons?" Thus, efforts to solve the prison overcrowding problem generally have focused on the supply side, or the amount of space for inmates.

Proposals abound that would increase the amount of space, or cells, to meet the number of convicts sentenced to prison. But the cost of prison construction and operation is high and the political support for spending on prisons and prisoners is relatively low. The result is that insufficient additional space has been planned or budgeted, and less has been built, relative to present or projected prison populations.

This has led to a heretofore hidden but ominous cost of such shortfalls: early release of inmates to make room for new arrivals. As the result of crowded conditions, Florida correction system officials expected to release 30,000 inmates early in FY [fiscal year] 1988-89. Early releases will increase as the prison population grows. . . . Indeed, the average portion of sentences served by Florida prisoners has already fallen from its long-term level of about 50 percent to 35.4 percent as of October 1988. Such reductions in the actual time convicts spend behind bars exposes the public to the criminality of such convicts for the time they would otherwise have been confined. This cost has been tragically experienced several times already. In addition, early releases can only encourage more crime by those who gain such release and others who are aware of it, as they see the costs of crime decrease relative to the benefits.

A Mistake to Focus on Supply

The supply-side emphasis on prison expansion, we contend, is mistaken. The correct question should be, "How can we alter the incentives within the criminal justice system and thereby improve the efficiency and effectiveness of the system?" When the question is asked this way, it implicates demand as well as supply.

Proposals to reduce the demand for prison space (the number of convicts reaching prison) can relieve overcrowding as much as proposals to increase the supply of prison space by construction of additional facilities. Thus, given the failure of the supply-side approach to date, we propose a demand-side solution. Our aim is to clarify the responsibility for the crisis and to stimulate the public debate necessary for constructive reform.

Many would argue that justice should not be rationed. But the process of justice requires the use of scarce resources, including police, courts *and* prisons. When resources are scarce there will be competing demands for their use and some means of discriminating between those demands (rationing) must be devised. Under the current system, prisons are treated as a free common pool resource and prisoners are sentenced with little regard for the existing level of use. After prisoners are sentenced, prison space is rationed on a first come, first serve basis and through complex early release programs.

The Sources of Demand

The first step in a demand-side analysis is identification of the source of the demand for prison space. Prisons are part of a *system* of publicly-produced criminal justice. Thus, the demand for prison space reflects what is going on throughout the system. But sources of demand for prison services are not as easily identified as those for, say, a public beach.

Judges Can Also Reduce Jail Overcrowding

Judges make more decisions affecting jail population than anyone else; this often makes them leaders in seeking jail-crowding solutions. Judges can issue summonses instead of arrest warrants; provide guidelines authorizing direct release by police, jail, and pretrial staff; and provide bail setting outside normal court hours. Evaluators of the 4-year Jail Overcrowding Reduction Project of the former Law Enforcement Assistance Administration found that the project's most successful sites were those with strong judicial leadership. . . .

Many judges have worked to extend the range of nonjail sentencing options, using probation supervision, suspended sentences, fines, community service and restitution, halfway house placements, and specialized treatment facilities as true alternatives to incarceration.

A growing number of courts now defer service of jail sentences, when the jail is at capacity, in cases in which jail is believed an appropriate sentence but immediate jailing is not essential for the community's safety.

Andy Hall, National Institute of Justice *Research in Brief*, January 1987.

Superficially, criminals "demand" prison space by committing crimes which call for prison sentences. At another level, legislators decide what actions are to be considered criminal in the first place. There has been an expansion in the types of activities that are legislatively defined as crime and in those subjected to minimum prison sentences. The effect is bringing more offenders within the categories eligible for prison. Thus, the same group (legislators) sets the budgets for prisons and determines the need or demand for prison space. At still another level, however, legislators are simply reflecting the demands of voters and taxpayers.

At yet another stage of the criminal justice process, and most directly of all, are the judges who sentence criminals to prison. They, especially, are responsible for the growing demand for prison space. Their responsibility is shared, however, with prosecutors, who decide what criminal charges to file and what sentences to seek. In fact, the vast majority of (over 90 percent) negotiate, usually through counsel, and agree upon sentences, rather than go through a trial. Judges, however, must at least ratify such plea-bargained agreements. Our demand-side proposal focuses therefore on the incentives of judges, but it has ramifications for other groups influencing demand.

The Concept of the Commons

The key to understanding prison overcrowding is the concept of the "commons." Analysis of the commons problem has been extensively applied to publicly or commonly owned grazing land. When several individuals are free to graze cattle on the same land, each individual has an incentive to use up as much grass as possible before other owners do the same. Thus, the commons becomes crowded with cattle and the grass land deteriorates in quality as the result of overgrazing. This has been called "the tragedy of the commons." Each user has an incentive to overuse or crowd the land because he is not liable for the full cost of his actions. None has an incentive to reduce the size of herds or to consider other ways of maintaining them (for example, supplementing the grass with feeds grown on private land.) Thus, all of them—doing what they think is in their individual interest—turn out to be losers in the end.

This contrasts with privately-owned grazing land or grazing land to which access rights are assigned or otherwise limited. If an individual crowds and overgrazes land to which he alone has access, he bears fully the consequences of actions which cause the land to deteriorate in quality. Thus, his incentive is to graze at a level which allows the land to maintain its productive value. He either maintains smaller herds compared to the size that would graze a commonly-used parcel of land of similar size, or he substitutes other feeds for the grass so that the quality of the land is not eroded.

The point is that assignment of access rights to individuals creates very different incentives from those which exist with common access. When rights to use a resource are assigned to an individual, that individual will use the resource in ways that are consistent with the maintenance of future value, since he bears the consequences of destructive overuse. However, when a resource is subject to common access, destructive overuse results because individual users are unable to capture the potential value from wise conservation. There is ample evidence that common access results in destructive overuse. For example, when buffalo were subject to common access, they were very nearly eliminated. Similarly, certain species of whales subject to common access today face the same threat of extinction. In contrast, privately-owned beef cattle in a system of limited-access land have never been in danger of extinction.

Judges and Prison Crowding

Judges have common access to the prison system. In their sentencing, they have virtually no incentive to limit the number of prisoners they "herd into the commons," or to consider alternatives to imprisonment. The effect is that judges as a group crowd the common-access prisons much as cattle owners crowd common-access grazing land.

Crowding is only one consequence of a commons problem. Indeed, although crowding may be the most easily observed result of common access, it is not the most significant. When grazing land is overused, it rapidly deteriorates in quality and is used up inefficiently. Thus, the output of the grazing land (fatter, healthier cattle) diminishes.

The same consequence results from common-access prisons. Imprisonment serves several purposes (produces several outputs), including punishment of convicted criminals, deterrence of potential criminals (the punished offender and others as well), incapacitation of dangerous criminals, and rehabilitation of criminals who can be reformed. These outputs of the prison system decline in quality because of crowding. Early release programs mean that criminals are not punished to the degree that judges, victims, and the public feel justice requires. Potential criminals recognize that prison sentences are rarely served fully, so deterrence is diminished. Criminals may be released who require further incapacitation. Finally, when corrections budgets are consumed by efforts to accommodate large prison populations, resources are not available for rehabilitation programs.

Thus, the tragedy of the commons occurs with common-access prisons just as it does with common-access grazing land. And the judges are liable for the costs, which are borne instead by (a) taxpayers who must pay for more prisons, (b) prisoners in crowded prison conditions, (c) victims and the public who feel that criminals who are released early have not been punished sufficiently, (d) citizens victimized by prematurely released criminals who are not rehabilitated and other criminals who are insufficiently deterred, and (e) corrections officials whose budgets are used up by coping with crowding.

A Solution to the Prison Crowding Problem

There have been demand-side proposals before. Some reduce the demand "at the back door," such as early-release programs. "Front door" proposals would rely more heavily on alternative forms of punishment. Some would limit the types of offender who could be imprisoned. Still others would adjust sentencing guidelines (where they exist), limit prison sentences or trigger across-the-board reductions in time yet to be served, or oblige judges themselves to control the prison population level. Our approach to prison overcrowding and its associated inefficiencies is the last mentioned because it arises most directly out of the commons analysis. As in the grazing commons, access rights to prison space would be limited by assignment. A limited-access system in its simplest form could allocate to each judge a certain amount of prison space. Literally, this would provide each judge with his or her own prison cells and supportive resources (guards, meal service, laundry, and so forth). But we do not have to go as far as providing judges with their own prisons, in order to alter their incentives. Rather, we simply need to individualize and thereby limit access to "parcels" of the prison system through correctional bookkeeping.

The prison system which we now have could be sub-divided into units with a certain number of cells for each individual judge, who would then be responsible for assigning space in his unit to those he sentenced. Each judge would have to determine who should be in his prison unit and for how long. If a judge crowded his unit, he would be responsible for deciding which prisoners to release. This clearly would create incentives for judges to consider alternative forms of punishment where appropriate and to take care in imposing prison sentences for relatively minor crimes, in order to assure that space is available for criminals who commit more serious crimes.

Access to Prisons Must Be Limited

As was the case with grazing land, access must be limited if we are going to deal with the prison overcrowding problem. This could be accomplished by providing each judge a certain number of cells. Once each judge "owned" a limited amount of space, the judge would have a strong incentive to consider alternative forms of punishment in order to husband the limited quantity of space. Convicts would be assigned to prison only when it was absolutely necessary for retribution, deterrence, or protection of the public. Criminals would no longer be assigned to prison simply because it was a convenient and easily assignable form of punishment. Judges themselves—rather than formulas, early-release programs, and wardens—would decide which criminals were most in need of incarceration. This system would both lead to more efficient use of prison space and provide judges with a strong incentive to use punishment alternatives like intense supervision, electronic monitoring, fines, and restitution.

"The two factors most responsible for our current crowded prisons [are] changed sentencing practices . . . and the so-called 'war on drugs.' "

Sentencing Reform Can Reduce Prison Overcrowding

Alvin J. Bronstein

Alvin J. Bronstein is the executive director of the National Prison Project of the American Civil Liberties Union. In the following viewpoint, Bronstein attacks traditional responses to prison overcrowding, such as building more prisons. He contends that these responses are futile because they do not address the two major causes of prison overcrowding, harsher sentences meted out to offenders in recent years and the vast numbers of arrests made in the war on drugs. Bronstein advocates sentencing reform to reduce the length of most prison sentences, and to end the war on drugs, which he believes is a costly failure.

As you read, consider the following questions:

1. What are the two other traditional responses to prison overcrowding identified by Bronstein?
2. According to the author, what are the problems associated with each of the traditional responses?
3. Why does Bronstein believe that U.S. drug policy is absurd?

Alvin J. Bronstein, "A Response to Prison Overcrowding." An attachment to the statement of Claudia Wright before the Subcommittee on Courts, Intellectual Property, and the Administration of Justice of the Committee on the Judiciary of the U.S. House of Representatives, September 27, 1989. Public domain.

145

Traditionally, there have been three responses to prison overcrowding at the state and federal level, adopted separately or in combination. They are:

1) *The prison construction response.* Large states like California are spending billions of dollars on new prison space and, at the end of 1988, California's prisons were 65% over capacity. A small state, Rhode Island, tripled its prison capacity between 1979 and 1989. . . . On May 15, 1989, President George Bush announced his "anti-crime package" which included one billion dollars in new federal prison construction to triple the planned spending on expansion of prison capacity. In light of the projected prison population increase resulting from the 1986 Drug Act and the new federal sentencing guidelines, this expansion will have no impact on overcrowding in the federal system, which was 72% over capacity in 1989.

2) *The alternative response.* Various states, wary of the cost of building new prisons, have developed large programs of alternatives to incarceration. Kentucky has a large Intensive Community Supervision program, Florida has the greatest number of people in house arrest supervision and both states experienced 1988 prison population increases at or above the national average.

3) *The do nothing response.* A number of jurisdictions, most noticeably the District of Columbia, watch their prison population soar and are bureaucratically frozen into doing nothing. The result of this approach is often a replay of the tragedies of Attica in 1971 or Santa Fe in 1980.

None of These Responses Will Work

I submit that none of the responses above will have any significant impact on our nation's growing problem of prison overcrowding. The new prison construction model is costly and doomed to failure. It represents the "Willie Horton" approach to public policy. It reflects the willingness of this country's political leadership to place short-term goals, getting elected to public office, above rational, long-term policy-making. We are experiencing a net increase nationally of 800 prisoners a week. That is the average size of a new prison which, conservatively, will cost 240 million dollars when you add debt financing and operating costs to capital construction costs. Thus, we would have to spend one billion dollars a month to build prisons just to accommodate the current increase in prisoner population, with no impact on current overcrowding. And, contrary to assertions by our state and national political leadership, this bankrupting of the future of this country will have no significant impact on crime rates. The public is confused into thinking that locking up more criminals is the same as reducing crime rates. They are

146

not, and no jurisdiction has every successfully built its way out of overcrowding or had an impact on crime rates by an expanded incarceration policy.

The increased use of alternatives, difficult to achieve in today's political climate, will have no long-term impact on prison overcrowding. Many alternative programs merely widen the net of social control. People who would ordinarily receive a prison sentence still receive a prison sentence and others, who were traditional candidates for probation, now go into alternative programs. And the less harsh alternatives are often reserved for the white and middle class offender thereby increasing the percentages of poor men and women of color who already disproportionately fill our nation's prisons.

Harsh Sentences Cause Prison Overcrowding

It is indisputable that American prisons are dangerously overcrowded, but new construction is not the solution. The reason for the rapidly growing prison population is not the "crime wave", but rather the rash of new stiff sentencing laws that have been recently passed by state legislatures. In the past, trial judges retained wide discretion in imposing sentences. Now, [most] states have replaced discretionary sentencing with minimum prison sentences for many crimes. In Indiana, for example, burglars and rapists are serving 100 percent more time than in the past and armed robbers 30 percent more. . . . In New York City between 1971 and 1980 the percentage of defendants sentenced to more than three years rose from 26 percent to 85 percent. Critics of the new sentencing laws rightly say they were passed in a climate of public hysteria without careful examination of their impact on the criminal justice system or public debate.

Alvin J. Bronstein, comments before the U.S. House of Representatives Subcommittee on Courts, Civil Liberties, and the Administration of Justice, 1985.

To do nothing about prison overcrowding is uncivilized and quite often a deliberate policy choice of elected officials. They can brag about being tough on criminals while saving taxpayers dollars and then scapegoat federal judges who intervene when the overcrowding results in unconstitutional conditions of confinement.

The Real Causes of Prison Crowding

None of the current responses are addressing the two factors most responsible for our current crowded prisons: changed sentencing practices which focus on longer prison sentences and mandatory minimum sentences; and the so-called "war on drugs." Although admittedly difficult in the current mood of the country, my proposed responses have the advantage, at least, of

147

being honest and realistic. We must develop new sentencing practices which punish as many people as are now being punished, perhaps more, but for much shorter periods of time. We must abandon the futile task of trying to solve our serious drug problem with our criminal justice system and deal with it as a public health and social welfare problem.

We already have the longest prison sentences in the Western world and they are getting longer. Our prisoners *serve* an average of two to ten times longer than in any country in Western Europe. We must begin to consider prison space as a scarce resource, reserving it in the main for short prison terms for those offenders who we feel must be punished by incarceration and we must begin to tell the public the truth that prisons have nothing to do with crime control.

> Although the criminal justice system deals with only a fraction of the crime that is committed, the public mistakenly looks to the criminal justice system to eliminate the crime problem. Better public understanding of both the causes of crime and the important, but limited, role that the criminal justice system plays in its control is essential to meaningful change in our approach to the crime problem.
>
> Findings, *Criminal Justice in Crisis,*
> Special Committee on Criminal Justice in
> a Free Society of The American Bar
> Association Criminal Justice Section,
> Nov. 1988.

My first response then is to eliminate most mandatory minimum sentences, eliminate most repeat offender enhanced sentences and shorten our sentences to lengths comparable to other industrial democracies. If we have one prison bed for the next three years, I would rather use it to sentence 12 burglars to three months each than one burglar for all 36 months.

Drop the War on Drugs

My second response has to do with our absurd drug policy. Between 1981 and 1989, while we have conducted our national "war on drugs," so much cocaine has come into this country that the wholesale price has dropped by 80% even as the retail purity of a gram of cocaine has quintupled from 12% to about 60% and the trend with heroin has been similar if less dramatic. During each of the last few years, police made about 750,000 arrests for drug violations, mostly for possession and not manufacturing or dealing. The result has been the overwhelming of most urban criminal justice systems. The greatest beneficiaries of our current drug policies are organized and unorganized drug traffickers. We are seeing rising levels of corruption in federal, state and local criminal justice systems largely attributed to the powerful allure of illicit drug dollars. We see more and more drug related crime. . . .

Our current drug policies are proving highly costly, ineffective and counterproductive just as the prohibition of alcohol did 60 years ago. We can make a huge impact on prison overcrowding by adopting rational new drug policies. We must remove drugs from the criminal justice system and, as with alcohol and tobacco, deal with drugs as a public health problem diverting the huge amounts of money now going into ineffective law enforcement programs into education, treatment and other social welfare programs.

"States known for their massive prison populations can use restitution to reduce prison crowding and the costs of incarceration, without compromising public safety."

Victim Restitution Can Reduce Prison Overcrowding

Richard Lawrence

Richard Lawrence is an assistant professor of criminal justice at St. Cloud State University in Minnesota. In the following viewpoint, Lawrence argues that restitution programs, through which offenders pay back their victims and society for their crimes, are a useful prison alternative and a viable solution to the problem of prison overcrowding. Furthermore, he continues, restitution programs also seem to fulfill the sentencing goals of retribution, deterrence, rehabilitation, and the reintegration of offenders into society.

As you read, consider the following questions:

1. Do you agree with Lawrence's argument that restitution programs fulfill sentencing goals better than prisons?
2. What benefits did the state of Texas gain from its Restitution Center Program, according to the author?

Richard Lawrence, "Restitution Programs Pay Back the Victim and Society," *Corrections Today*, vol. 52, no. 1, February 1990. Reprinted with permission of the American Correctional Association.

Crowded prisons have led to countless lawsuits against departments of corrections, forcing states to build more prisons and find other ways to punish offenders.

Expense is another factor that has forced states to seek alternatives, in addition to expanding their prisons. The cost for new prison construction ranges from $50,000 to $150,000 per bed. The annual cost to keep an inmate in prison averages about $15,000.

Probation has been the traditional alternative, but caseloads have become so enormous that probation officers cannot maintain reasonably close control and supervision. New alternatives must reduce prison populations, preserve public safety, and punish and deter offenders. Many forms of community corrections have not met these goals.

Paying Back the Victim

Restitution as a criminal sanction in the American judicial system is a fairly new development. Restitution sentences may require the offender to pay money to the victim and/or the justice system or perform some public or community service.

Minnesota developed a restitution program in 1972, allowing convicted property offenders a chance to avoid prison if they worked and paid restitution to their victims. Courts throughout the United States began adopting the idea. A survey estimates there are from 500 to 800 restitution programs for juvenile offenders in this country, and an estimated 250 to 500 restitution programs serving the criminal courts.

Restitution seems to be gaining popularity and acceptance among the public, legislators, judiciary and corrections personnel because it seems to fulfill sentencing goals as well as or better than other punishments.

• Retribution—Restitution requires that offenders pay for crime, the damages and loss incurred. Court-ordered monetary and community-service restitution helps satisfy victims' and the public's needs for "just desserts."

• Deterrence—Restitution programs require greater demands and offender accountability than probation alone. Many believe that paying more for crime will be a greater deterrent.

• Rehabilitation—Restitution aims to confront offenders with the consequences of their crime. It often changes criminal thinking and behavior patterns. Victim-offender restitution programs (VORP) bring the victim and offender together to resolve losses and damage. Such programs often result in greater offender responsibility.

• Reintegration—Offenders who pay restitution often get more positive responses and acceptance from the victim and community. Restitution programs benefit the offender by maintaining community ties. Eliminating the problems of post-prison adjustment and overcoming the "ex-con" label may reduce subsequent criminal behavior, making it one of restitution's greatest benefits.

Making It Work

Is restitution really an effective alternative to prison? Can it achieve the goals of sentencing, reduce prison crowding, and still avoid risk to public safety? An examination of one state's program may help answer these questions.

The Texas Restitution Center Program began in 1983. Since then, it has grown to 17 centers with a combined bed capacity of more than 700 residents. The primary purpose of the program is to serve as a cost-effective form of punishment. The Texas program is applicable to other states with large, crowded prison populations, which tend to have high incarceration rates.

Texas was faced with a crowded prison system, decreased state revenues, and a federal court order to reduce crowding (Ruiz v. Estelle, 1982). The courts divert non-violent felony offenders to the centers, where they repay victims and the community while continuing to work and pay taxes.

Restitution Helps Victims and Offenders

We need to make sure that offenders repay their victims whenever possible.

One obvious benefit of this approach is that it takes care of the victim. Those hurt by crime deserve more than just the satisfaction of seeing their offender convicted. (Often they don't even get that satisfaction.)

But offenders benefit from assuming personal responsibility and performing purposeful work as well. Paying back someone they have wronged allows a criminal to understand and deal with the consequences of his actions. Psychologist Albert Eglash argues, "Restitution is something an inmate does, not something done for or to him. . . . Being reparative, restitution can alleviate guilt and anxiety, which can otherwise precipitate further offenses."

Charles Colson and Daniel Van Ness, *Convicted: New Hope for Ending America's Crime Crisis*, 1988.

The bill emphasized community protection and community input in developing the centers. Residents' activities are carefully monitored by the center's staff and by the probation department. During the day, the residents go to work in the community and return to the centers afterwards. The residents use their wages to pay for room and board, transportation, court and probation costs, victim restitution and child support. They perform community service restitution during evening and weekend hours.

From 1983 to 1988, more than 3,000 offenders who would have been sentenced to Texas prisons were diverted to the restitution centers. For the five-year period from 1984-1988, an average of 60.5 percent of the residents were successfully discharged or successfully participating in the centers. The average percentage of residents discharged for technical or rule violations from 1984-1988 was 11.7 percent. Only 1.9 percent of the residents were discharged for a new offense, and 65 percent of those arrests were for misdemeanors. The vast majority of the diverted offenders did not increase the risk to public safety.

Most of the offenders got jobs during their stay at the restitution centers. While 75 percent were unemployed when they arrived at the centers, only 25 percent were unemployed at the time of discharge. Thousands of hours of community service restitution are performed by the residents each year. From 1984-88, nearly half a million hours of community service were performed by the residents—an average of 96,900 hours per year. Translated into savings to the community at the minimum wage rate, those hours would equal over $1.6 million.

Monetary Restitution and Reduced State Costs

The residents also pay a considerable amount of monetary restitution. From 1984-88, a total of $480,866 was paid to crime victims; $376,548 went for court costs, fines and fees; and $368,440 was paid for probation fees. The residents paid a total of $931,454 to support their dependents and personal savings; and $340,924 to other financial obligations in the community.

The operating cost to the state was reduced significantly by the total of $4,530,081 paid by the residents (1984-88) for room, board and transportation.

Considering the incarceration costs in the Texas Department of Corrections, the restitution center program is a success. The operating cost for Texas prisons is reported to be $37.50 per day per inmate. This figure includes only operating expenses, not the more than $50,000 per cell for new prison construction. Cost to the Texas Adult Probation Commission for operating the Restitution Center Program averages $30 per day per bed space. In addition to lower operating costs, the monetary restitution paid by the residents helps make a strong case for the program.

Restitution programs have grown rapidly in the past decade. The program in Texas has shown that states known for their massive prison populations can use restitution to reduce prison crowding and the costs of incarceration, without compromising public safety. Many citizens, judicial and probation personnel seem to have readily accepted the idea of restitution as a unique method of meting out punishment with a visible benefit to the community.

Recognizing Statements That Are Provable

We are constantly confronted with statements and generalizations about social and moral problems. In order to think clearly about these problems, it is useful if one can make a basic distinction between statements for which evidence can be found and other statements which cannot be verified or proved because evidence is not available, or the issue is so controversial that it cannot be definitely proved.

Readers should be aware that magazines, newspapers, and other sources often contain statements of a controversial nature. The following activity is designed to allow experimentation with statements that are provable and those that are not.

The following statements are taken from the viewpoints in this chapter. Consider each statement carefully. *Mark P for any statement you believe is provable. Mark U for any statement you feel is unprovable because of the lack of evidence. Mark C for any statement you think is too controversial to be proved to everyone's satisfaction.*

If you are doing this activity as a member of a class or group, compare your answers with those of other class or group members. Be able to defend your answers. You may discover that others will come to different conclusions than you do. Listening to the reasons others present for their answers may give you valuable insights into recognizing statements that are provable.

P = provable
U = unprovable
C = too controversial

1. In 1989, correctional institutions in the U.S. held about twice as many inmates as they did in 1980.

2. New construction is critical to meeting the prison overcrowding dilemma.

3. In 1987, the General Accounting Office estimated that the number of federal inmates could quadruple by 2002.

4. Increasing the use of incarceration has not solved and will not solve the crime problem.

5. To put people behind walls and bars and do nothing to change them is to win a battle but lose a war.

6. In eighteenth-century England, criminals were shipped off to Australia, a far-off, desolate, uncrowded continent.

7. The jails in Los Angeles County were originally built to hold 13,464 inmates. They now hold 22,000.

8. The premise underlying the public attitude toward criminal justice seems to be, "Better to lock up one hundred innocent men than to let one guilty man go free."

9. Building and operating jails is expensive, with costs continually rising.

10. Building more jails is the most expensive and least effective way to eliminate overcrowded jails.

11. Recreational opportunities for inmates have been severely curtailed because of overcrowding. Gymnasiums and other rooms once used for recreation are now packed wall to wall with beds.

12. In 1989, thirty-five states, the District of Columbia, the Virgin Islands, and Puerto Rico were operating some or all of their prisons under court order.

13. In America, prisoners serve an average of two to ten times longer than in any country in Western Europe.

14. Our current drug policies are proving highly costly, ineffective, and counterproductive, just as the prohibition of alcohol did sixty years ago.

15. Between 1981 and 1989, the wholesale price of cocaine dropped by 80 percent.

16. George Bush's anti-crime package is an ineffective, weak attempt at easing an overwhelming national crime problem.

17. To do nothing about prison overcrowding is uncivilized and quite often a deliberate policy of elected officials.

Periodical Bibliography

The following articles have been selected to supplement the diverse views presented in this chapter.

George M. Anderson
"American Imprisonment Today," *America*, May 8, 1982.

Ted Gest
"Personalized Penalties," *U.S. News & World Report*, November 20, 1989.

Ted Gest
"U.S. Jails: 'Bombs Waiting to Go Off,'" *U.S. News & World Report*, June 9, 1986.

Ted Gest et al.
"Why More Criminals Are Doing Time Beyond Bars," *U.S. News & World Report*, February 26, 1990.

Ronald W. Jackson et al.
"Prison Crowding: A Policy Challenge for Parole," *Corrections Today*, August 1989.

Dana C. Joel
"Time to Deal with America's Prison Crisis," The Heritage Foundation *Backgrounder*, November 15, 1989. Available from The Heritage Foundation, 214 Massachusetts Ave. NE, Washington, DC 20002.

John M. Klofas
"Jail Crowding: What We Need to Know," *American Jails*, January/February 1991. Available from the American Jail Association, 1000 Day Rd., Suite 100, Hagerstown, MD 21740.

Richard Lacayo
"Our Bulging Prisons," *Time*, May 29, 1989.

Richard L. Madden
"Out of Space: Prison Crowding in New York, New Jersey, and Connecticut," *The New York Times*, September 30, 1984.

Francis T. Moore and Marilyn Chandler Ford
"A Model to Reduce Jail Overcrowding," *American Jails*, Fall 1989.

Norval Morris
"Filling the Vacuum Between Prison and Probation," *The World & I*, April 1991. Available from 2850 New York Ave. NE, Washington, DC 20002.

Barry J. Nidorf
"Community Corrections: Turning the Crowding Crisis into Opportunities," *Corrections Today*, October 1989.

Daniel Seligman
"Housing Shortage," *Fortune*, November 20, 1989.

Michael S. Serrill   "A Growing Crisis Behind Bars: Tough Justice Is Causing the Nation's Prisons to Bulge," *Time*, December 5, 1983.

Jonathan Turley   "Solving Prison Overcrowding," *The New York Times*, October 9, 1989.

Bill Turque et al.   "Why Justice Can't Be Done," *Newsweek*, May 29, 1989.

Tom Wicker   "An Ungrand Total," *The New York Times*, October 13, 1989.

Should Prisons Be Privatized?

Chapter Preface

For many years, public prisons have contracted with private firms to provide essential services, including medical and mental health care, staff training, vocational training, and drug treatment. In the 1980s, the role of private firms expanded to include prison ownership and operation. This development was heralded as a potential solution to overcrowding. However, private prisons soon became mired in controversy. Opponents of private prisons, such as the American Civil Liberties Union, argued that punishment should remain a government function and should not be delegated to private firms under any circumstances. These critics also feared that the welfare of prisoners would be jeopardized because private companies would place profit ahead of all other considerations. When challenging the privatization of prisons, opponents were able to draw on the sordid history of the private prison in America to bolster their arguments.

Throughout much of the nineteenth century and well into the twentieth, many American prisons were privately owned and operated. According to Sean McConville, a professor of criminal justice at the University of Illinois at Chicago, the private administration of prisons was gradually overtaken by federal and state governments for two main reasons. First, living conditions in many private prisons were appalling. Prisoners were little more than slave laborers, subject to the brutality and greed of the jailer and the turnkeys, and were housed and maintained in cramped and filthy conditions. The American public was simply no longer willing to tolerate these kinds of conditions inside penal institutions. The second factor McConville credits with the demise of private prisons was the growing desire to use prisons to rehabilitate criminals. The public gradually came to believe that prisoners could not be rehabilitated in the squalid environment of the private prison.

Today, proponents of private prisons argue that things have changed and that modern private prisons bear no resemblance to those of the past. Firms like the Corrections Corporation of America, which runs several private institutions, contend that contemporary private prisons are bright, modern, and substantially more efficient than their public counterparts. In addition, they are effectively monitored by government regulations and high industry standards. Proponents further insist that the development of private prisons is absolutely essential to alleviate overcrowding in public prisons, and that the sordid reputation of the private prison in history should not unfairly taint the reputable private firms involved in this field today.

The viewpoints in the following chapter examine the modern private prison in both theory and practice.

"The profit motive is not necessarily in conflict with the pursuit of justice; it can, in fact, be conducive to it."

Private Prisons Are Just

Charles H. Logan

Charles H. Logan, a professor of sociology at the University of Connecticut in Storrs, is the author of *Private Prisons: Cons and Pros.* In the following viewpoint, Logan argues that there is no reason to assume that private prisons will be less just than public prisons. As long as private prisons are accountable to the people and subject to state and federal laws, he continues, we should give them a chance to prove themselves. By comparing the performances of public and private prisons, taxpayers can obtain the best value for the money they devote to prisons, he concludes.

As you read, consider the following questions:

1. What does the author mean when he argues that the state "does not *own* the right to punish"?
2. How does Logan justify his belief that conditions would not deteriorate in private prisons?
3. Do you agree with the author that competition between private and public prisons can improve prison conditions?

Charles H. Logan, "The Propriety of Proprietary Prisons," *Federal Probation*, September 1987. Public domain.

Can the "Invisible Hand" administer criminal sanctions as well as the "Iron Fist"? Dispensing justice is generally regarded as one of the primary functions of the state. And yet, a small but growing number of penal institutions, such as prisons, jails, detention centers, and reformatories, are now privately owned or managed under contract to local, state, or Federal government agencies. These "proprietary" correctional facilities appear to push the limits of privatization to an extreme. However, what seems at first to be a radically conservative proposal—private ownership of the means of state punishment—can be shown to be fully consistent with the principles of classical liberalism.

Only a few anarchists believe that the state should totally abdicate its penal authority in favor of private companies. While the state may *delegate* to a private agent its authority and responsibility for administering penalties, it cannot *relinquish* them. Thus, what is now under serious consideration around the country is not a corporate takeover of the legislative and judicial functions of the state, but the subcontracting of some aspects of the executive function.

The Source and Delegation of Authority to Imprison

The most principled objection to the propriety of commercial prisons is the claim that imprisonment is an inherently and exclusively governmental function and therefore should not be performed by the private sector at all, even under contract to the government. How can it be proper for anyone other than the state to imprison criminals? Perhaps the place to start is by asking what makes it proper for the state itself. By what right does the state imprison?

In the classical liberal (or in modern terms, libertarian) tradition on which the American system of government is founded, all rights are individual, not collective. The state is artificial and has no authority, legitimate power, or rights of its own other than those transferred to it by individuals.

Why does this transfer take place? John Locke argued that individuals in the state of nature have the right to punish those who aggress against them. However, there will always be disagreement over interpretations and applications of natural law; people cannot be unbiased in judging their own cases; and those in the right may lack the power to punish. For these reasons, said Locke, people contract to form a state and completely give over to it their power to punish. Thus, the power and authority to imprison does not originate with the state, but is granted to it. Moreover, this grant is a conditional one. Citizens reserve the right to revoke any of the powers of the state, or indeed, the entire charter of the state, if necessary. . . .

Whatever the reasons for placing the power to punish in the

hands of the state, however, the major point is that it must be transferred; it does not originate with the state. The power and authority of the state to imprison, like all its powers and authority, are derived from the consent of the governed and may therefore, with similar consent, be delegated further. Since all legitimate powers of government are originally, and continuously, delegated to it by citizens, those same citizens if they wish can specify that certain powers be further delegated by the state, in turn, to private agencies. Because the authority does not originate with the state, it does not attach inherently or uniquely to it, and can be passed along.

Private Prisons Facilitate "Comparison Shopping"

Private prisons will not, and should not, reduce the responsibility of government for imprisonment. Nor is it likely for the foreseeable future that they will significantly replace government in the total volume of prisoners held and facilities managed. Their most important contribution will be to provide a market test of costs and to serve as a comparative standard by which to measure government performance. Competition can be good for government agencies just as it is for private businesses. When government must compete with the private sector in the provision of a public service, that competition provides a powerful mechanism of evaluation, accountability, and control.

Charles H. Logan, *The American Prison: Issues in Research and Policy*, 1989.

The state does not *own* the right to punish. It merely *administers* it in trust, on behalf of the people and under the rule of law. There is no reason why subsidiary trustees cannot be designated, as long as they, too, are ultimately accountable to the people and subject to the same provisions of law that direct the state.

Legitimation of Authority

In any prison, someone will need authority to use force, including potentially deadly force in emergencies. Questions of legitimacy in the use of that force, however, cannot be resolved simply by declaring that for state employees some use of force is legitimate, while for contracted agents none is.

In a system characterized by rule of law, state agencies and private agencies alike are bound by the law. For actors within either type of agency, it is the law, not the civil status of the actor, that determines whether any particular exercise of force is legitimate. The law may specify that those authorized to use force in particular situations should be licensed or deputized and adequately trained for this purpose, but they need not be state employees.

The distinction between a contractual relation and salaried state employment, in terms of the derivation in authority, may be more apparent than real. In both cases, the authority of the actor, say a guard, derives from the fact that he is acting, not just on behalf of the state, but within the scope of the law. Consider the case of a state-employed prison guard who engages in clearcut and extreme brutality. We do not say that his act is authorized or legitimate, or even that he is acting at that moment as an agent of the state. In fact, we deny it, in spite of his uniform and all the other trappings of his position. We say that he has overstepped his authority and behaved in an unauthorized and unlawful fashion. The state may or may not accept some accountability or liability for his act, but that is a separate issue. The point here is that the authority or legitimacy of a position does not automatically transfer to the actions of the incumbent.

There is, in effect, an implicit contract between a state and its agents that makes the authority of the latter conditional on the proper performance of their roles. This conditional authority can be bestowed on contractual agents of the state just as it is on those who are salaried. Where contractually employed agents, such as guards, have identifiable counterparts among state-salaried agents, there is no reason why their authority should not be regarded as equivalent. Thus, the boundaries of authority for contracted state agents should be no less clear than those for state employees and they could be even clearer, if they are spelled out in the conditions of the contract.

Inside the Private Prison

What about authority inside the prison itself? Would private prisons lack authority in the eyes of inmates? Some critics [including Ira Robins] worry about that prospect:

> When it enters a judgment of conviction and imposes a sentence, a court exercises its authority, both actually and symbolically. Does it weaken that authority, however—as well as the integrity of a system of *justice*—when an inmate looks at his keeper's uniform and, instead of encountering an emblem that reads, "Federal Bureau of Prisons" or "State Department of Corrections," he faces one that says "Acme Corrections Company"?

I suspect that prisoners will be more concerned about practical, not philosophical, distinctions. They will care more about how the guards treat them, than about what insignia grace their uniforms. To the extent that they are treated with fairness and justice, inmates will be more inclined to legitimate their keepers' authority and to cooperate with them.

This is especially important to a private prison. The exercise of naked power is extremely costly; cooperation is much more cost-effective (and therefore profitable) than is coercion. Commercial prisons, unlike the state, cannot indefinitely absorb or pass along to taxpayers the cost of riots, high insurance rates, extensive litigation by maltreated prisoners, cancellations of poorly performed or controversial contracts, or even just too much adverse publicity. These are some of the potential costs of the unfair treatment of inmates.

Efficiency Not Synonymous with Exploitation

To be sure, private prison entrepreneurs are in business to make a profit and will operate their facilities as efficiently as possible. But efficiency is not synonymous with exploitation. Private operators will be required to make substantial front-end commitments of capital and other resources. They will have to balance their desire to cut costs with their need for long-term contracts. Furthermore, many of the companies seeking private prison contracts want to operate facilities in several states. Such companies will not wish to jeopardize future contracts by running substandard institutions. Reputable private prison operators have a vested interest in promoting strict enforcement of government standards in order to deter fly-by-night outfits that could, by association, taint the entire industry.

Charles R. Ring, *The Wall Street Journal*, May 8, 1987.

Legitimation constitutes one of the most effective methods of cutting the costs of power in all forms of social organization; prisons are no exception. Since legitimation is generally granted in exchange for the fair exercise of power, a profit-seeking prison has a vested interest in being perceived by inmates as just and impartial in the application of rules. Moreover, the state is more likely to renew a contract with an organization that has a good record of governance than with a contractor who generates numerous complaints and appeals from inmates. Thus, economic self-interest can motivate good governance as well as good management. At the least, there is no inherent incompatibility between the making of profit and the pursuit of justice.

Due Process Under Contracting

Certain aspects of prison administration have a quasi-judicial character. Controversial examples would include imposing solitary confinement or other disciplinary actions, "good time" sanctions that affect the date of release, and classification procedures that significantly affect the conditions of confinement. Moreover, even where a commercial prison's actions are purely administrative, the coercive environment in which they occur makes the question of their fairness all the more important.

164

Being suspicious of authority in the hands of commercial prison managers is an example of having the right attitude for the wrong reasons. It is not because they pursue profit that we should be vigilant, but because they wield power. A constructive response to this suspicion would be to require as part of a contract that commercial prisons codify the rules that they will enforce, specify the criteria and procedures by which they will make disciplinary decisions, and submit to review by a supervisory state agency. In short, the requirements of due process should be built into the conditions of the contract. This is no different from the attitude we should have toward the state itself, and its employees.

Our focus should be on the procedures that will best protect the due process rights of inmates regardless of whether they are applied by government employees or by contracted agents. The procedures that will do this best will probably be the same in either case. It should be treated as an open, empirical question whether these procedures are adhered to better under one system or another. Therefore, it is no solution to propose, as some have, that all decisions having implications for due process should simply be left in government hands. The whole point of having procedures is to reduce our reliance on being in "the right hands.". . .

Justice and the Purpose of Punishment

In addition to due process, justice requires clarity as to the purpose of punishment. It is the state's job to ensure that private prisons pursue a proper penology. This may be difficult, since states themselves are rarely clear and consistent in penal philosophy. One of the services private contracting will render is to require state agencies to specify their goals as clearly as possible, along with criteria by which their attainment is to be assessed. This is just one more way in which contracting makes visible, and therefore more solvable, problems of penology that are always there but usually overlooked.

One critic has cited the case of a transcendental meditation group that wanted to build and run a prison with the requirement that all prisoners practice meditation. Lest it be thought that this proves the irresponsible extremes to which only the private sector is prone, let us remember how the penitentiary got its name: through the Quaker-inspired but state-imposed requirement that prisoners spend their time in solitary, silent contemplation of the evil they had done. Indeed, the contractor so worrisome to this critic already operates a meditation program inside one of Vermont's state-run prisons. Other state prisons, such as Folsom, also have TM programs. In fact, it is hard to imagine a private company subscribing to penological beliefs so bizarre that they have not been implemented already in some state system. Nonetheless, it is still true that it is the mandate of the state to define the parameters of justice and to see that they are fulfilled. It would seem, however, that this is at least as likely to occur under contractual arrangements as otherwise.

The Profit Motive

Before we look at motives, we should note one point of logic at the outset. Strictly speaking, the motivation of those who apply a punishment is not relevant either to the justice or to the effectiveness of the punishment. It is true that for punishment to be a moral enterprise, it is important that it be done for the right reasons. This, however, is a stricture that applies more to those who determine and decree the punishment than to those who carry it out—to legislative and judicial more than to executive agents. The immediate agents of punishment may be humans with motives virtuous or venal, or robots with no motives at all; that does not affect the requirements of justice.

Still, the matter of motives—or rather, one particular motive—seems to be of such great importance to so many opponents of proprietary prisons that it must be dealt with. These critics believe that "criminal justice and profits don't mix." The ACLU [American Civil Liberties Union] in particular has complained repeatedly that "the profit motive is incompatible with doing justice."

If it is legitimate to examine the motives of interested parties, then to be consistent we ought to examine the motives of *all* parties, including state agencies, public employee unions, prison reform groups, and "public interest" groups. All these parties, like private vendors, have motives that reflect self-interest as well as altruism, and agendas that are hidden as well as overt. For example, the ACLU's National Prison Project may really be as much opposed to prisons *per se* as to running them like a business. They may be afraid that more efficient prisons will mean more imprisonment. They do not object to the profits that are made from the private administration of community correctional programs that serve as *alternatives* to prison.

A consistent objection to the existence of vested interests in punishment would have to focus as much on the public sector as on the private. Is it wrong for state employees to have a financial stake in the existence of a prison system? Is it wrong for their unions to "profit" by extracting compulsory dues for those employees? Is it wrong for a state prison bureaucracy to seek growth (more personnel, bigger budgets, new investment in human and physical capital) through seizing the profits of others (taxation) rather than through reinvestment of its own profits? Are the sanctions of the state diminished or tainted when they

166

are administered by public employees organized to maximize their personal benefits? If not, why would it tarnish those sanctions to be administered by professionals who make an honest profit? I admit I have posed these questions in prejudicial language, but I have done so to make a point. The notion that any activity carried out for profit, *as compared to salary and other benefits*, is thereby tainted, is simply an expression of prejudice. Both are economic motivations. . . .

Replacing "public servants" with "profit seekers" in the management of prisons will not trade those whose motives are noble for those whose motives are base. Rather, it will replace actors whose motives we suspect too little with actors whose motives we are inclined to suspect perhaps too much. . . .

The Benefits of Competition

In the case of prisons, the existence of competition, even potential competition, will make the public less tolerant of facilities that are crowded, dirty, unsafe, inhumane, ineffective, and prone to riots and lawsuits. Indeed, the fact that these conditions have existed for so long in monopolistic state prisons is a big part of what makes private prisons seem attractive. The possibility of an alternative will make the public, quite rightly, more demanding in its expectations.

Without competition, the state has had a monopoly over both service and supervision, over both doing justice and seeing that it is done properly. With competition, there will be a proliferation of agencies having a direct stake in both, without detracting at all from the state's role as the final arbiter of justice.

For these reasons, among others, the profit motive is not necessarily in conflict with the pursuit of justice; it can, in fact, be conducive to it.

If we want to have prisons that do justice and follow due process, then here's what we should do. First, we should define what we mean by these concepts and decide how to measure them. Then, we should shop around. Where can we get the most, or the best, of these values for our money? It may turn out to be the department of corrections and its public employees, or it may turn out to be a provider competing on the open market. We cannot know which unless we are able to make comparisons. What we should *not* do is beg the question by declaring proprietary prisons to be either unjust by definition or improper on principle.

"Helpless men and women have never fared well in the hands of profit-seeking entrepreneurs."

Private Prisons Are Unjust

Michael Walzer

Michael Walzer is an editor of *Dissent* magazine and a contributing editor for *The New Republic*. A professor of social science for the Institute of Advanced Studies at Princeton University in Princeton, New Jersey, Walzer is the author of several books, including *Spheres of Justice: A Defense of Pluralism and Equality* and *Exodus and Revolution.* In the following viewpoint, Walzer argues that while private firms may be able to operate prisons more efficiently and economically than the state, privatization is likely to make prison conditions unjust. Abuses will occur, he contends, because private prisons are interested in making money, rather than protecting prisoners' rights. Because the state sentences people to prison, it should take responsibility for their treatment, he concludes.

As you read, consider the following questions:

1. According to Walzer, what is wrong with private prisons?
2. An argument for private prisons is that they will be more competitive than their state and federal counterparts. The author believes this is inaccurate. Why?

Michael Walzer, "Hold the Justice," *The New Republic*, April 8, 1985. Reprinted by permission of *The New Republic*, © 1985, The New Republic, Inc.

The idea of "privatization". . . has evidently taken hold—and it has taken hold in a strange place. One somehow imagined that even a minimal state, stripped of all its welfare functions, would still have a police force and a prison system of its own. But private prisons, so the argument goes, are much cheaper to run than public prisons, and the owners can still make a profit; we need such men and their good works. Here are our convicts: *enrichissez-vous!*

We ought to be talking about the barbarous conditions that exist in many prisons, the swelling population of young and minor offenders, alternative forms of custody and control. But the argument from cheapness, in these mean times, is not surprising; it may even be true. Entrepreneurs in the incarceration business will probably be bound by less rigorous building and safety codes; they won't have to pay union wages and pensions; they will more easily skimp on the training of guards and the care of (more and more) prisoners. But if all this makes for economic efficiency, what does it do to justice?

Economic Issues Not Crucial

I am inclined to concede the cheapness issue. It is not unimportant; but economic arguments cannot be the crucial ones. The Vietnam War could probably have been fought more cheaply if General William Westmoreland had fielded a private army, without 20-year retirements, short-term tours of combat duty, extensive rest and recreation facilities and without nagging reporters and nervous politicians. The idea is, nonetheless, unattractive. The U.S. government could conceivably raise more money if it farmed out the income tax to the private sector. Entrepreneurs in the collection business might well display what one supporter of private prisons claims for their eager operators: "a vitality that is sometimes lacking in civil servants." The degree of vitality would presumably depend upon the likelihood of profit. But once again the idea is unattractive. Encounters with the tax collector would be even more difficult than they are today if we knew that our deductions were also his profit margin. He would be nothing more, in that case, than another competitor, another market antagonist, grasping for our money.

Difficulties With Private Prisons

Private prisons pose similar difficulties but in a much sharper form: for imprisonment, unlike taxation (or conscription), is a way of punishing people, singling out some but not others, not only for painful but also for dishonorable and degrading treatment. How do we ever acquire a right to do that? The question goes to the heart of the state's legitimacy; it is a moral and political—not economic—question.

The strongest democratic defense of the right to punish goes roughly like this. When we agree to the laws (participate in making them or in electing representatives who make them) we accept the proposition that if we ever break the law we ought to be punished. Criminals are punished, then, with their own consent. And if this isn't active and explicit consent, then it is constructive and tacit: for the criminal has lived under and enjoyed the benefits of the laws, and could have participated in the making of those laws. Criminals are fellow citizens; when we punish them we presume upon the fellowship. (When we punish aliens or visitors we presume upon a kind of guest fellowship.)

Privatization Furthers Exploitation

Racial and ethnic minorities and low social-class whites are disproportionately represented in the American prison population. Today they are under the care and control of a government in which blacks, Hispanics and others are gaining a small share of power, at least a foothold. Corporate America is upper-class white. Only a few of its hirelings are minority people. Privatization places in the hands of the haves a tool to exploit and further enrich themselves at the expense of the have nots.

Edward Sagarin and Jess Maghan, *The Angolite*, January/February 1986.

But if this is right, then it is crucial that the agents of punishment be agents of the laws and of the people who make them. Though it may sound paradoxical, the criminal is punished by his own agents—who are ours too. That's why private punishment is ruled out. We can't be judges or police or jailers in our own name or for our own purposes. It is only some public purpose, which the criminal could share—which as a fellow citizen, he does share—that justifies punishment. Men and women who have been injured by a criminal may have good reasons to want him punished, but he isn't punished for those reasons or by those people but rather for reasons we all share and by representative officials.

Police and prison guards are our representatives, whose activities we have authorized. The policeman's uniform symbolizes his representative character. When he puts on his uniform, he strips himself bare, so to speak, of his private opinions and motivations. Ideally, at least, he is equally energetic in enforcing laws that he does and doesn't like and he treats all citizens, and all criminals, in the same way, whatever his personal prejudices. When the police behave in this way, impersonally enforcing the general will, their coercive powers are justified. They may annoy us or frustrate us or even, sometimes, frighten us, but they don't oppress us.

Consider a trivial but useful example: if, speeding down the highway, I am stopped by someone I can recognize (though I know nothing else about him) as a uniformed representative of the democratic state, I should not and probably will not feel resentful. But if I suspect that I have been stopped because of the color of my skin or the political tone of my bumper stickers, or because the policeman hopes for a bribe, then resentment and anger are the right response. Policemen with private motives are dangerous.

Not only private motives: corporate motives are dangerous too. If the group of policemen, or any subgroup among them, has purposes in mind different from the purposes we had in mind when we created a police force, justice is corrupted. Obviously, then, justice is often corrupted; our impersonal representatives turn out to be ordinary persons; they have careers, interests, feelings of their own. But we are protected against their selfishness and against their private angers and resentments, at least to some degree, by the professional ethic and internal safeguards of the civil service, by legislative oversight committees and civilian review boards, and finally by the courts, which uphold the law even, or especially, against the agents of the law.

What's Wrong with the Private Prison?

We can now see clearly what is wrong with the private prison. It exposes the prisoners to private or corporate purposes, and it sets them at some distance from the protection of the law. The critical exposure is to profit-taking at the prisoners' expense, and given the conditions under which they live, they are bound to suspect that they are regularly used and exploited. For aren't the purposes of their private jailers different from the purposes of the courts that sent them to jail? All the internal rules and regulations of their imprisonment, the system of discipline and reward, the hundreds of small decisions that shape their daily lives, are open now to a single unanswerable question: Is this punishment or economic calculation, the law or the market?

There are bound to be other questions too, not only about corporate profit-taking but also about private willfulness and caprice. Theorists of free enterprise insist that the market is a disciplinary agent, enforcing rational if not benevolent behavior; but the history of the pre-union factory suggests how ineffective this discipline is at the local level, how much room it leaves for petty tyranny. It is in part because prisoners can't form unions that we, who put them in prison, must accept responsibility for their treatment. How can we teach them their own responsibilities if we evade ours, leaving them to endure what is bound to

171

feel like one more racket?

Even if the market provided some initial control over the treatment of prisoners, it is unlikely to be effective for very long. Once a large private company has built and is operating a number of "facilities," holding thousands of men and women, the state is hardly in a position to break the contract and turn to some upstart entrepreneur with nothing to offer but a bid and a plan. At that point, competition won't do its work: the prison industry will turn out to look very much like the defense industry. This suggests that cost effectiveness may well be a short-term business, but that's not, again, the crucial point. It's more important that cleanliness, safety, and ordinary decency will almost certainly decline over the years. Helpless men and women have never fared well in the hands of profit-seeking entrepreneurs. The incentive system is all wrong. Who will look after the interests of prisoners? Who will be watching the prison owners as they run their "own" business?

Conditions in a Private Facility

In Houston, TX, we visited the Houston Processing Center, an institution operated by America's largest investors in private prisons, the Corrections Corporation of America (CCA). This institution is a 350-bed detention facility operated on behalf of the U.S. Immigration and Naturalization Service. The facility is used for the detention of suspected illegal aliens.

The institution demonstrated what are possibly the worst conditions we have ever witnessed in terms of inmate care and supervision. The inmates were contained in large dormitories each containing between 50 and 60 beds with no privacy whatsoever, no lockers, no screening around the toilets or showers which were open to view by both male and female staff. Inmates dined in these dormitories.

The [British] Prison Officers' Association, *Jericho*, Fall 1987.

Perhaps the courts will be watching. There are already indications that the courts will treat public and private prisons as legally identical institutions. How can they do otherwise? Imprisonment is a state action, and so is every decision made, whoever makes it, about the course and character of imprisonment. All such decisions are subject to constitutional norms, and the courts will do what they can to enforce those norms. The enforcement will probably be more roundabout, and will take longer and be harder to monitor, in private than in public prisons. It is not all that effective now, but at least it offers the hope of legal protection.

This is probably the chief economic advantage of privatization —that it shuts down this hope, that it offers a (temporary) escape from the enforcement of constitutional norms. The resulting savings are like the profit added when a factory moves from union to non-union territory. If the union catches up, the old situation is restored. Similarly, if the courts catch up, we will find ourselves again where we are now, with judges struggling to do what state legislatures and Congress ought to do—reform the prison system. It will turn out that we haven't privatized the prisons so much as deputized the "owners" and all their employees.

The Present System

Perhaps, indeed, we should deputize nongovernmental agencies to perform some prison-like functions. The present system is so awful that we all might benefit, prisoners too, from a little flexibility, unorthodoxy, experimentation. But this will have to be the work of nonprofit agencies, with publicly recognized programs and explicit authorization. We should not be contracting out, as if these were not *our* prisoners; we should be bringing new ideas into the orbit of the public service. The argument from democratic theory need not commit us to prisons as they now exist or to a single pattern of bureaucratic organization. The argument commits us only to political responsibility. So long as we send men and women to prison, we have to pay attention to what happens to them once they are there. It may be a sad truth, but it is a truth nonetheless: in a democracy, the prisons belong to the people.

"Under private ownership and operation of adult facilities, operating costs can be reduced with no decline in the quality of life for inmates."

Private Prisons Are More Efficient than Public Prisons

Randall Fitzgerald

Randall Fitzgerald is a staff writer for *Reader's Digest* and the author of five books on domestic public policy issues. In the following viewpoint, Fitzgerald argues that private prisons can help to alleviate the overcrowding crisis within the prison system. He contends that private firms will be able to run prisons more efficiently and humanely than the public sector, and that the government can monitor the performance of private prisons.

As you read, consider the following questions:

1. According to the author, what are the drawbacks to federally- and state-funded prisons?
2. How did private prisons evolve, according to Fitzgerald?
3. Do you agree with the author when he argues that private prisons could not be any worse than public prisons?

Excerpted, with permission, from *When Government Goes Private* by Randall Fitzgerald, © 1988 Pacific Research Institute for Public Policy. Published by Universe Books, New York, 1988.

Faced with a court-ordered ceiling on the city's jail population, Washington, D.C., officials in early 1986 bused 55 inmates to a privately owned prison in Cowansville, Pennsylvania, north of Pittsburgh. The misdemeanants spent less than a week in the minimum-security facility before a Pennsylvania state judge ruled that they must be returned because the District of Columbia had failed to consult with Pennsylvania state government authorities about using that state's private jail. As the inmates were rounded up for their trip back to the nation's capital, a *Washington Post* reporter on hand for the occasion detected their considerable resentment at leaving the center's simple brick and concrete facility. They bombarded the reporter with praise for the center's roomy cells, relaxed atmosphere, catered food, and friendly guards. "It's like the difference between night and day," said a 51-year-old inmate, Luther McGee, comparing the private prison with the D.C. Jail. "It doesn't feel like a prison. They give you a feeling of being a human being." By contrast, the D.C. Jail was "built for chimpanzees," remarked an inmate serving time for driving with a suspended license. "The guards (at D.C. Jail) ignore everything you say; the place is filthy. It was a nightmare for me."

Pennsylvania officials apparently could not summon the inmates' enthusiasm for privately owned and operated prisons. The private facility, known as the 268 Center, had been conceived when nearby Pittsburgh fell under a court-ordered population ceiling at its jail and a facility was desperately needed to handle those inmates and the overflow from neighboring county prisons. Other private prisons were being developed by the firm of Buckingham Security, founded by a former state prison warden. These developments galvanized opposition from the union representing state and local prison guards, which feared the competition of private prisons, and from the American Civil Liberties Union, which said it had to protect inmates from mistreatment by "profit-hungry" private operators. Pennsylvania Governor Richard Thornburgh responded to this political pressure by asking for the court order to return the D.C. inmates, as members of the state legislature improvised legislation placing a moratorium on the operation of private prisons.

America's Correctional Crisis

The dilemma confronting our nation's capital city underscores the severity of the crisis that grips penal systems nationwide. Prisons in 33 states and the District of Columbia have been under federal court orders to reduce overcrowding that resulted when the state and federal inmate population increased by 66% between 1980 and 1986 to 546,000 prisoners. In Pennsylvania 14,000 prisoners were squeezed into facilities designed for only

9,500. A frustrated Tennessee county sheriff with an over-crowded jail handcuffed inmates to a state prison fence all day in 1985 to protest a federal court order barring their entry into the already burgeoning state system. Too little space in Texas state prisons produced the highest prison homicide rate in the nation. (It was three times *safer* to drive on Texas highways than to spend time in a Texas jail.) Violent prison uprisings caused by cramped conditions struck prison systems in nearly every state. A maximum-security prison in Pittsburgh erupted, and 24 in-mates, three prison guards, and two firefighters lay injured. Four buildings burned to the ground and 32 persons were in-jured at the District of Columbia's Lorton Reformatory, and three died and several dozen were injured at a West Virginia penitentiary.

An obvious remedy would have been the construction of more prisons and larger jails. But most states require public referen-dums to authorize the issuance of bonds to finance prison and jail construction, and during the 1980s an average of 60% of jail-bond proposals were being defeated at the polls in local elec-tions. These defeats combined with constitutional and statutory debt limitations on general obligation bonds forced governments to attempt new approaches. Some responded to overcrowding by prematurely releasing convicts. The result was more crime in the streets. Of 613 prisoners given early release from New York City jails in 1983, two-thirds either were arrested for new of-fenses or skipped bail. Public outrage rapidly eliminated early releases as a safety valve to relieve overcrowding.

The Problems in the Public System

The corrections field suffers from outmoded facilities, rising staff costs, a failure to innovate, increasing judicial demands for improved services, and public clamorings to incarcerate even more prisoners less expensively. From these pressures sprang both budgetary and credibility gaps, as prison officials scram-bled to quell inmate revolts that erupt each time overcrowding reaches unbearable limits. To relieve these pressures, the pri-vate sector, beginning in earnest about 1983, began its rush into the prison construction and operation business, with at least ten companies forming or expanding to meet the demand.

Our nation's first prison built in 1814 turned out to be the most expensive building constructed in this country through the early 19th century. Little innovation has occurred in prison con-struction since that time. "Because of the character of the way that these buildings are built, there is little or no incentive to in-troduce new technologies or new ideas, because there is no profit motive on either the part of the user or the builders to consider an alternative," testified Paul Silver, a New York architect and prison designer, in a 1984 appearance before the Joint Economic Committee of Congress. Privatization of prison construction, according to Commissioner Thomas Coughlin of the New York State Department of Correctional Services, is "the quickest, most inexpensive way to go."

The First Truly Private Detention Facility

In 1983 the Immigration and Naturalization Service desperately needed a new detention facility in the Houston area to hold illegal aliens before their deportation. Lacking the funding for either construction or the staffing for a new facility, INS solicited bids from the private sector. Corrections Corporation of America (CCA), based in Nashville and backed by some of the same investors involved in the Hospital Corporation of America, won the contract. In April 1984, at a cost of $8.2 million for land and construction, the first wholly designed, built, owned, and operated private detention facility in the world opened— just six months after construction started. Had INS undertaken the construction project, it could have taken two years and cost in excess of $12 million.

Private prison builders lower their costs by 15% and more below government costs by using more innovative design and building techniques, taking advantage of flexibility, and avoiding the time-consuming multi-agency contract-negotiation processes that characterize government construction. If during construction a government agency needs to make a design alteration, approval must be sought in the form of a change order that must drift back through various layers of bureaucracy, a procedure that could take months. Private firms can make such changes immediately. During construction of the Houston detention facility, CCA discovered the need for a significant modification in door design. A decision was made and the new doors were ordered within six hours, whereas it could have taken six weeks or more in government. Private firms avoid overdesigning buildings, while government prison designs often suffer from too much complicated detail and not enough attention to functional needs (meaning more guards than necessary must be retained). Private builders also select only the most appropriate materials to meet goals of economy, construction speed, and security.

"The checks and balances within government have become too paralytic and self-defeating," contends Gay E. Vick, CCA vice-president for design and construction, who formerly designed prison facilities for the State of Virginia. "Government tends to lose sight of the goals. There are so many regulations the goal becomes how to get around the regulation rather than solving the problem. Industry lets the process be flexible in pursuit of the goals, while government is overly concerned with the process."

A creative form of prison financing and construction has been pioneered by the National Corrections Corporation, based in Denver, a firm involved in jail construction since 1972. If a county needs a new jail, this company builds it, then leases it back to the county. Such a maneuver enables local governments to circumvent voters who otherwise would have to vote on bonds or taxes for new jail construction. In 1985 the company expanded into prison operations, signing a contract to build, staff, and operate a jail for three New Mexico counties.

The Evolution of Prison Privatization

Prison privatization began as an evolutionary process when support services like medical care and food provision were contracted out several decades ago, followed later by contracting for pre-release, work release, and halfway-house facility operation. Residential supervision of juvenile offenders became the next phase of contracting, followed by federal contracting for the construction and operation of illegal-alien detention centers.

The Benefits of Private Enterprise

Privatization of corrections has the potential to expose the public penal sector to the vitality and flexibility of private enterprise—to private sector management efficiencies and principles of competitive business; to methodologies designed to meet and respond to ever-changing penological circumstances; to experimentation with new modes of corrections, uninhibited by the bureaucracies and politics inherent in the management and operation of public penal facilities; and to address and satisfy special penological needs with an economy of scale that may not be possible in a single sector jurisdiction.

W. James Ellison, *Cumberland Law Review*, 1987.

Privatization of health-care services within jails was pioneered by Prison Health Services, which brings nurses, physicians, dentists, and psychiatrists into prisons for a monthly fee of $90 to $120 per inmate. Only 160 of the nation's 4,000 jails are accredited by the National Commission on Correctional Healthcare, and of that number 31 have health services provided by Prison Health Services, which guarantees its clients accreditation within one year. In 1979 the Federal Bureau of Prisons began contracting-out all of its 300 halfway houses to nonprofit agencies and private for-profit companies; today at least 1,500 privately operated facilities for juveniles can be found nationwide;

and since 1983, the Immigration and Naturalization Service has turned over a dozen illegal-alien detention centers to private operators. Concludes a study by the National Institute of Justice, "Private sector participation in correctional programs is thus a relatively old idea which is being expanded and reconsidered in the face of modern needs and pressures."

California in 1986 became the first state to allow its corrections department to contract-out for care of state prisoners, utilizing two firms—Eclectic Communications, Inc., and Management and Training Corporation of Ogden, Utah—to operate return-to-custody facilities for parole violators. Eclectic, of Ventura, California, operates 13 corrections facilities under contract with state and federal agencies, including work-furlough, alien-detention, halfway-house, and parole-violator centers. In 1983 it opened the first privatized federal juvenile detention facility in America at Hidden Valley Ranch in La Honda, California.

Private Sector Efficiency

Behavioral Systems Southwest of Pomona, California, founded by a former San Quentin prison guard, Ted Nissen, after he became disenchanted with traditional approaches to corrections, operates 12 halfway houses and detention facilities which brought in revenues to the company approaching $5 million in 1985. Six of the minimum-security prisons are designed to prepare inmates for their reentry into society. States and the federal government are charged from $14 to $33.50 a day per detainee, about 15% less than what the State of California spends on similar programs. Nissen believes that a perverse set of bureaucratic incentives have helped overfill our prisons and raise the costs to society. "Status in the corrections system goes to those who run the highest-security prisons, so the whole system promotes classifying people as more of a security risk than they are. We have built a prison industry based on concrete walls, guard towers, and the overclassification of inmates." Nissen and other reformers among the private prison entrepreneurs see this bureaucratic inertia as an opportunity to build better, cheaper prisons, while developing programs behind bars that prepare inmates for survival outside prison.

Under private ownership and operation of adult facilities, operating costs can be reduced with no decline in the quality of life for inmates. Private firms say they generally can obtain a better price on supplies using bulk-purchasing arrangements, require fewer employees because of innovative building designs, and function with greater flexibility than can government.

CCA operates its Houston detention facility for nearly $3 per detainee a day cheaper than the Immigration Service can run its own facilities, a gap which is probably much higher because

179

CCA includes construction costs in its per diem while the INS uses only operating costs in figuring its rates. Lowering costs need not come at the expense of corrections employees. The starting salaries of guards at the Houston center are higher than those of personnel performing comparable jobs in other government detention centers in the region. When CCA took over operations of the Panama City, Florida, jail in late 1985, each jail employee received an immediate 7% pay raise plus a $500 bonus. As additional motivation, CCA provides its employees with stock-ownership and profit-sharing plans, something government can never duplicate. Private companies also lower costs by reducing dependence on bureaucracy. "Government is so easy to beat because it is so inherently inefficient," argues Tom Beasley, president of CCA, which has seven former state commissioners of corrections on its payroll. "So much of prison budgets is allocated to bureaucratic overhead that has nothing to do with the institution. We don't have that layer.". . .

The National Institute of Justice Study

A comprehensive study of private prisons released in 1985 by the National Institute of Justice, compiled a list of possible benefits from private ownership. Funding for new jail construction would be easier to obtain with private providers, taking the capital-appropriation burdens off government. Much bureaucratic red tape would be eliminated along with the political considerations and patronage connected with the public system. Using private companies would allow government more flexibility to experiment with new models of corrections facilities and programs. Private companies would be more cost-effective and efficient, and would pay taxes on their profits, thus providing additional returns to taxpayers. Eliminating civil-service restrictions allows private providers to control employee performance more closely and to tailor staff to changing program needs. "Independence from the bureaucracy also gives the private provider greater freedom to innovate and to deal more rapidly with problems in the management or delivery of services. Finally, unlike government providers, the private sector is under competitive pressure to perform—pressure that can provide significant incentive to deliver high-quality services.". . .

Factories with Fences

Prisons could be organized around various industrial activities—creating real factories with fences instead of just warehouses with walls—to be managed by the major corporations already involved in prison construction and operation. Under our current system, instead of prisoners paying their "debt" to society, they increase the debt of American taxpayers by consuming public resources without offsetting the expense of their incarceration, which averages more than $20,000 a year per inmate.

Wages earned by working prisoners could be divided three ways: to contribute toward the cost of their confinement; to make restitution to the victims of their crimes; and to help support their own families during imprisonment, or accumulate funds for use on their release to lessen any temptation for a return to a life of crime. Productive work behind bars would also reduce prisoner idleness, which is a major cause of gang warfare and other violence in our prisons. . . .

The System Needs Innovation

Creating and maintaining efficient, fair, and humane correctional facilities will never be possible unless innovation from beyond traditional prison models is allowed to play a role. "Only true innovation will address the larger problem of why our system of incarceration is such a mess," concludes Peter Greenwood, the Rand Corporation's chief criminal-justice researcher. "And when you're looking for innovators you don't look to government; you look to business." Bringing about experimental models of institutional corrections practice, new ideas with concrete improvements, should be the goal of privatization innovators, rather than simply attempting to jumpstart an outmoded and decaying system into a momentary flicker of efficiency.

Private Prisons Couldn't Do a Worse Job

It is a great misfortune that prison reform lobbies are largely from the political left. They recoil at the idea of profits for companies invariably described as multi-national, and they seem to believe 'commercial prisons' would dilute the right of the state's courts to decide sentences. Market alternatives can scarcely get worse results than the present state system; so it is an illustration of how far liberal economics has yet to be applied that intelligent people can still regard private prisons as an idea unworthy of experiment.

Peter Clarke, *Economic Affairs*, December/January 1989.

Private prison operators can be financially penalized by government for jail violence and escapes, and rewarded for programs behind bars that succeed at reducing recidivism rates. Neither approach can be duplicated within government. Using private operators may also give the public sector a new ability to enforce correctional standards, since the contractor can be held accountable for any deterioration in prison operations or conditions. Government can afford to operate unconstitutional facilities, and continue to do so despite court orders. The private sector will not have that luxury since the threat of fines and contract severance would hit where it hurts most—in the pocketbook. Government confronts the real costs of incarceration, and the impact of stiffer sentencing laws, only when a private contractor bills it on the basis of the number of inmates housed.

"Prisons and jails have been operated as public monopolies for so long that there is no alternative to which they can be compared," argues Charles R. Ring, author of a report on private prisons for the American Correctional Association. He answers critics who believe that in cutting costs, private prison operators would ignore the welfare of the inmates, and that since profit might depend on expanding inmate populations, private operators would lobby for harsher laws, longer sentences, and more prison beds. Ring is not convinced they could manipulate public opinion and lawmakers that easily, especially since "given current levels of overcrowding and public sentiment already in favor of stricter sentencing, there will be no shortage of inmates to fill new facilities." Efficiency is not synonymous with exploitation, he argues, and the primary advantage of private correctional services is their ability to adjust the level of services more quickly to meet changing needs. "By establishing and enforcing population limits and operating standards, the government can, in fact, require much better conditions at private prisons than currently exist at many public institutions."

Give Private Prisons a Chance

Some civil-rights advocates question the propriety of government delegating any of its police powers over what they perceive is a quasi-judicial function of criminal justice. Answers CCA's president Tom Beasley: "We're not policymakers; we implement. Ours is a care and custody function. We provide better facilities, better inmate care, better working conditions and higher pay for employees—all at less cost to the taxpayer. Now give me a moral impropriety in that!"

If anything, the focus of civil rights concern over moral propriety seems misplaced. Other policy questions deserve greater attention. Does it truly serve the cause of justice, for instance, to incarcerate in detention centers mostly hard-working, honest people who happen to be in this country illegally in search of a job? Is it humane to imprison victimless crime offenders with hardened criminals convicted of offenses against people and property? Can we call any system fair that refuses to allow the perpetrators of crimes to labor behind bars to compensate their victims?. . .

A Russian novelist, Fyodor Dostoevsky, wrote that "the degree of civilization in a society can be judged by entering its prisons."

Government at all levels has simply failed to confront the problems of our prisons in a cost-effective and humane way. "It is hard to imagine that the private sector could do any worse a job than government has done," Claudia Wright, an American Civil Liberties Union lawyer, admitted in a *Dun's Business Month* interview. As the *Chattanooga Times* newspaper has put it, endorsing the prison privatization trend, "Private enterprise should be given a chance to find the corrections solutions that have eluded the public sector."

"When we examine the particular constraints operating on the prison industry, we discover serious flaws in the standard arguments for the inherent efficiency of private enterprise."

Private Prisons Are Not More Efficient than Public Prisons

Christine Bowditch and Ronald S. Everett

Christine Bowditch is an assistant professor of sociology at the University of Southern Maine in Portland. Ronald S. Everett is an assistant professor of sociology at Louisiana State University, Baton Rouge. During 1990 and 1991, Everett served on the United States Sentencing Commission, an agency of the federal government charged with evaluating federal sentencing guidelines. In the following viewpoint, Bowditch and Everett dispute claims of the superior efficiency and flexibility of private prisons. The privatization debate, they conclude, serves only to deflect attention from the fundamental problems facing the American criminal justice system, particularly an overreliance on prisons.

As you read, consider the following questions:

1. How do the authors support their belief that privatization would not result in better efficiency?
2. What do Bowditch and Everett mean by "hidden costs"?
3. According to the authors, what are the public policy implications of prison privatization?

Christine Bowditch and Ronald S. Everett, "Private Prisons: Problems Within the Solution," *Justice Quarterly*, vol. 4, no. 3, 1987, pp. 441-453. Reprinted with permission of the Academy of Criminal Justice Sciences.

Concern about the serious overcrowding in prisons and the current fiscal constraints of public budgets has prompted a number of public officials and private investors to consider an expansion of the private sector's role in corrections. As with the privatization of other public services, the appeal of private-sector involvement rests on the belief that private firms, especially for-profit firms, can outperform the public sector in the delivery of goods and services. Private financing, delivery, and management of prisons and prison services seem to offer a solution to the immediate, pressing problems facing our nation's prison system. In this viewpoint we examine the proposed benefits of private prisons and explore some of the possible problems accompanying this solution.

The Problem

A review of the factors that led to the current problems of prison overcrowding and fiscal constraint helps explain the appeal of privatization. Policies concerning prisons and prison populations change in response to a number of external factors, including economic pressures, demographic fluctuations, legal decisions, and ideological changes. During the 1970s all these factors worked together to produce a critical shift in criminal justice policy.

When liberals became disillusioned with the effectiveness of rehabilitation and when the recession eroded public support for "lenient" prison programs, the goals of incapacitation, deterrence, and retribution resurfaced in criminal justice policy. Public sentiment as well as the emergence of the justice model focused attention on sentencing policies. Sentencing reform had the political appeal of appearing relatively costless while responding at the same time to the public demand for "get tough" policies. The harsher mandatory and determinant sentences that resulted, however, helped create the current overcrowding in prisons.

The prison population in the United States tripled between 1970 and 1985. As of June 1985, federal and state prisons held 490,000 inmates, with another 230,000 in jails. In 1985, at least one correctional institution in each of 33 states was under court order to reduce overcrowding. Pennsylvania, although not under court order, reported its state prison system as 33 percent over capacity. Many observers, however, noted that public resources lack the flexibility to respond to this crisis within the time and budget constraints that exist presently.

The Private Solution

Various advocates of privatization claim that the private sector can provide the flexibility and cost efficiency needed to meet current demands for prison space and to improve prison conditions. Privatization addresses the problem of prison space without challenging the underlying justifications for sentencing policies. In addition, private initiatives in corrections follow the more general movement to shift public functions to the private sector. In view of this situation, private-sector involvement has broad public and private appeal.

Tom Hachtman for INX. Reprinted with permission.

Although the private operation of adult prison facilities is a recent move, the private sector has long been involved in the correctional system. Public institutions have contracts with private firms for the operation of prison work programs. Private vendors supply health care services, educational and vocational training, drug treatment programs, and an array of other services to public institutions. Private contractors provide community-based programs, such as half-way houses and rehabilitation services, and operate a range of juvenile facilities.

Even so, the recent attention given to the privatization of corrections has focused not on these long-standing private services, but on the development of for-profit corporations designed to finance and/or operate private detention and correctional institutions. The most prominent of these corporations are Corrections

Corporation of America (CCA), Behavioral Systems Southwest, Buckingham Security Limited, and American Corrections Corporation. All these corporations pursue contracts for the construction and/or management of prisons and detention facilities. Most of the contracts awarded to these and other firms have been for small, low-security facilities for the Immigration and Naturalization Service, the U.S. Bureau of Prisons, or county jails. CCA, however, operates both the Silverdale work farm in Hamilton County, Tennessee, and the first private, high-security facility in Bay County, Florida.

Although most private detention facilities currently operate on a small scale and with minimal security, the ultimate goal of these private corporations is the operation of adult state institutions. However, the controversy over private prisons has thwarted these efforts. In Tennessee the CCA proposal to take over the operation of the entire state system was rejected by the legislature. In Pennsylvania the state moratorium on private prisons stopped Buckingham's plans to build a 715-cell maximum-security facility for protective custody inmates. Yet the current crisis of prison overcrowding and the continuing difficulties with financing and constructing public institutions may well create a more receptive atmosphere for these private initiatives. Thus, we must consider carefully the potential advantages and disadvantages of private, for-profit prisons.

The Views of Privatization Proponents

Proponents of privatization cite a number of advantages to private prisons. Such institutions could provide a greater diversity of programs and facilities than those currently available within the public system. Small facilities within the state, or regional facilities serving several states, could handle special inmate populations or offer special rehabilitative or training programs. Contracts for services could specify maximum inmate populations, facility conditions, standards of performance, perhaps even treatment outcomes, and thus avoid the serious problems currently plaguing the public system. Lobbies, sponsored by the private firms, could exert political pressure on state legislatures and thereby secure the necessary support for a humane correctional system.

The weight of the argument supporting privatization, however, rests on the belief that private industry can respond quickly and cost-efficiently to the current pressures for more prison space. With so many prison systems under court order to reduce overcrowding, the speed at which private corporations respond makes privatization an attractive solution. The 1985 report prepared by the Legislative Budget and Finance Committee of the Pennsylvania General Assembly, for example, cites as a key benefit the shorter time required for private corporations to expand or construct prison facilities. Both public and private sources agree that the private sector can act faster than government bureaucracies in providing prison space. In addition, several authors note that private provision allows the state to cancel contracts for services and space as population demands decrease.

Private Services in Other Sectors

Proponents of privatization frequently refer to the success of private services in health care, education, parcel delivery, or food service as support for their argument of cost efficiency. When compared to the services available in the public sector, these private alternatives appear more efficient in both cost and performance. From this evidence, proponents argue that private industry could also operate prisons more efficiently than the public sector.

Although different authors cite different cost advantages to privatization and some authors raise the issue of hidden costs, advocates of private prisons report savings over public institutions. The state, they believe, gains in two ways. First, the private corporation makes the initial capital investment in facility construction. As with private financing arrangements, this arrangement enables states to avoid debt ceilings and voter approval on bond issues. Second, the private prison charges the state less per day to hold each inmate than does the publicly operated facility. These savings come from several sources, such as reduced building costs, reduced labor costs, and economies of scale. Finally, the most powerful argument cites the inherent efficiency created by the profit motive. . . .

Problems with the Private Solution

Although some proponents of privatization acknowledge the limitations of a free-market model or admit that prisons carry out a task fundamentally different from other government services, they assess the advantages of private prisons as though these restrictions and differences did not affect potential gains in efficiency. Yet, when we examine the particular constraints operating on the prison industry, we discover serious flaws in the standard arguments for the inherent efficiency of private enterprise.

Proponents of privatization point to the success of the private sector in delivering other formerly public services. Typically the private sector offers the greatest gains in efficiency when it specializes in a particular, limited service. Thus private vendors can offer cost-effective, efficient services to public institutions, as in the case of food, medical, or maintenance services now contracted out by prisons. It also seems reasonable that the private sector could offer certain advantages in providing services to special inmate populations.

Yet, examples of private efforts to operate total institutions provide less support for increased efficiency through the private management of an entire prison. When a private corporation takes over a total institution, such as a psychiatric hospital, medical hospital, nursing home, or school, concerns for profitability often restrict or eliminate services to underprivileged groups or those with special needs. Difficult or unprofitable cases typically receive no service. In such cases, public hospitals and schools must provide programs for these people. Therefore comparing costs between private and public institutions disguises important differences in the type and range of services provided.

Prisons Are Different

Unlike those institutions, however, prisons do not have a clientele that can select among alternative firms. Instead the state, as consumer, would select a private firm to provide prison space.

Contracts might well specify the type of prisoner accepted and thus create special institutions for the least troublesome groups of inmates. If a private corporation, however, assumes responsibility for a mainstream population or for an entire state adult system, that firm would be forced to provide the full range of services and conditions mandated by law. The savings gained in other institutions by dropping unprofitable cases would not be possible in these prisons. Instead, savings could arise only through the internal efficiency promoted by a competitive marketplace.

Some of the most frequently cited ways to save costs through privatization are sidestepping government red tape and reducing labor costs. Much of that red tape, however, assures public participation and review of policy decisions. Voter approval on bonds, public hearings on service changes, and legislative reviews on policy options cannot be reduced to mere inefficiency. In the words of M. Wayne Huggins, spokesman for the national sheriffs' group, "Red tape, in a lot of cases, is there to protect the public."

We should not assume that the lower labor costs of private firms necessarily represent an advantage. Even in the public sector, the average correctional officer earned only $10,780 per year in 1986. In view of such a low salary, the retirement benefits offered to civil service employees do not seem excessive. Yet private corporations target both salaries and benefits for reduction. Planned savings on labor costs also include reductions in training and in staff size. CCA's plans for correctional staff at the Bay County facility included less than 50 hours of training, compared to the 320-hour program mandated for public employees. Sheriff Huggins reported that his guards receive 14 weeks of training, compared to CCA's 120 hours during the first year and 80 hours in a year thereafter. CCA also reported that it designed its facilities to reduce staff requirements. These cutbacks should be weighed against the reported benefits of cost reductions.

Market Failure

Other cost-saving mechanisms of privatization rely on the inherent efficiency of a competitive marketplace. In a model of the economy as a fully competitive system, the consumer enforces a private firm's efficiency. If the service or product offered by a firm drops in quality (or rises in price), the consumer either patronizes another firm or complains to the management. Albert Hirschman defines these options as "exit" and "voice." According to this model, deterioration in a firm's performance will affect its profits and hence inspire greater efficiency. Hirschman argues, however, that a number of factors can limit the consumer's exit and voice options and thus violate the assumptions of a free-market model.

Private Firms Shouldn't Make Prison Policy

With profit-making prisons, the Wall Street companies, the architectural firms eager to build new facilities, the contractors who will be paid per prisoner have a vested interest in seeing that the incarcerated population of America increases. Whether that increase should take place is a matter of public policy and should be decided without the propaganda barrage of billion-dollar firms like E.F. Hutton and Shearson-American Express, two of the major corporations seeking a foothold in this business.

Edward Sagarin and Jess Maghan, *The Angolite*, January/February 1986.

Unlike this model of a completely competitive free market, the real marketplace includes forces that limit competition. Although many of the private detention facilities already constructed are small or dual-function structures, a maximum-security adult institution would require such an enormous capital investment that it would limit the number of firms able to compete for contracts. When one or several firms made these investments in capital, they would gain an advantage in the marketplace and would have a vested interest in limiting competition. In the face of restricted competition, the state would have limited exit options. Even with the available options, practical considerations could easily limit the state's ability to turn over contracts often enough to ensure a competitive market for adult high-security institutions. According to Hirschman even firms that ostensibly offer competition "can learn to play a coopera-tive, collusive game" which can limit the power of the con-sumer's exit option.

Indeed, experience demonstrates that private industry does not always provide the most cost-efficient services when given opportunities to reduce competition and exercise greater con-trol. The most obvious examples come from recent publicity over waste and mismanagement in defense contracts. We have no reason to expect that the same situation would not occur if a few corporations became the major suppliers of prison facilities.

Privatization could also make the state dependent on the pri-vate sector for the provision of prison facilities and services. If the private sector expands its investment in new prisons and if the state relinquishes control of existing facilities to private man-agement, private operators would assume a more dominant posi-tion in negotiating contracts and determining costs for services.

Hidden Costs

In addition to overestimating the gains in efficiency that com-petition would create, proponents of privatization give only lim-ited attention to many potential indirect or hidden costs. Even the administration of contracts would create a new cost to the state; one estimate places this cost as high as four percent of the total contract. The biggest potential cost, however, stems from the necessary creation of a regulatory bureaucracy. Even when private industry controls prison management, it must uphold federal and state guidelines on the custody and care of inmates. To ensure compliance, the state must develop a system for moni-toring private prisons. In addition to the traditional problems re-lated to control within the prison, the profit incentive of private firms could introduce new forms of abuse or corruption, such as cost-cutting methods in the delivery of services and the manipu-lation of release mechanisms to maintain maximum population.

The state would also have to provide means of dealing with emergencies that could endanger the public or the inmate popu-lation. Escapes, riots, fires, natural disasters, public health prob-lems, employee strikes, or bankruptcy would require some form of state intervention. Despite privatization, the state apparently would retain its responsibility for protecting the constitutional rights of prisoners. Provision for these state services would have to be calculated as costs to the private firms and written into the contract.

The problem of regulating a private prison industry would ex-tend beyond the costs of a state bureaucracy. Even without a profit incentive, history demonstrates the potential for abuse in the management of a total institution. Prisoners suffer the disad-vantage of having few advocates outside the state itself; regulation of prison conditions, prisoner treatment, and public safety would depend upon what systems the state could establish to monitor private prisons. Yet experience indicates the limit of the state's ability to monitor and control powerful, entrenched economic interests. Critics of the nuclear power industry, the Environmental Protection Agency, and the Occupational Safety and Health Administration, for example, have drawn attention to the problems and even the impotence of regulatory agencies.

Three major factors can limit the state's regulation of a private industry. First, if the state supports the goal of the industry, as in the development of nuclear power, the state regulatory mechanisms could suffer from a conflict of interests. Second, if industry lobbies depict their interests as the national interest or manipulate their political power to limit recognition of other options, as in the case of the auto and chemical industries, lobbyists could effectively influence state policy and regulation. Finally, if the regulatory agency uses personnel trained within the industry, the agency would share the industry's perspective on organization, goals, and priorities. We see no reason to expect that these factors would not influence the regulation of prisons. . . .

Policy Implications

In addition to the issues of cost, public accountability, and regulation, the expansion of the prison system made possible by privatization could ultimately influence criminal justice policy. Privatization advocates either do not address the consequences of expanded prison capacity for future policy or they credit a private competitive market with the flexibility to shrink as the demand for services declines.

Arguments for private prisons assume that we need only a cost-efficient means of providing prison space. Yet asking "Can for-profit prisons save us money?" moves us farther away from asking "Why do we use prisons?" Indeed, creating private interests in prisons may take us past a point where we can easily reconsider the goals of imprisonment implicit in the current sentencing policies.

Perhaps, however, we should question the rationale for these policies. Existing studies offer little evidence for the effectiveness of incapacitation or deterrence. Therefore we can see current policies only as a mechanism for punishment. Our resources might be spent better on programs that address the problem of criminality directly. Although no consensus exists on the causes of crime, the criminological literature suggests a number of factors related to criminality. Policies or programs that respond to these factors might do more for society than does our current system of retribution.

The development of for-profit prisons would create an industry with economic and political interests in prisons and therefore in policies concerning imprisonment. The availability of private prison space might encourage a continued reliance on prison sanctions; in addition, industry lobbies, concerned with maximization of profits, might promote policies that sustain or increase the demand for that space. In a less obvious and potentially more powerful way, a private prison industry could influence policy by participating in and funding the research organizations that formulate policy options. Because limiting consideration of alternative responses to crime would represent industry interests, research and discussion would focus on the benefits and even on the necessity of an extensive prison system. If this happens, profits—not theoretical justifications for imprisonment—would determine our use of prisons as the primary sanction for criminal behavior.

a critical thinking activity

Distinguishing Between Fact and Opinion

This activity is designed to help develop the basic reading and thinking skill of distinguishing between fact and opinion. Consider the following statement as an example: "The proposal of Corrections Corporation of America to take over the operation of the entire state prison system in Tennessee was rejected by the state legislature." This is a factual statement because it could be checked by examining the record of the Tennessee legislature or newspaper coverage of the issue. But the statement "Corrections Corporation of America should have been allowed to take over Tennessee's prison system because private firms are more efficient at running prisons than government" is an opinion. Many people may not agree that private firms are more efficient than the government at running prisons.

When investigating controversial issues it is important that one be able to distinguish between statements of fact and statements of opinion. It is also important to recognize that not all statements of fact are true. They may appear to be true, but some are based on inaccurate or false information. For this activity, however, we are concerned with understanding the difference between those statements that appear to be factual and those that appear to be based primarily on opinion.

Most of the following statements are taken from the viewpoints in this chapter. Consider each statement carefully. *Mark O for any statement you believe is an opinion or interpretation of facts. Mark F for any statement you believe is a fact. Mark I for any statement you believe is impossible to judge.*

If you are doing this activity as a member of a class or group, compare your answers with those of other class or group members. Be able to defend your answers. You may discover that others come to different conclusions than you do. Listening to the reasons others present for their answers may give you valuable insights into distinguishing between fact and opinion.

O = *opinion*
F = *fact*
I = *impossible to judge*

1. A small but growing number of penal institutions are privately owned.

2. John Locke argued that individuals in the state of nature have the right to punish those who aggress against them.

3. The state does not own the right to punish.

4. Prisoners are more concerned about practical considerations, like the quality of their food, than with who owns the prison.

5. Transcendental meditation programs exist in several state prisons.

6. Criminal justice and profits don't mix.

7. The American Civil Liberties Union's National Prison Project is opposed to private prisons.

8. Helpless men and women have never fared well in the hands of profit-seeking entrepreneurs.

9. Racial and ethnic minorities and poor whites are disproportionately represented in the American prison population.

10. State legislatures and Congress ought to drop the idea of prison privatization, and focus on reforming the prison system as it currently exists.

11. In early 1986, officials in Washington, D.C. bused 55 inmates from the city jail to a private prison in Pennsylvania.

12. The first wholly designed, built, owned, and operated private detention facility in the world was opened in 1983 in Houston, Texas.

13. Harsher mandatory and determinant sentences helped create the current overcrowding in prisons.

14. No consensus exists on the causes of crime.

15. With profit-making prisons, the contractors who will be paid per prisoner have a vested interest in seeing that the incarcerated population of America increases.

Periodical Bibliography

The following articles have been selected to supplement the diverse views presented in this chapter.

Kevin Acker	"Off with Their Overhead: More Prison Bars for the Buck," *Policy Review*, Fall 1989.
Lisa Belkin	"Rise of Private Prisons: How Much of a Bargain?" *The New York Times*, March 27, 1989.
Samuel Jan Brakel	"Give Private Firms a Greater Role," *The Wall Street Journal*, March 21, 1989.
Deborah Davis	"Prisons for Profit: Crime Pays If You Own the Jail," *In These Times*, August 17-30, 1988.
Randy Fitzgerald	"Free-Enterprise Jails: Key to Our Prison Dilemma?" *Reader's Digest*, March 1986.
David H. Folz and John M. Scheb II	"Prisons, Profits, and Politics: The Tennessee Privatization Experiment," *Judicature*, August/September 1989. Available from the American Judicature Society, 25 E. Washington, Suite 1600, Chicago, IL 60602.
Robert Lekachman	"The Craze for 'Privatization': Dubious Social Results of a Reaganite Dogma," *Dissent*, Summer 1989.
Charles H. Logan	"Incarceration, Inc.: Competition in the Prison Business," *USA Today*, March 1986.
H. Laws McCullough and Timothy S. Maguigan	"PRICOR: Proving Privatization Works," *American Jails*, November/December 1990. Available from the American Jail Association, 1000 Day Road, Suite 100, Hagerstown, MD 21740.
Allen L. Patrick	"Private Sector: Profit Motive vs. Quality," *Corrections Today*, April 1986. Available from the American Correctional Association, Inc., 8025 Laurel Lakes Court, Laurel, MD 20707.
The People	"Capitalists Find Profits in Prisons," November 19, 1988. Available from *The People*, 914 Industrial Ave., Palo Alto, CA 94303-4911.
Charles R. Ring	"Private Prisons Need a Fair Trial," *The Wall Street Journal*, May 8, 1987.
Ira P. Robbins	"Privatization of Corrections: Defining the Issues," *Judicature*, April/May 1986.
Julia Ward	"Bay County Jail and Jail Annex: A Case for Private Enterprise in Corrections," *American Jails*, November/December 1990.

What Are the Alternatives to Prisons?

AMERICA'S
PRISONS

Chapter Preface

The overcrowding crisis in America's prisons has renewed interest in the development of alternative forms of punishment. These alternatives, usually reserved for nonviolent offenders, include community service, home incarceration, electronic monitoring, victim restitution, and closely supervised probation.

Advocates of such alternatives contend that they are essential, not only to alleviate prison overcrowding, but also because of the destructive effects of prisons on criminals. Proponents of alternative sentencing can point to many success stories to bolster their views. For example, in 1989 the *Washington Post* recounted the story of a Maryland man charged with drug possession in the 1970s. Instead of sentencing the man to jail, the judge gave him a suspended sentence and required that he devote time to community service as a handyman at a home for the elderly. The judge described how the man returned to the courtroom a year later, accompanied by a half-dozen elderly residents of the home. "They told me he'd finished his hours months and months earlier, but he'd continued to work there," the judge explained. "They loved him." This story exemplifies the purported benefits of alternative sentencing programs. Not only did society save on the cost of incarcerating this offender, but it benefited from the unpaid services he performed during and after the completion of his sentence.

Opponents of such programs caution against their widespread acceptance, however. For instance, Richard B. Abell, a former assistant attorney general of the United States, contends that 95 percent of those incarcerated in state prisons are recidivists or are there for the commission of violent crimes. At most, then, only 5 percent of the total number of offenders could safely be given alternative sentences, Abell believes.

The authors in the following chapter discuss the benefits and drawbacks of some alternatives to prison.

"Although many of these [creative sentencing] programs are still relatively young, the early indications of their success are impressive."

Creative Sentencing Is Effective

Marc Mauer

Marc Mauer is the assistant director of the Sentencing Project, a national, nonprofit organization which promotes sentencing reform and the development of alternative sentencing programs. In the following viewpoint, Mauer argues that imprisoning more criminals in an attempt to reduce crime is a futile endeavor which only worsens prison overcrowding. As an alternative to prison, Mauer advocates developing sentencing programs that are specifically tailored to suit the needs of the individual offender. Such alternatives, he contends, can include a combination of supervised probation, fines, restitution, community service, drug treatment, and others. Early evaluations of creative sentencing programs have shown them to be popular with judges and effective in reducing prison overcrowding, he concludes.

As you read, consider the following questions:

1. Why does Mauer believe that locking up offenders is an ineffective method of crime control?
2. How does Mauer define client-specific planning?
3. According to the author, why is alternative sentencing sometimes viewed as a "soft" approach to crime?

Marc Mauer, "Doing Good Instead of Doing Time," *Business and Society Review*, Summer 1988. Reprinted with permission.

In 1987, in Greensboro, North Carolina, Jack Bookman (not his real name) was convicted on several counts of breaking and entering and larceny. Because of his prior criminal record, he faced several years in prison. But Yvonne Johnson of a Greensboro alternative sentencing program proposed a comprehensive alternative to prison for Bookman. Her plan included participation in an outpatient drug program, restitution to the victims of his crimes, 150 hours of unpaid community service, mental health counseling, and full-time employment. The plan was accepted by the sentencing judge, and Bookman is serving his sentence in the community.

The Greensboro sentencing received far less attention than did the high-visibility cases of Ivan Boesky, Dennis Levine, and other Wall Street traders. It is, however, part of a growing movement that is creating a "quiet revolution" in America's criminal courtrooms. Sentencing advocates like Yvonne Johnson are helping the courts and corrections systems develop new sentencing options for indigent defendants such as Bookman—the kinds of defendants inundating our nation's prisons and jails. Their numbers are growing, and they are forcing us to change the way we look at our system of justice.

A Quiet Revolution

What has brought about this "quiet revolution"? Many factors have contributed to the movement for alternative sentencing, but most significant by far has been the "dollars and cents" motivation—the soaring cost of our prison system caused by an unprecedented rise in our incarcerated population. The dimensions of this crisis are profound:

• The number of people locked up in our state and federal prisons has almost doubled . . . rising from 307,000 in 1978 to 600,000 in 1988.

• Local jail populations have increased at a similar pace, climbing from 158,000 to 300,000 between 1978 and 1988. . . .

• The cost of this massive increase in the prison population has been staggering, with state and local governments bearing the greatest burden. Corrections costs now total $13 billion annually.

• Overcrowding in prisons and jails has led to lawsuits challenging conditions of confinement in almost every state. In 1988 more than thirty states [were] under court order requiring them to reduce overcrowding and improve conditions.

• Our prisons are increasingly becoming homes for minorities and the poor. Nearly half of all new prison admissions are non-white, and the vast majority of all prisoners are poor or under-employed.

The prison system is becoming increasingly costly and unmanageable. Some would say that these problems and costs may be a necessary evil, merely a response to a rising rate of crime. An analysis of the system, though, shows that this is not the case. Criminologists have been closely studying the rising numbers of prisoners for the past decade. Most experts in the field now believe that the primary reason for the increased incarcerated population is not higher rates of crime but a "tougher" system—harsher sentencing and parole policies. Although this tougher sentencing has come about partly through judicial decision making, it is most often a result of legislative action. Legislators have enacted mandatory minimum prison terms, fixed sentencing, and more severe penalties for a range of crimes, all of which have resulted in more people being locked up for longer periods of time.

We Must Expand Creative Sentencing

We tried soft on crime, and that didn't work. Now we've tried tough on crime, and the results have been just as unimpressive. Maybe we should try smart on crime. As state and federal lockups approach gridlock, the challenge to our criminal justice system is to take the elegant, custom-tailored sentence and start marketing it retail.

James Bennett, *The Washington Monthly*, January 1990.

The primary argument offered in support of the high incarcerated population is that although costly, it is an effective method of crime control. There is little empirical evidence for such a conclusion. Although it might seem obvious at first that locking up more criminal offenders would reduce the crime rate, the reality of crime and its causes is more complex. First, only a small percentage of all felony crimes are even reported to the police, and fewer still result in arrest and conviction. As great as the numbers of prisoners are, they represent only a fraction of the crime-committing population. Second, many crimes are committed in pairs or groups, as is the case with drug or car theft rings. Convicting and removing one of the group members may only result in recruitment of new members or continuation by a smaller group. A 1978 report by the National Institute of Sciences documented the futility of trying to achieve significant increases in crime control through incarceration. The Institute estimated that in order to achieve a 10 percent reduction in crime, California would have to increase its prison population by 157 percent, New York by 263 percent, and Massachusetts by 310 percent.

Finally, it is claimed that the threat of imprisonment deters potential offenders from committing crimes. This impact, though, has never been shown to be as strong as its proponents claim. For most of the inhabitants of our nation's prisons—minorities and the disproportionately poor—the opportunities presented for a "legitimate" life-style often seem so remote as to hardly offer an attractive alternative to crime.

A New Approach

More and more, public policy leaders and criminal justice officials are beginning to realize that we cannot build our way out of the prison overcrowding crisis. This has led to a series of experiments in alternative sentencing and new programs designed to enhance the effectiveness of the sentencing process itself. One of the more successful models has been called "defense based" sentencing. It is an approach to sentencing that combines the skills of the defense attorney with the creativity of a new breed of sentencing professionals in an attempt to offer sentencing judges a greater range of options than have traditionally been available.

The defense-based sentencing model dates back over twenty years in some locations, involving the use of social workers to assist attorneys in finding social services for their clients that can be used to argue for reduced prison terms. Its most immediate impetus, though, dates from the introduction of the client-specific planning (CSP) model of sentencing, pioneered by the National Center on Institutions and Alternatives (NCIA) in 1979. The basic premise of the CSP model is that each defendant coming before a judge for sentencing is a unique individual. He or she has a particular family background, social history, and set of circumstances that led to the commission of the crime. Although this set of concerns does not excuse the criminal activity, it serves as a starting point for consideration of a sentence that will be tailored to the individual.

Working with a defense attorney, a sentencing specialist then develops a sentencing plan that speaks directly to the needs of the victim, the offender, and the community. The sentencing plans vary according to the case but generally involve some or all of the following elements:

- *Supervision.* Placement on probation with specified conditions; the defendant may also be required to report to a community third-party sponsor.
- *Fines or restitution.* Payment of fines and/or restitution to the court or victim of the crime.
- *Community service.* Unpaid community service for a specified number of hours in a community agency.
- *Treatment.* Placement in drug, alcohol, mental health, or other

counseling program.

- *Residence*. Confirmed residence at home, a halfway house, or an approved site.
- *Employment/education*. Maintaining verified employment or school attendance.

The sentencing plan is then presented to the judge as an option for sentencing that is more restrictive than probation but less restrictive than imprisonment. The judge is free to accept the proposal in whole or part or to reject it and sentence the offender to prison.

Creative Sentencing Saves Money

Creative sentencing or alternative sentencing or innovative sentencing—the concept has many names—is being tried by judges throughout the land as hard-core criminals—the rapists and muggers and drug dealers—fill up our prisons.

Drunk drivers and teen-age drug dealers are sentenced to watch autopsies. A marijuana smuggler is told to work with AIDS patients. Criminals are given the option of going to jail or facing public humiliation by buying ads of apology. A slumlord is forced to live in one of his own buildings. Juvenile delinquents are ordered to join the Boy Scouts. Felons are being sentenced to do good deeds—community service—for the aged or the poor or the churches or the schools in their towns.

All of this saves money. It costs upward of $40,000 a year to keep some prisoners in prison. It costs more to build one jail cell in some cities than it does to build a whole house. And the wrongdoers who aren't sent to jail get to keep their jobs and earn their salaries—and pay their taxes.

Michael Gartner, *The Wall Street Journal*, October 12, 1989.

As Jerry Miller, one of the founders of NCIA, has remarked, "We should treat offenders as if they were our sons and daughters who had been convicted of a crime." He and other proponents of alternative sentencing feel that the $20,000 a year we spend to lock up each prisoner could be better used in a community-based setting. In addition to helping the offender, the possibility for restitution and community service offers a payback to the community that incarceration can never achieve.

Numbers Speak for Themselves

Since the introduction of the CSP model, programs patterned on it have spread rapidly. In 1979, there were fewer than twenty defense-based sentencing programs in the country. In 1988 there [were] over 100. A survey conducted by The Sentencing Project found that the more than eighty programs existing in 1986 handled over 11,000 cases in one year. The figure is substantially larger today. Although many of these programs are still relatively young, the early indications of their success are impressive. Of more than 6,000 cases handled by NCIA since its inception, over two-thirds have resulted in sentencing plans being accepted by the courts. Similar success rates have been achieved by most other programs.

Studies of several state programs have demonstrated that the defense-based programs are having a substantial impact on the number of offenders being sentenced to prison. In North Carolina, researchers at the Institute of Government of the University of North Carolina at Chapel Hill have conducted sophisticated studies of the state's defense-based sentencing programs, called community penalties programs. In one of the local programs studied, they found that program clients were sentenced to prison only two-fifths as often as was a control group. In another program, 46 percent of the program defendants received a prison term, compared with 63 percent of a control group. A 1987 study of a New Mexico public defender sentencing program conducted by The Sentencing Project concluded that the program had resulted in the freeing up of sixty-two prison cells over the course of one year, at a value of $1.4 million.

In some ways the most important indicator of success is the reaction of the sentencing judges, for no matter how good a sentencing plan is developed, it is ultimately a judicial decision as to what sentence will be imposed. Here, too, the response has been almost uniformly favorable. Judges throughout the country praise alternative sentencing programs for providing them with new options—options that fall between traditional probation, often viewed as inappropriate, and incarceration, viewed as overly harsh for many offenders. As Superior Court Judge Coy E. Brewer, Jr. of Fayetteville, North Carolina, has said: "The greatest concern I have had in sentencing is the paucity of sentencing options that I would face in a particular situation. These programs create a continuum of punishment options with more gradations in them, so we have the possibility of meaningful community-based punishment."

Looking Ahead

What does the future hold for alternative sentencing? It is difficult to predict and will depend in part on economics, politics, and the success of these programs in "selling" themselves. Although many alternative sentencing specialists have proved their value to the system, they still must compete for funding with other needs in our ever-increasing corrections budgets.

Perhaps the greatest problem that proponents of alternative

sentencing face is the tendency to categorize crime policies as either "tough" or "soft." As columnist Colman McCarthy has written, though, the issue is not quite so simple: "Nothing is hard-line about the so-called get-tough judges who think jail is the only punishment and stiff sentences the only justice. They only deal in weakness. They put off to another time and probably for another court the obligation of treating the criminal as something other than a hopeless case. They postpone until another day the danger created when the offender is released as a greater menace than when he went in."

Our overburdened court system is faced with serious problems. It must be able to take advantage of the resources being brought to bear on the sentencing process by sentencing specialists around the country. If this is done successfully, we may begin to see the development of an improved decision-making process, one that provides greater benefits to victims, offenders, and the community at large.

VIEWPOINT

"[Creative] sentences . . . are designed by largely unaccountable judges who seek not 'to let the punishment fit the crime' but rather to let it fit the criminal."

Creative Sentencing Should Be Limited

Steven G. Calabresi

Steven G. Calabresi is a research associate at the American Enterprise Institute for Public Policy Research in Washington, D.C. In the following viewpoint, Calabresi argues that creative sentences, which tailor punishments to fit individual offenders, present many problems. Such "designer sentences," he continues, allow judges too much discretion in varying the punishments given to people convicted of similar crimes. While Calabresi argues that there are viable alternatives to prison, creative sentencing is not one of them.

As you read, consider the following questions:

1. According to the author, what is wrong with creative sentencing?
2. Why does Calabresi believe that America needs more prisons?
3. What prison alternatives does the author support, and why?

Steven G. Calabresi, "Designer Sentences and the Justice System," *The American Enterprise*, January/February 1990. Reprinted with permission of The American Enterprise Institute for Public Policy Research, Washington, D.C.

When millionaire industrialist Victor Posner was convicted in federal court of tax evasion, he, like most criminals, faced the prospect of spending some time in jail. Unlike most criminals, however, Posner did not receive a jail term but was sentenced instead to, among other things, set up a $3 million fund to assist the homeless. The first $267,000 was used to pay for an 800-page study directed by David Fike of Barry University that provided "guidelines for changes in community action, funding, and policy to ease the plight of the homeless in South Florida." The rest of Posner's $3 million will not go to the U.S. Treasury or to any program established by Congress or the Executive Branch. Instead, a committee appointed by Posner's sentencing judge will distribute the funds according to the Barry University plan.

Celebrities Oliver North and Rob Lowe had similar alternative sentencing experiences. When Lt. Col. North was convicted after a controversial trial in May 1989 on three of 12 criminal counts growing out of the Iran-Contra scandal, he faced a maximum sentence of ten years in jail and $750,000 in fines. The sentence North actually got, however, included two years' probation, a $150,000 fine, *and 1,200 hours of community service* in a drug program for inner-city youths. The confused message from the criminal justice system was that North's misdeeds warranted criminal conviction but did not disqualify him from being drafted to serve as a role model for impressionable adolescents. At least that must have been the view of the sentencing authority, U.S. District Judge Gerhard A. Gesell.

Community Service

Even more remarkable was the deal struck with local prosecutors in Atlanta by actor Rob Lowe, star of such films as "St. Elmo's Fire" and "Oxford Blues." Lowe faced a possible 20-year prison sentence and a $100,000 fine for sexually exploiting a minor. The 25-year-old actor had seduced a 16-year-old girl during the 1988 Democratic National Convention and videotaped himself having sex with her and another girl. What sentence did Georgia's Fulton County Court and district attorney impose on Lowe for committing this crime? Plea-bargaining produced a sentence of 20 hours of community service to be spent warning *high school students* about the dangers of drugs. Georgia's district attorney even suggested that Lowe could serve his sentence by speaking at high schools in Los Angeles, where he lives, and in Ohio, his home state. Jackie Goldberg, president of the Los Angeles Unified School District Board, was outraged: "We will want a guarantee for parents . . . that children are protected. . . . [Rob Lowe] has, at minimum, dubious judgment. I would want to know who is monitoring his talks for appropriate behavior and who is monitoring him for appropriate behavior."

Unfortunately, the Posner, North, and Lowe cases are far from unique. In the last 15 years, federal and state courts have increasingly suspended the imposition or execution of regular criminal sentences in order to impose conditions of probation or "alternative sanctions." Even the more sober area of antitrust law has been affected. According to testimony before the U.S. Sentencing Commission, one defendant's community service involved coordinating an annual rodeo for a charity. A defendant in another antitrust proceeding was required to organize a golf tournament fund-raiser for the Red Cross. This experience proved so pleasant that he quickly agreed to organize the golf tournament again the next year! These alternative sentencing arrangements have less to do with the traditional goals of criminal sentencing than with judges' own ideas about fairness for individual defendants and for society at large.

The Problems of Creative Sentencing

Judges, or some of them anyway, are using their ingenuity when they sentence criminals. The convicted slumlord is required to live in one of his tenements. The big-time tax cheater must donate millions to helping the homeless. The New York City racketeer is exiled from the city. Punishment is becoming creative. But is this a promising reform? . . .

Made-to-order penalties . . . tend to be reserved for the affluent. The ordinary burglar cannot be sent to a tenement; he often lives in one already. It is also not clear whether the customized sentence really reduces the use of incarceration. When the slumlord, racketeer or tax cheater receives a specially designed sentence, is it in lieu of prison or of probation? That depends on a hypothetical: whether the judge would have otherwise opted in favor of confinement or of probation. Even the judge may not be certain which option he or she would have chosen.

Andrew von Hirsch, *The Nation*, June 25, 1988.

The problem with these nontraditional alternative sentences is not simply the absence of incarceration or fines. Indeed, there is much to be said in defense of contemporary legislative efforts to develop alternatives to incarceration for nonviolent offenders as long as those alternatives are sufficiently punitive to accomplish the objectives of criminal law. The problem instead is that the alternative sentences described are all sentences of a particular kind: they are "designer sentences." Alternative sentences of this genre are designed by largely unaccountable judges who seek not "to let the punishment fit the crime" but rather to let it fit the criminal. These are highly individualized sentences, fashioned with a particular individual's misdeeds (and redeeming characteristics) very much in mind. Because such sentences are so exquisitely and creatively tailored, they seem in theory to hold the promise of greater fairness than traditional sentences. In fact, designer sentences are highly problematic on several grounds.

What's Wrong with Designer Sentences?

First, the essence of designer sentences is that they give judges much more discretion in sentencing than they have traditionally had. This is no small feat because judges have historically had a great deal of leeway. Recent trends in sentencing have been in the direction of trying to reduce discretion—indeed, the U.S. Sentencing Commission was created with that goal in mind.

Discretion in sentencing creates a host of problems. It greatly increases the likelihood that race and class bias will affect sentencing decisions. It puts those with unpopular political, religious, or other beliefs at risk. It undermines deterrence by making it less certain that an individual who commits a particular criminal act will receive a specific punishment. Finally, the presence of discretion, and the concomitant reduction in certainty of punishment, makes it less likely that individuals will know what the law expects.

Second, designer sentencing confers too much power on judges by allowing them to both design the laws and apply them in particular situations. The framers of our Constitution believed that the essence of the separation of powers principle was to keep legislative power (the power to devise rules of general applicability) apart from the judicial power (the power to apply the general law to particular cases). Designer sentencing effectively violates the separation of powers principle by concentrating in the judiciary the effective authority to both devise sanctions and apply them. This concentrates too much power in an institution that is not directly accountable to the electorate.

Third, designer sentencing allows judges too much power to identify sentencing beneficiaries and to tailor punishments. As one critical appellate court explained: *Creative sentencing of the kind here undertaken, for example, necessarily involves the court in selecting particular third persons to become beneficiaries of the probationer's assets—presumably acting in some way as "surrogates" for the public as the actually "aggrieved party." Such selections of course carry financial benefits for which there may be quite legitimate rival claimants among potential "surrogates," whether known or unknown to the court. Where the sums imposed for payment are also fixed by the court without reference to any measurable losses or damage, the court exposes itself to possibly justifiable and unanswerable criticisms, both with respect to the particular beneficiaries selected and the specific sums awarded them.*

Fourth, many of the designer sentences imposed by trial judges in recent years are unlawful in that legislatures have not delegated to courts the power to impose those sentences for the crimes that have been committed. Many sentences are ultimately overturned on appeal for this reason. Judges have no inherent power to impose criminal sentences, but must instead apply sentences that have been authorized by legislatures as punishments for particular acts. Generally, legislatures in this country have authorized only the most limited alternatives to incarceration and the imposition of fines. While community service sentences are available in some circumstances, many of the more creative designer sanctions plainly are not. Some of these sanctions involve the judiciary in the exercise of powers that Congress might be unable constitutionally to delegate to courts. The appropriation of federal treasury funds, for example, is ordinarily a legislative function. Transferring to a private entity funds that would otherwise have gone, in the form of a fine, into the Treasury (as happened in the Posner case) seems to involve the federal courts in the appropriation process unconstitutionally.

Fifth, at least some designer sentences raise other constitutional problems. Sentences that require an individual probationer to give public speeches may raise First Amendment issues if the sentencing judge attempts to dictate the content of what is said. Moreover, harsher or more vindictive designer sentences raise Eighth Amendment concerns of cruel and unusual punishment. For example, one 28-year-old cocaine dealer was prohibited from getting married or having children for four years, a sentence that he rightly describes as "kind of odd."

Designer Sentences Are Insufficiently Punitive

Finally, many designer sentences seem problematic because they are insufficiently punitive: that is, they fail to accomplish the purposes for which we have criminal laws. Traditionally, scholars have identified four objectives of criminal punishment: retribution, deterrence, incapacitation, and rehabilitation. To that list, we have recently added victim compensation, formerly more a goal of the civil law. None of these objectives is adequately served by individually tailored designer sentences.

• Retribution. Sentences imposed frequently reflect a judge's, not the community's, notion of what punishment "fits" a particular crime. Given the subjectivity of determining that "fit," it seems most unwise to take the choice of sanction away from the governmental bodies closest to the people. The discretion associated with designer sentencing also makes the criminal law less "fair" by increasing the chance that the public will decide that "like cases are not being treated alike." Such an undermining of the public's confidence in the criminal law's fairness is especially likely if discretion in sentencing leads to a reality or even a perception of race or class bias.

• Deterrence. Designer sentences undermine deterrence because the certainty of punishment is reduced. Certainty and severity of punishment are the two great pillars of any deterrent scheme.

• Incapacitation. Keeping a criminal out of circulation is frequently undercut when designer sentences are imposed in lieu of prison. Certainly, many people in Los Angeles felt this was true when Rob Lowe's commission of statutory rape resulted in his being sentenced to lecture high school students rather than in his being put in jail.

•Rehabilitation and Restitution. These objectives of the criminal law may appear to be satisfied by the imposition of alternative designer sentences. But there is no guarantee that a criminal who has not first been "punished" will be rehabilitated by the imposition of a creative or lenient sentence. Indeed, the opposite may be true if the criminal concludes that society's tepid response to his misdeeds indicates a lack of serious disapproval. Similarly, designer sentences will compensate actual victims only if judges design them that way. Most of the designer sentences cited here have benefitted third parties rather than benefitting victims or the government.

The Prison Problem

Justifiable concerns about prison overcrowding and the high financial and human costs of incarceration are certainly contributing to creative alternative sentencing schemes. The nation's combined federal and state prison population has been steadily increasing: from 218,466 in 1974 to 673,565 by June 1989. Indeed, in the first six months of 1989, the combined U.S. prison population expanded by 46,004 inmates, or 7.3 percent, requiring nearly 1,800 new beds a week! This expansion is alarming because prisons are expensive to build and operate. Rand criminologist Joan Petersilia estimates that: "Construction costs typically range between $50,000 and $75,000 per cell and the expenses to incarcerate [average] $14,000 per year." Given that . . . "our rate of imprisonment is twice as high as Canada's, three times as high as Great Britain's, and four times as high as West Germany's," we obviously need to consider seriously at least some alternative punishments to incarceration.

We also need to expand greatly our prison capacity to isolate more violent offenders. A Bureau of Justice Statistics study strongly suggests that our prison system is failing to isolate many who would be unable to commit crimes if they were still incapacitated, serving their maximum prior sentences. This failure to incapacitate obviously and justifiably creates a crisis of public confidence in the ability of leaders to handle the basic responsibilities of government. This problem must be addressed, in part by a program of rapid prison construction, regardless of what alternative sanctions are developed for offenders who do not need to be incapacitated.

Creative Sentencing Confuses Proportionality

Proportionality of sentence is a . . . serious concern. During the past two decades there has been increasing recognition of the importance of making sanctions proportionate to the gravity of the crime. Punishment conveys our disapproval of criminal conduct, and should be graduated to reflect that conduct's degree of reprehensibility. Maintaining proportionality requires an ability to compare penalties' severity. The more idiosyncratic the sentence, the more difficult the comparison becomes. How does one compare the onerousness of having to live for fourteen days in a tenement flat with being forced to give large sums to charity or being exiled from New York City to Vermont?

Andrew von Hirsch, *The Nation*, June 25, 1988.

There are, however, at least some alternative sanctions that might be appropriate for certain prisoners. These would help address the problems of prison overcrowding without the problems associated with designer sentences. These include:

• House Arrest. Programs to incarcerate some offenders in their homes, either with or without electronic monitoring, are well under way. Both California and Florida have apparently successful programs. To the extent that the sanction is applied based on the acts that criminals commit rather than on who they are, it need not raise the problems associated with designer discretion.

• Shock Incarceration or Boot Camps. Under these programs, young offenders spend a relatively short time (90 to 180 days) in a highly regimented prison program involving strict discipline, physical training, and hard labor, resembling some aspects of military training. Again, offenders are sentenced for the acts they commit and not because of who they are, so the problem of discretion is minimized.

• Scarlet Letter Punishments. Some have suggested that offenders be socially stigmatized without being incarcerated. Example: offenders who are convicted of drunk driving might be required to place a bumper sticker on their car warning the general public that they have been convicted of drunk driving.

Again, the designer problem does not arise so long as the penalty for a criminal act is defined in general terms in advance of the act being committed.

• Intensive Supervision Programs. These programs are a highly supervised and regimented form of probation and parole. They have proven successful in some circumstances and can avoid the problem of excessive discretion if rules are applied so that offenders who commit similar acts are supervised and restricted in similar ways.

• Community Service Programs. Of all alternative sanctions that do not involve explicitly designed sentences these may raise the most problems. There is an enormous temptation to let judges prescribe what community service is warranted for what offense and more importantly for what offender. Legislators can mandate community service in a fashion that minimizes the problem of discretion. Doing so requires spelling out terms of service in advance for particular criminal acts. If the task is too detailed for a legislative body, then the assistance of a sentencing agency or commission may be needed. As long as the choice of penalties is not left to individual judges, problems can be avoided.

The Goals of Criminal Law

The problem of how to sentence criminals justly is a perennial one, requiring continual reform. The prison system itself is, after all, one such reform, having been introduced in its present incarnation only 200 years ago as a humanitarian alternative to corporal and capital punishment. Alternative sanctions must accomplish the goals of the criminal law, but they also must comport with our aspiration to live under a government of laws and not of men. Designer sentences fail that test by giving sentencing judges too much discretion unguided by rules of law. We want our judges to be able to boast, as Justice Felix Frankfurter once did, that they are members of: *a court of review, not a tribunal unbounded by rules. We do not sit like a kadi under a tree dispensing justice according to considerations of individual expediency.*

"Electronic monitoring is available [and] it works."

Electronic Monitoring Is Effective

Russell Carlisle

Russell Carlisle is a judge in the State Court of Cobb County, Georgia. In the following viewpoint, Carlisle recounts his experience testing an electronic monitoring device used on offenders sentenced to probation or home incarceration. While he was initially skeptical about the usefulness of electronic monitoring, Carlisle's experience changed his mind about this new technology. He now advocates the wider use of electronic monitoring as an alternative sentencing tool.

As you read, consider the following questions:

1. According to the author, how does electronic monitoring work?
2. How are sentencing and probation procedures affected by the availability of electronic monitoring devices, according to Carlisle?
3. What does the author mean by psychological imprisonment?

Russell Carlisle, "Electronic Monitoring as an Alternative Sentencing Tool," *The Georgia State Bar Journal*, February 1988. Reprinted with permission.

For months I had been hearing on radio and television and reading in the newspaper of judges throughout the country who were sentencing defendants to home incarceration as an alternative to jail, but like everyone else I only knew what I read in the papers. The most publicized case I had seen involved an alleged slumlord in the San Francisco area who was confined to one of his own tenement buildings as part of his sentence. However, in July, 1987 I was invited to attend a presentation by the firm of Security Guild International, Inc., a private company in the business of providing electronic monitoring services for courts, hospitals and businesses. This organization presented the Contrac electronic monitoring device to a group of judges, prosecutors and probation officers from our circuit. Everyone was, of course, interested in the latest gadgetry; and the questions that followed seemed to express both curiosity about the mechanism and concern as to its reliability when used as a basis to revoke someone's probation.

As the meeting ended, I continued to press the representatives of Security Guild International for answers and even began to make some humorous suggestions as to how I might try to defeat such a system. My bluff was quickly called when they offered to place a unit in my home and strap a monitor to my ankle, thus allowing me all the time I needed to try to defeat the machine. Having never learned in my youth to refuse a dare, I readily accepted and plans were made to place me on probation when I returned from vacation.

Word quickly leaked out that there was some "fool" at the courthouse who was going to sentence himself to probation and become a guinea pig for the latest electronic equipment. It was either a slow news week or else the American public has a tremendous interest in this type of alternative sentencing, because within days I was deluged with calls from the media, requesting more information. Stories began to appear in the local press and soon the national media were beating a path to my chambers. All of this curiosity over a device that was already in use in a number of states, including California, Michigan and Florida, was surprising; but perhaps the added novelty of a judge first trying out his sentencing on himself had something to do with it.

The Monitoring Device

By the time the day arrived to strap on my ankle bracelet, there were three news cameras in the courtroom and CNN had already filmed a piece that was being broadcast nationwide. Now that all the hoopla has died down, I thought it might be a good idea to look at the more serious side and report on my week of living with this monitoring device.

The device I used is known as the Contrac Electronic Monitor and was developed by Mr. Tom Moody of Boca Raton, Florida. The equipment consists of a blue box that is about the size of a clock radio with a small antenna, and a sealed grey plastic box which is attached to the defendant. The blue box connects to one's telephone line by use of a standard jack and is also plugged into a standard electrical outlet. The display panel on the box consists of a key slot for turning the machine on and several monitoring lights, which indicate the mode in which the machine is presently operating. This monitor contains a back-up battery system which will provide power for up to eight hours should there be an electrical failure. Also, the monitor reports AC power outages and any interruption of telephone service, whether intentional or otherwise. The machine will internally store this information and all other violations until such time as the telephone line is restored. The information can then be reported to the main computer.

Electronic Monitoring Is Growing in Popularity

As crime rates continue to tax our already burdened correctional facilities, electronic home detention programs are gaining in popularity as an intelligent alternative to incarceration.

In 1988, more than 2,300 offenders were enrolled in such programs—representing a 300 percent increase from 1987. The programs' popularity can be attributed to high compliance rates, low operating costs, and badly needed reductions in jail populations. . . .

Electronic monitoring is easy to use, requires little maintenance, and allows for expansion.

Jerry Silvia, *Corrections Today*, July 1989.

The device which is actually placed on the defendant is 2 3/4" long x 1 3/4" wide x 1" thick. This device is a sealed grey plastic box which can be opened only by literally tearing it to pieces, and is placed on the defendant by means of a plastic hospital or jail type bracelet, although this bracelet has some specialized properties. It is mounted on the ankle for anatomical reasons: although many people can compress their hand and wrist in such a manner as to allow this bracelet to be slipped on or off, it appears virtually impossible to do the same with the human ankle and foot. Making that last turn around the ankle raises the [greatest] difficulty. This I can personally attest to, having attempted to stretch the bracelet and use the resulting slack for removal.

My first problem in attempted removal was a small tear in the bracelet that came from my constant stretching. Naturally, one of the rules of probation is that the defendant will do nothing to damage the equipment. Thus, I was technically in violation of my "sentence" at this point, although I had not actually severed the bracelet. On a normal probationer, the condition of the equipment would be checked on a regular basis by his probation officer. Any normal wear and tear could be quickly corrected on long-term probationers by simple replacement of the bracelet, which is riveted in place with a special riveting device and can be removed only by cutting the bracelet. It would be fruitless for a probationer to attempt to cut or drill the rivets with the hope of replacing them. Even if the probationer could obtain rivets identical to those used, he would have difficulty finding a riveting tool that would match the exact identifying marks placed by the special tool of the Security Guild.

I might add that I also tried both heat and cold on both the ankle device and the bracelet, and quickly learned that a special liner inside the bracelet will contract when subjected to a heat lamp. If enough heat is applied, the bracelet could possibly cut off one's circulation. Naturally, I had no punishment awaiting me should I violate the system intentionally, and therefore I had more leeway than the average probationer in making my experiments. The same experiments, if tried by a probationer, could result in incarceration for the balance of the probationary period.

Computer Tracking

A computer actually records the activity of the defendant. While this computer can be located anywhere, in my case the location was in Boca Raton, Florida, and the computer monitored my movements from the home unit over an 800 WATS line at a distance of several hundred miles. The WATS line was used because I was the first "defendant" in Georgia to be placed on this device. It would not be economically feasible to have a base computer in place locally until a sufficient number of defendants are being monitored to warrant the expense. However, a local program can be monitored in the same way as mine. Once the expense can be justified and a local unit is in place, all probationers then on the long distance system can merely be transferred to the local unit. The cost remains the same whether the defendant is monitored locally or by long distance.

The accuracy rate of the machine appears to be excellent. The machine even recorded brief electrical outages from a series of storms that swept through our area the first night I was on the monitor. After approximately three power brownouts I received a phone call from Boca Raton, inquiring if I were attempting to move the machine within my house. During the week that I wore the device I kept a daily log of each and every time I left the house to go to work or for any other activity. A comparison at the end of the week between my log and the computer print-out, allowing for the few minutes' delay for transfer of the information, proved to be accurate without exception.

Sentencing and Probation Procedures

Before I comment further on the individual impact of the use of such a device, I think it would be helpful to go through the procedures that would normally be followed both before and after placing a defendant under electronic surveillance. To begin, a pre-sentence investigation is almost always necessary in any case that might be a candidate for home confinement. If only from a purely logistical standpoint, the investigation must determine in what type of dwelling place or workplace the instrument will be installed, whether or not a telephone is readily available, and if the place itself has any surrounding temptations that are within the range of the monitor (e.g., a defendant living in an apartment over a bar). Additionally, the probation officer conducting the pre-sentence investigation can assess whether the defendant is psychologically receptive to cooperating in this type of program. If the individual is one likely to cut off the band and flee the jurisdiction at the first sign of trouble, then he is not a suitable candidate. Remember, this machine is not a restraining device, but merely a monitoring device. Therefore, offenders of a violent nature should usually not be considered unless there are some extraordinary circumstances, such as compelling medical disabilities or a perceived danger to prison personnel or inmates (e.g., AIDS).

Once the pre-sentence investigation is completed, a brief conference with the prosecution and defense can reveal if there are any strenuous objections to this sentencing tool. This is also an excellent opportunity to clear up any questions as to the exact procedures that will be implemented, so that once the case is before the court for sentencing the judge can inquire of defense counsel if he has fully advised his client concerning the program.

While the actual sentencing can be handled in a number of ways, the most common is to make the monitoring program a special condition of probation. Another alternative is to sentence a defendant to incarceration, allow a "work release" during certain daylight hours, and place a monitoring device at the defendant's place of employment with his employer's consent. Many times the employer comes to court with the defendant to state how valuable his employee is and to offer to cooperate with the court in any way. This cooperation can be used to ensure that the defendant is incarcerated every night and monitored at the workplace every day.

Once the sentencing is completed the defendant will then meet with his probation supervisor and execute the necessary documents allowing the installation of the monitor in his home (or workplace, with the consent of the employer). The defendant must also agree to abide by all the rules of the program, including a stipulation that the computer records of the defendant's movements will be admissible in a revocation proceeding to establish a prima facie violation. These contractual agreements are provided by Security Guild International and can, of course, be modified if needed.

The defendant will also submit a work schedule, which will be verified with his employer. This work schedule is to be used by the monitoring service to program the base computer in those cases in which the defendant is allowed to leave home and report to work. Of course, any number of other exceptions can be put into the program, such as regular medical treatments, church attendance, community service. Also, the program can be varied at any time to allow the court or the probation supervisor to provide greater degrees of freedom to a defendant as he proves worthy. Thus, the program is completely flexible and can be tailored to the needs of each individual case.

All violations that occur during the monitoring period are reported to the probation supervisor on whatever priority basis he has specified. For instance, there may be certain cases in which the probation supervisor will wish to be informed even in the middle of the night. But in most cases, a report at the beginning of the next business day will suffice. The probation office can then, through regular channels, investigate the violation and determine whether any revocation proceedings are justified. In most cases, the monitoring agency will have attempted some telephone verification of the problem before notifying the probation supervisor. A good example was the power outage at my home, which I was able to explain in a subsequent telephone conversation with base monitoring personnel. Additional verification can be made through the power company and telephone company in the case of interruption of either service.

Paying for the Program

The finances of the program may be approached from many directions. It would not seem cost effective for an individual jurisdiction to purchase its own equipment and operate it with regular probation staff. Ownership of the equipment not only has very costly start-up expenses, but can also lead to delays in repair or replacement of equipment, require the probation department to maintain costly unused inventory, and tie up the same probation officers that such a program would normally free for other duties.

On the other hand, a private company can bear the start-up cost, maintain its inventory, repair its equipment, and use the same base unit to monitor defendants in a number of jurisdictions up to the capacity of each base monitor (approximately 500 defendants). The initial cost is an installation fee of $50.00 for each defendant and a per diem cost of $8.00. Obviously, the optimal method is to require the defendant to bear the cost, since he is receiving the benefits of such program. He would do this from his earnings, if the defendant is allowed to leave home and go to work, and the expense can be paid as part of a regular probation supervisory fee.

Use Electronic Monitoring to Pre-Release Prisoners

It would be monetarily beneficial for the taxpayers to let individuals, with less than six months left, who are on minimum security, to be put on electronic monitors. . . .

Allowing the individual to establish community and family bonds, pay taxes, ease overcrowding, pay restitution, and also incur the cost of his own incarceration, (i.e., the electronic monitoring device) are direct benefits of this type of program.

Tim Smith, *The Prison Mirror*, January 26, 1990.

The installation fee includes a crew to install the monitor in each defendant's home and to fine-tune and test the equipment in each case to assure maximum performance. The costs are usually paid by the defendant in advance for each month of use. If a defendant fails to pay for the next month's usage within a stated number of days prior to the beginning of the next month, then the machine is removed from his home and he is no longer eligible for the program. In this manner the court does not become a surety for the defendant's payment and does not have any financial obligation whatsoever to the monitoring agency.

There appear to be a number of other devices on the market designed in some way to monitor a defendant without incarceration. Some of these require the defendant to place a device attached to his body into a receptacle attached to his telephone at certain specified times of the day. Others require the defendant to telephone a computer or to answer a computer call at certain hours of the day. The main advantage that I have seen in the Contrac system is that it acts independently of the defendant and does not require the defendant to do anything other than stay in a particular location during a particular time frame. The defendant has no idea how the machine actually works or how he might defeat its purpose. He knows only that if he travels a certain distance from the base monitor, he is likely to be in violation of his sentence and subject to incarceration. It is simple state-of-the-art technology that puts the burden upon the defendant not just to obey the rules at certain times of the day but to obey the rules continuously.

Psychological Imprisonment

I stated earlier that I would review my psychological impressions of the unit, and I would like to close with these observations. There has been talk of reducing the size of these units with future advance in electronics. Yet I think that further miniaturization would detract from the psychological effectiveness of the unit. The unit is now small enough that its weight does not bother an individual. It can be concealed under a sock or pants leg, but it is still large enough that an individual cannot ignore its existence as he could something as small as, say, a wristwatch or a ring. Every time one bathes, dresses or props up his feet to watch television he is reminded that the court sentence is still in effect and that he is paying the price for his criminal action. This psychological impact cannot be discounted when judging the overall effectiveness of the program. Finally, there will come a time with each individual, just as there did with me, when he feels the bracelet to be physically confining even when it is not. This is much the same feeling one gets upon awakening in the middle of the night, discovering one has fallen asleep with his wristwatch or ring on and feeling that he must take it off immediately. Yet this bracelet cannot be taken off without violating probation, and that very fact is part of the punishment.

With increased community awareness and demands for greater punishment for certain types of offenses, the problem of overcrowding of prison facilities is a reality that will eventually face even the smallest of jurisdictions. So it is not a question of whether or not alternatives such as this are going to be used—it is only a matter of when. We will either be on the cutting edge of this technology or be made to follow in its path. It seems to be far better to pick and choose now the cases that are amenable to this type of system, rather than to be forced at some future time to use it indiscriminately just to make space in our overcrowded jails. . . .

I hope this information will satisfy the curiosity of those who have seen or heard news stories about these devices. Electronic monitoring is available, it works, and it is now in use in Georgia.

"[We are concerned about] the 'Orwellian overtones' of electronic monitoring."

Electronic Monitoring Is Dangerous

Richard A. Ball and J. Robert Lilly

Richard A. Ball is a professor of sociology at West Virginia University in Morgantown, and J. Robert Lilly is a professor of sociology at Northern Kentucky University in Highland Heights. Ball and Lilly, who were formerly enthusiastic advocates of home incarceration, argue in the following viewpoint that it now poses a major threat to personal liberty. Individual freedom is endangered, according to the authors, because home incarceration programs tend to use electronic devices, rather than community volunteers, to monitor offenders. The authors fear the widespread use of these electronic devices, envisioning an Orwellian future in which the state monitors every move of its citizens.

As you read, consider the following questions:

1. What are the advantages of home incarceration, according to the authors?
2. Why are Ball and Lilly concerned about the spread of electronically monitored home incarceration?

Richard A. Ball and J. Robert Lilly, "Home Incarceration with Electronic Monitoring," in *Controversial Issues in Crime and Justice*, Joseph E. Scott and Travis Hirschi, eds., pp. 147-156, 158-161, © 1988 by Sage Publications, Inc. Reprinted by permission of Sage Publications, Inc.

Within the past two decades, the need for alternatives to institutional incarceration of offenders has become more and more pressing, and the problem has gained international attention. In the United States, this trend has been referred to as "the new justice." Jails and prisons have become too costly to build and maintain, and there is a persistent and dangerous problem of overcrowding. More recently, there has appeared a new trend toward an alternative we have termed "Home Incarceration."

Although we have been instrumental in the development of such programs, we have become increasingly concerned with their larger implications for the changing nature of social control. Our intention here is to examine home incarceration as an alternative, to consider its possible advantages, and to investigate certain of these larger issues with respect to major trends in the ideology and strategy of social control. . . .

Advantages of Home Incarceration

Home incarceration seems to have both theoretical and practical advantages. The problem with many alternatives to institutional incarceration is that the public is deprived [according to D.E. Aaronson and colleagues] "of the symbolic value of an official finding of offender accountability." Home incarceration takes account of this symbolism. According to our theoretical perspective, punishment is a symbolic statement of reprobation in the form of an official denunciation of an offense. As such, it combines aspects of retribution, social utilitarianism and the hope of reformation. Key to this theoretical perspective is the goal of reconciliation of offender and community.

Official confinement to the home for a specified period would appear to provide, at least for certain offenses, a clear statement of retribution, a utilitarian form of incapacitation, and the possibility of reformation within a more "normal" environment.

We have proposed, for example, that home incarceration be considered as a sentencing alternative for drunken drivers. This proposal is based upon an analysis indicating that, while the current "slammer laws" mandating jail time for those convicted of DWI (Driving While Intoxicated) are counterproductive, public sentiment demands that something more effective than the typical fines or license suspensions be employed to deal with the problem. Home incarceration for a reasonable period of time would seem to offer sufficient retribution to satisfy the sense of public indignation by "grounding" the offender. It would serve the incapacitation function and thereby protect the community. And it would allow the community to deal with the "drinking problem" of the offender in a setting that might be expected to add to the probability of "rehabilitation" and "reintegration."

Whether such advantages outweigh a number of possible disadvantages must be left for later consideration. The fact is that the trend toward home incarceration rests upon its perceived *practical* advantages. . . . Home incarceration has a good *degree of fit* to a variety of circumstances in such a way that it could be employed alone or in concert with other programs, tailored to certain hours of the day, and perhaps even combined with incarceration in a traditional jail with home incarceration on weekends in certain cases. It also offers the possibility of practical use at various *stages* of the correctional process from pretrial detention through parole. Our early hope was that this alternative might be structured to allow for initiation either by the court or by the offender, especially in the case of offenders with such special problems as mental retardation or terminal illness, which could be faced much more easily while confined to the home rather than jail. This we considered an alternative that might be made available by law to certain offenders and not simply an alternative to be used only at the discretion of the court.

Electronic Monitoring Destroys Privacy

With the [electronic] beeper, the State can monitor its citizens in the last bastion of privacy, the home. Traditional probation, to be sure, entails a reduction in the offender's privacy at home. In 1987, the U.S. Supreme Court went so far as to rule that probation agents may conduct warrantless searches of their clients' residences. But unlike old-fashioned probation, electronic monitoring empowers the government to control a population from *within* the halls of authority. That is a qualitative increase in police power.

A few years ago, polygraph examinations and drug tests appeared to be isolated incursions into the privacy of a handful of unfortunate individuals. Today, such probing is commonplace, at least in the private sector. We become inured to losing bits and pieces of ourselves to this or that greater good or technological imperative. The beeper blurs the line between freedom and imprisonment, and further erodes the sphere of self.

Keenen Peck, *The Progressive*, July 1988.

Home incarceration appeared from its earliest development to possess practical features that would provide a high likelihood of actual adoption. According to the National Advisory Commission on Criminal Justice Standards and Goals (1973), these include communicability, a satisfactory complexity level, a reasonably clear potential impact, reasonable cost, reversibility, divisibility, compatibility with existing programs, and perceived relevance to organizational goals. Such an alternative is simple to explain and is certainly not of forbidding complexity. Its potential impact in terms of reduction of jail overcrowding, protection of the community through the effective incapacitation of selected offenders such as drunken drivers, and avoidance of the "crime school" effects of jailing seems fairly obvious. As to reversibility, any agency adopting home incarceration as we had originally envisioned it would have been in position to retreat if significant public sentiment arose against the policy, if offenders failed to cooperate, or if other unforeseen problems appeared. . . .

From the beginning of our own efforts, however, we have assumed that the most crucial advantage of home incarceration as an alternative to jailing lay in its relatively low cost. If community volunteers were used to monitor compliance by telephone and occasional unannounced visits, the savings would be enormous. This is an especially important consideration given the fact that many communities face increasingly severe fiscal problems. Even if there were doubts as to potential impact, questions as to relevance to organizational goals, or simply reluctance to try something new, the lure of cost reduction appeared to give home incarceration good prospects for adoption. . . .

Potential Problems

By early 1986, at least 30 states were experimenting with home incarceration, with offenders in home incarceration programs numbering as many as 4,750 in Florida. Although some jurisdictions were following the model advocated in our early work, employing volunteers as monitors, the trend was clearly toward electronic monitoring. This issue deserves closer examination.

The use of volunteers to monitor compliance was suggested for both practical and theoretical reasons. In practical terms, volunteers could reduce the pressures on probation officers, who tend to be caught between the surveillance and counselor roles. It is difficult to provide guidance to an offender who resents the probation officer as someone who is constantly "checking up on" or "spying on" him or her. With the surveillance and monitoring function in the hands of volunteers with a home incarceration program, the probation officer might find this problem less troublesome. And the low cost of employing volunteers appeared as another very important practical inducement.

The use of community volunteers was also considered of significant value in terms of our theoretical perspective, which seeks to facilitate the reconciliation of offender and community. Under these conditions, the offender would be involved with representatives of his or her community rather than only with official functionaries representing some governmental bureaucracy. At the same time, the use of volunteers would contribute to the further involvement of the public in the systems of juvenile and criminal justice, fostering community penetration into these rather closed systems. According to this perspective, home incarceration ought to provide a powerful symbolic denunciation of the offense in community rather than bureaucratic terms, saying in effect, "If you continue to endanger the community (e.g., by driving while intoxicated), your liberty to participate in the community will be restricted, even while you are permitted to remain within the boundaries of that community (i.e., inside your own home)." Such a reaction was regarded as fitting our theoretical perspective in that it symbolized a repudiation of the act rather than the actor. Given these advantages in the use of community volunteers, the extent to which the home incarceration has tended to use electronic monitoring is something of a puzzle. . . .

The Current State of Electronic Monitoring

Several electronic monitoring systems are now on the market. In general, they involve a "bracelet" that attaches to ankle or wrist, serving as a transmitter emitting signals to a receiver located in a telephone within the home. If the offender wearing the bracelet moves further than a specified distance (e.g., 150 feet) from the telephone, this signal is broken and another signal alerts a central computer, located perhaps in the local probation agency, which provides a printout indicating a violation. The computer can be programmed with the incarceration parameters set for that particular offender so that if, for example, he or she is permitted to leave the home during specified time periods, the computer will take account of this and disregard any break in the bracelet signal during these approved time frames. As of 1983, Albuquerque, New Mexico, was paying $100,000 per year for 25 GOSSline monitor/bracelet sets with additional sets leasing at $1,000 per year.

Because we expected that cost reduction would be the most attractive advantage of home incarceration to those willing to consider it, we have been struck by their eagerness to embrace the more expensive electronic monitoring systems in lieu of the use of volunteers. Much of our theoretical perspective has rested upon the concept of reconciliation between offender and community, and we had been troubled by data suggesting that the community might resist such reconciliation, calling into question the entire enterprise of community-corrections. The rapid development of electronic monitoring now suggests that the systems of juvenile and criminal justice may be more interested in maintaining bureaucratic control over offenders than in involving the community in the monitoring of compliance with home incarceration, even at the cost of sacrificing other goals to the budget squeeze. But if the public resists reconciliation and reintegration of offenders and if the bureaucracies charged with offender surveillance and control prefer to remain aloof, this lends substance to the argument that the very term "community" is often meaningless rhetoric.

Potential Abuses of Electronic Monitoring

Some civil libertarians are concerned about the potential abuses inherent in this electronic monitoring. One suggested variant of the bracelet would "gently remind" the wearer that he has left the approved zone by transmitting a small electric shock back to the bracelet. This shock technology is currently being used to train dogs not to leave the family yard. Variations on this "Clockwork Orange" behavior modification aren't difficult to imagine.

Alan Dershowitz, *The Washington Times*, February 13, 1986.

Home incarceration may be caught in the common pattern of the "dialectics of reform" in which the entrenched agents of social control, such as judges, sheriffs, prosecutors, and the like, permit reforms only at the expense of certain libertarian traditions. The question of a possible "widening of the net" so as to place even more people under official social control is only one of the issues here. Despite the assertion of the National Advisory Commission on Criminal Justice Standards and Goals for Corrections (1973) that "the humanitarian aspect of community-based corrections is obvious," developments within the home incarceration movement suggest otherwise. There is the additional danger that the use of the home as a jail may contribute to the further erosion of the distinction between the private and public realms, which some have argued would leave the community more and more open to the extension of control by the state.

Electronic Monitoring Is an Affront to Personal Privacy

It is important to note that the very concept of a private self appears to have developed in conjunction with the emotional seclusion made possible by the construction of the home in such a way as to separate certain areas from the public domain. This sense of self is sustained by a zone of personal space extending about an arm's length from the body. Thus it is that the elimination of opportunities for privacy has been associated with various techniques for breaking down the self. What does this imply for a policy that converts the private dwelling place into a mode of official incarceration and monitors compliance by attaching an electronic device to the body of the individual so incarcerated?

As G.T. Marx has shown, "It would appear that modern society increasingly generates ironic outcomes, whether iatrogenic effects . . . unintended consequences of new technologies . . . or the familiar sociological examples found in prisons and mental hospitals, or in the careers of urban renewal and various other efforts at social reform." This increase in ironic outcomes stems from the increasing complexity and interdependence of social life and the increased effort at intervention based upon the expansion of professionalism and expertise. As others have shown, the legal concept of the right of individual privacy is based on the person's right to challenge invasion rather than the institution's responsibility to avoid it. Defense of privacy would thus seem to require considerable self-identity and a strong sense of personal autonomy on the part of those threatened. If it is true that individual autonomy is being eroded by more general social trends, then this tilt in favor of the institutions of social control may greatly reduce possibilities for the "negation of potential power-relationships between a person or group and others." Such a possibility would make a mockery of the famous quotation from William Pitt:

> The poorest man may in his cottage bid defiance to the crown. It may be frail—its roof may leak—the wind may enter—but the King of England cannot enter—all his force dares not cross the threshold of the ruined tenement.

What is so sacred about the home? The answer is that it has come to represent the social significance of the nuclear family and the personal dignity of the individual. The home is much more than an organized pile of bricks and mortar; it is a phenomenological domain. Thus it is of vital importance that the law give more attention to the phenomenological experience of the perceiver, especially with respect to legal conceptualizations of privacy. What the law takes for the "facts" of the matter may correspond not at all to the experience of the individual concerned. To breach the walls of the home electronically is to alter the nature of interpersonal boundaries and hence the nature of intersubjectivity within society. . . .

Home Incarceration

From the beginning of our own work with home incarceration, we have been concerned about the social psychological impact of employing the home as a surrogate jail. Even the use of volunteers to monitor compliance by telephone presents problems, for it is clear that the intrusion of the telephone itself into the home represents a more complex phenomenological situation than may be apparent at first glance. But the electronic bracelets are of a different level of intrusion, not only because they operate continuously and impersonally, but because they are actually strapped to the *body* itself, which is even more intimately associated with the sense of selfhood than is the home. . . .

Expectations about the future of home incarceration depend largely on how one reads the history of corrections over the past century. Several interpretations are possible, and it is likely that there is some degree of validity to each. But which is most valid? Is it fundamentally a history of progress, of benevolent intent leading to unanticipated consequences, or the inexorable outcome of deeper structural trends toward total social discipline and suppression of individuality? Such social control techniques as torture, branding, mutilation, flogging, and hanging represented brutal, public spectacles of the past. Although social control has tended to become less coercive in a physical sense, it has become both more specialized and technical, as well as more penetrating and intrusive, and thus more subtly coercive in a different sense. . . .

The Repudiation of Corporal Punishment

The repudiation of corporal punishment and capital punishment in favor of imprisonment was regarded as an immensely progressive step. The much later movement from institutional to community-based correction was regarded as even more progressive. Yet there are more and more data suggesting that the potential problem of "widening the net" to bring an increasing proportion of the population under state control has become a reality. S. Cohen argues that official social control is being extended through both the *exclusion* and the *inclusion* of offenders. Policies of exclusion lead to the use of institutional incarceration to the point of severe overcrowding of jails and prisons and great pressure from the public and from correctional authorities for construction of more and more such facilities. These pressures lead to a search for "alternatives" by which the offender can be included within the "community" at the price of surrendering certain personal autonomy. Because the inclusive policy is perceived as less harsh, its use is encouraged. Thus it is extended to include a larger and larger proportion of the population. . . .

Even in our earliest papers dealing with home incarceration, we expressed concern about the possibility of widening the net to include a greater percentage of the population and gave special attention to the "Orwellian overtones" of electronic monitoring and the implications of home incarceration for the "Anglo-American tradition of 'home as castle' in which the private dwelling place is regarded as sacred ground off limits to the state except under extreme conditions." Developments since then have done nothing to reduce these concerns.

"IPS [Intensive Probation Supervision] is an essential element of the complete pattern of a restructuring of criminal justice."

Intensive Probation Is Effective

John P. Conrad

John P. Conrad was formerly a visiting fellow at the National Institute of Justice in Washington, D.C., and a visiting professor at Simon Fraser University in Burnaby, British Columbia. Now retired, he continues to write and consult on corrections issues. In the following viewpoint, Conrad argues that while prison is necessary for violent offenders, the vast majority of nonviolent criminals do not require imprisonment. Instead, Conrad contends, these offenders can be effectively punished in the community by participating in supervised probation programs. Because Intensive Probation Supervision [IPS] has already demonstrated its success in reducing both prison populations and recidivism among program participants, Conrad continues, it should be introduced throughout the entire country as a cost-effective alternative to prison.

As you read, consider the following questions:

1. What problems does the author see in the current system of criminal justice?
2. How does intensive probation work, according to Conrad?
3. What benefits does the author see in intensive probation?

John P. Conrad, "Return to John Augustus," *Federal Probation*, December 1987. Public domain.

Years ago I was invited to sit in on an impromptu session of chief probation officers and academics considering the preparation of candidates for careers in probation and parole. It was the kind of occasion of which there should be more. No prepared papers, but everyone present was loaded with ideas and anxieties that they'd lived with for a long time. We were deeply concerned professionals thinking together about our frustrations and the future of correctional field services.

One of us, a chief probation officer who had administered a well established department in a northeastern state for many years, was poignantly candid. His confession was sad but honest, and I recall it vividly to this day:

> When I started out as a probation officer twenty-five years ago, I thought I knew what my job was all about and how it ought to be done. I was eager to get to work, and I think I was a good officer, as officers were judged in those days. Now I'm at the top in my department, and I don't know what to tell new men and women when I meet with them to do my bit for their indoctrination. I'm not at all sure what I can tell them about our objectives, how to do their jobs, or what I consider a good performance to be. I used to be positive about all these things.

I don't recall that anyone had any encouraging suggestions to raise his spirits. The ideas with which we had come to this session, the ideas which we had all entertained throughout our careers in this enterprise of field penology, didn't seem to be applicable. Our anxieties took over without leading to new thoughts. The baleful influence of [Robert] Martinson's [1974] report on the effectiveness of correctional treatment pervaded the room. We uneasily recalled that the "nothing works" message particularly applied to probation and parole. No one was ready to give up on the traditions of probation or on its practice, but confidence in its usefulness as it was practiced at that time was at a low ebb. The fundamental question lingers in my mind. What should judges, practitioners, probationers, and the public expect of probation in the administration of justice?

Probation, Past and Present

Until very recently there was a simple answer, even if its application was deceptively difficult. Probation officers were to investigate the personal circumstances of convicted offenders and report them to the court as an aid to fair but safe sentencing. Then, if the offenders were granted probation, they were to be supervised. The object was to assist the probationer to complete his probation without violation of its terms. Supervision included social services to assist the probationer to lead a lawful life and surveillance to make sure that he did. It was all so reasonable in criminology and social work seminars in graduate school, but all of us in that field seminar knew that what's reasonable in a classroom gets lost in the unreason of the streets.

What distressed the doleful chief at this think-session was the accumulation of evidence showing that what he and his staff were doing didn't make much difference. It was no secret. Support for probation was declining. Budgets were cut, and there was talk in some hard-pressed counties of doing away with it altogether. We might argue that probation was a good idea that wasn't getting a fair trial. After all, common sense should tell any layman that a probation officer responsible for upward of a hundred probationers could not be responsible for any. I don't think that message ever got through to the budget analysts or the public at large. After all, the public had also heard from Dr. Martinson that "nothing works."

Intensive Probation Works

Constant checks on crime-prone probationers, including surprise drug tests, are centerpieces of an "intensive probation" routine being tried in more than half the states. Instead of assigning officers the hopeless task of trying to keep track of 200 or more convicts, case loads are reduced to two or three dozen so officers can keep a better watch over their charges. In Georgia, which pioneered the idea, only 1 in 5 was arrested while under scrutiny, far lower than the average rate of 50 percent or more for those on traditional probation. Because so many stay on the straight and narrow, taxpayers save. It costs $2,700 a year for an intensive watch on a convict, compared with the $13,000 tab for confinement.

U.S. News & World Report, February 26, 1990.

The prospects [now] look more hopeful. We know that we have to use probation more effectively, and there are signs that we are learning how to do it right. High time, too. Any state persisting in the hard line that demands the incarceration of all or most felons invites eventual bankruptcy. Long before reaching this improbable catastrophe, correctional budgets would consume an alarming share, maybe the largest share of state revenues. Once a relatively minor item in the general budget of most states, correctional priorities begin to threaten universities, schools, and highways in some metropolitan states. At the present rate of commitment to state prisons, some states face the necessity of building a new 500-man prison every year—or discovering radically new ways of imposing meaningful sanctions on the less dangerous criminals.

The only relief in sight is the vastly increased use of probation and parole. That is an unpromising alternative if it means probation as usual, administered by overworked and often under-trained officers carrying unmanageably large caseloads and able to see only those probationers who have fallen into dire new trouble. . . .

Joan Petersilia and her colleagues should have set to rest any lingering hopes that there might be some value in preserving the practices required by the 100+ caseload. The gist of their seminal research was the finding of a 1985 Rand study of probation in the California metropolitan counties of Alameda and Los Angeles. This study showed that in a 40-month followup of 1,672 felons on probation only 35 percent managed to stay out of further trouble, the preponderant majority having been arrested for serious offenses. Fifty-one percent were convicted of new crimes. Eighteen percent of the sample were guilty of homicide, rape, weapons offenses, assault, or robbery. This is not the place to summarize again these alarming findings. The point is that we professionals in criminal justice should not be surprised and most of us are not. Petersilia and her colleagues argue forcefully for fundamental changes in the way we administer field services in corrections. The good news is that we'd already been changing rapidly and significantly. The bad news is that the changes in the management of probation haven't been formalized as yet by the changes of legislation and policy that innovation has clearly indicated.

Quite the reverse. The Federal sentencing guidelines shy away from innovations other than longer incarceration for more felons, with alarming consequences predictable for the Bureau of Prisons. If these guidelines are emulated by the states, desperate overcrowding of the prison systems in which they are applied can be confidently predicted. Long before this state of affairs is reached, alternatives to the traditional sanctions for nonviolent offenders must be adopted—not as experimental options but integrated in the law of sentencing.

In Plain Sight on the Streets

In the first place, I refer to Intensive Probation Supervision (IPS) which, in various forms, is in use in at least eight states. I will argue here that IPS is an essential element of the complete pattern of a restructuring of criminal justice. The design of this new structure depends on more experience than we now have. At this stage in the development of IPS, the most impressive model has been put into effect in Georgia. From its inception, systematic data have been compiled by the Office of Research and Evaluation of the Georgia Department of Offender Rehabilitation. IPS in that state is based on 25-person caseloads managed by a probation officer and a surveillance officer. Only felons are admitted, and only those who would be sentenced to prison if IPS were not an option to incarceration. Commitment to IPS is voluntary. In principle, the offender may choose prison instead of the fairly strict IPS regime—an option that has been very seldom chosen. Employment and community service are requirements, and a monthly fee (from $10 to $50), based on ability to pay, must be paid by participants. Probationers must also agree to daily visitations by probation or surveillance staff.

IPS outcomes have been promising. Of the 2,322 offenders placed with IPS from 1982 to January 1985, 15 percent completed their sentences, and probation has been revoked for only 16 percent. A firm figure on savings depends on the method of computing costs of incarceration. Disregarding the cost of prison construction (a legitimate factor in the calculation of incarcerative costs), the savings are estimated at $6,775 for each case diverted from prison, a saving to the state of about $13 million, assuming that each IPS participant would have been sent to prison if the program did not exist.

On the [basis of the available evidence] . . . we can declare a success of the Georgia version of IPS in its present form. I contend that it is a foundation on which criminal justice can build. This model, or a reasonable variant, should be legislated into the system throughout the country, not only in the interest of humane treatment of prisoners but also for the substantial savings to taxpayers that could be realized by reducing prison intake to a manageable flow of humanity. There are offenders for whom nothing but the hard line will do, but less expensive rigors for most will do much better. Can we discern the outlines of a common-sense system of criminal justice?

Intensive Probation Is Not for All Offenders

Let's begin with the recognition that there are some offenders who belong in prison. At the head of the list are the truly dangerous offenders. There are many ways of distinguishing them, ranging from arbitrary commitment to prison for certain classes of offenders, to clinical decisions about dangerousness, and on to the statistical calculation of probabilities; but this is not the place to decide on the most appropriate method. Opinions vary as to how many truly dangerous offenders there are, but even by the most sweeping estimate the numbers are far less than the present prison population. Dangerous offenders have in common the commission of a violent crime: homicide, rape, assault, and robbery, and a prediction that at liberty they would commit more violence. . . .

In addition to the obviously dangerous, there are others who should do some time to preserve the integrity of the system. Wholesale illegal drug distributors, scandalous violators of public trust, persistent major property crime recidivists, and flagrant probation violators fall into this category. With few exceptions sentences should be brief but exemplary, and some form of supervision should follow.

For the remainder of the offender population now clustered in the nation's prisons, field supervision should be the sanction of choice. IPS is more expensive than traditional probation, hard to administer and hard to conduct. For the offender it represents a sanction with irksome requirements, a considerable sacrifice of freedom, but some hope of restoration to the community as a productive citizen. For the community itself, IPS is a substantial saving when compared with incarceration and, if conscientiously administered, much better protection in the long run and probably in the short run, too.

Fuzzy thinking, whether on the soft or the hard line, is dangerous for public confidence in the system. As of these times, the fuzziness of hard-line thinking threatens the integrity of the public purse without affording the public protection it promises. The softer line, whether fuzzy or not, is getting little attention in these days of pervasive alarm about crime.

The Message of Surveillance

What does the nightly visit of the surveillance officer mean to the probationer in the Georgia version of IPS? No matter how we disguise the requirement as a reassurance to the community that all is well at the probationer's address, the contact is coercive, an implicit statement that the probationer is not trusted. The coercion inherent in corrections is mitigated by the companion role of the probation officer, who is supposed to offer counsel, assist with finding employment, help with family and neighborhood problems, and generally support the probationer in making peace with the community he or she has offended. To borrow from Charles Murray's succinct encapsulation of the two messages, surveillance tells the offender, "you can't do that any more because some very unpleasant things will happen if you do," while the service offered by the probation officer is positive: "you shouldn't do that any more because you have better options." And to be even more succinct, surveillance is punishment, whereas service is reformative, at least in intent.

What good is punishment? Leaving aside the possibility of general deterrence and the affirmation of values that are derived from the imposition of a sentence, there is pretty good reason to suppose that punishment can do little for the offender himself or herself. B. F. Skinner, the prophet of behaviorist psychology, has consistently denounced negative reinforcement as unproductive. I am no Skinnerian, but it seems like common sense to me that punishment and the threat of further punishment if misconduct is repeated will accomplish nothing with a man or woman who does not see any other choice to obtain necessities, pleasure, or the relief of the ennui of impoverished idleness. Incentives have to be realistic. For a product of the inner city under-class, the admonition that he will be punished even more severely if he repeats an offense is open to the response: "what else can I do?" If we can't tell him honestly, punishment won't make much difference. Education in prison and job opportunities on probation will fail with some, but if we stop trying we have no reason to suppose that we will succeed with any.

Intensive Probation Reduces Recidivism

The prison system does little but train and harden criminals to commit more crimes. But alternative sentences for those criminals who are not violent have proved remarkably successful where they have been tried.

In Georgia, only 16 percent of all participants in the state's Intensive Supervision Probation (ISP) program are rearrested within 18 months of completing the program. Seven percent of those are for technical violations and only 9 percent for new crimes.

In New Jersey, only 8 percent of ISP graduates are rearrested for new crimes. In Illinois, the rate of rearrests for new crimes is only 5 percent.

The ISP program saves Georgia $10,000 per offender per year compared to imprisonment. In New Jersey, the annual savings per offender amount to $11,000 and in Illinois, $13,000.

Cal Thomas, *The Washington Times*, May 14, 1990.

Intensive probation is conservatively administered, and properly so. No violent offenders, no persons presenting "unacceptable risks" to the community are admitted. All recruits to IPS know what they are getting into and must sign on of their own free will. At the same time, nearly all have been sentenced to prison as felons before they are considered for assignment to IPS. In the early years of such a seemingly radical program the risks of scandalous failure are real. To compromise it by accepting an offender whose record suggests even the possibility of a spectacular crime would be a disaster from which there might be no recovery.

Even as now administered the Georgia version of IPS has had a significant impact on the prison population. According to Billie Erwin and Lawrence Bennett, between 1982 and 1985 there was a 10 percent decrease in the number of prison commitments with a reciprocal increase of 10 percent in the number of persons placed on probation. In the jurisdictions with IPS teams (IPS does not cover the entire state), the percentage of offenders on probation ranged between 15 and 27 percent.

At the front end of the flow of felons into social control we can divert a significant 10 to 25 percent from prison, and with confidence born of experience, probably a good many more could make it on the streets without any cell time at all.

Supervised Intensive Restitution

At the other end, where felons trickle out of the joints, the flow could be commenced at an earlier point. Alabama cannot be considered a state where criminals are offered an easy go, but faced with an intolerable overcrowding situation a conservative administration opened the Supervised Intensive Restitution program, an inaccurate designation chosen to obtain SIR as its acronym for easy reference. Under SIR, prisoners with 6 months or less to go before their release dates and who have non-violent records, free of narcotics arrests, are eligible for release under much the same terms as IPS in Georgia, from which SIR was obviously derived. The program contains between 600 and 700 individuals at any one time and has drastically cut back the waiting list of felons awaiting movement to prison but held in a county jail. As with IPS, there have been recidivists and new commitments to prison, together with occasional complaints from Alabama's unreconstructed devotees of the hardest possible line. But like IPS in Georgia, SIR is enough of a success to deserve extension and emulation. . . .

Can IPS and SIR make a difference? The idea of teamwork between a service officer and a surveillance officer is plausible and attractive. At this point we don't know how far it can be pushed, but of all the possible ventures into the future of criminal justice, these surely deserve the most attention. There's not much time to spare. The expansion of prison populations cannot go on indefinitely without serious damage to the social fabric. That such damage is needless adds to the absurdity of our present system of sanctions.

"ISP programs that have been evaluated do not reduce recidivism rates, significantly reduce prison crowding, or save much (if any) money. "

Intensive Probation Does Not Work

Michael Tonry

Michael Tonry is the managing editor of *Crime and Justice: A Review of Research*. In the following viewpoint, Tonry argues that intensive probation programs do not achieve their stated goals of reducing prison crowding, saving money, or reducing recidivism. Despite these failings, he contends, these programs are very popular with the nation's probation officers because they are perceived as tougher and more effective than regular probation. This mistaken impression is wasting scarce tax dollars.

As you read, consider the following questions:

1. What are the stated goals of intensive probation programs, according to Tonry?
2. What three kinds of intensive probation projects does the author identify?
3. What does Tonry mean by latent goals, and how do they differ from the stated goals of intensive probation programs?

Michael Tonry, "Stated and Latent Functions of ISP," *Crime and Delinquency*, vol. 36, no. 1, January 1990, pp. 174-181, 183-186, 188-189, © 1990 by Sage Publications, Inc. Reprinted by permission of Sage Publications, Inc.

There is good, albeit preliminary, reason to doubt that intensive supervision probation (ISP) programs substantially reduce prison crowding, save public funds, or increase public safety. Yet over the last half dozen years they have spread across the United States, and they continue today to proliferate. This [viewpoint] examines the question of why these new programs are thriving.

The answer appears to be that ISP programs, despite their apparent failure to achieve their primary stated purposes, admirably serve a variety of other, latent, purposes. They serve bureaucratic and organizational goals by enabling probation administrators to be "tough on crime" and thereby increase the institutional and political credibility of probation. This brings more staff, more money, and new programs to probation. Bigger budgets and increased responsibilities are the traditional measures of bureaucratic success, and ISP programs are means to those legitimate organizational ends.

They serve administrators' normative goals. By being purposely more punitive than traditional probation, ISP programs permit administrators to express a reduced tolerance of crime and disorder that they share with the general public and political leaders.

They serve professional and psychological goals. By attracting new resources and new visibility, ISP programs put probation on the front lines of crime control and thereby enhance the esteem accorded probation and, vicariously, the professional and personal self-esteem of probation officers. This is not a cynical point. Every serious person wants to believe that his work is important and socially useful. If smaller caseloads managed by collaborating probation and surveillance officers promise both enhanced public safety and more effective service delivery, probation officers can quite reasonably believe that theirs is a socially important role. . . .

Thus, the argument to be made in this [viewpoint] is that the spread of ISP can be understood better in terms of its latent functions, which it can accomplish, than in terms of its patent functions which, in most places, it apparently cannot. . . .

The Stated Goals of ISP

Most people seem to agree that the primary formal goals of ISP programs are to reduce prison crowding, to save money, to protect public safety, and to provide a punishment that is more punitive and intrusive than ordinary probation. Here is how Frank Pearson, the evaluator of New Jersey's program, describes its goals:

> (a) To *improve the use of scarce prison resources* by releasing selected offenders from incarceration into the community after they serve three or four months of their prison term, thus

saving prison space in which to confine the more serious offenders.

(b) To have the program be *monetarily cost-beneficial and cost-effective* compared to ordinary incarceration.

(c) To *prevent criminal behavior* by those selected offenders while they are in the community. . . .

(d) To *deliver appropriate, intermediate punishment* in the community.

A statement similar to Pearson's could be made about most ISP programs. As I read the evidence from evaluation research, only Pearson's last goal, delivering "appropriate, intermediate punishment in the community," is being realized. Many evaluations show that punitive, intrusive policies—frequent urinalysis, unannounced visits, astonishingly high levels of contacts, official intolerance of violations of technical conditions—were implemented vigorously. Whatever else it may or may not be, in many places ISP *is* punitive. By contrast, the evidence to support realization of the other goals is exceedingly weak. . . .

Intensive Probation May Increase Incarceration

Intensive supervision programs easily fall into the pattern of detecting a large number of minor violations and generating revocations to an unmanageable degree. That can become almost as significant a problem in managing the program as the felony arrests and convictions that are bound to occur in any community-based program. For instance, when Georgia randomly tested probationers for drug use using urinalysis methods, 46% of those tested produced positive results. What is the appropriate response to positive drug screens? If incarceration is called for, then the county's incarceration rate could increase significantly after such intensive surveillance programs are implemented.

Joan Petersilia, *Controversial Issues in Crime and Justice*, 1988.

There have been a handful of major recent evaluations. Three different kinds of ISP projects have been examined. Some are caseload management efforts [which exist in Massachusetts, for example]; they are created and controlled by probation managers and by definition claim neither to serve as "alternatives to incarceration" nor as a direct means to reduce prison crowding or save public monies. . . .

The other two types of ISP projects have been inelegantly described as front-door and back-door programs. The doors are prison doors. Programs of the former type operate as diversions from prison and thereby notionally keep offenders from entering the prison's front door. Programs of the latter type offer early release from prison, on condition of the intense supervision of ISP, and thereby notionally hasten prisoners' exit through the prison's back door. Both types of programs seek their justification in claims that they reduce prison crowding and save public funds by replacing expensive imprisonment with less expensive ISP, all the while protecting public safety by means of unrelenting and unforgiving surveillance.

Georgia's ISP program, the best known front-door project, has been emulated in many states including Illinois, Arizona, and New York. In Georgia, ISP operates as a sentencing option. Ideally, ISP probationers are first sentenced to imprisonment and then diverted to probation; in practice, many judges sentence directly to ISP. . . .

New Jersey's is the best known back-door project. Offenders apply to admission from within the prison. Eligibility standards eliminate those who pose significant threats of public relations embarrassment or serious new offending; several stages of subjective screening eliminate many more. . . .

Reduced Jail and Prison Crowding

There is little reason to believe that most ISP programs, by diverting offenders from prison, do much to reduce crowding. The argument is different for each type of ISP program, so I address them one by one.

Front-door ISP programs like Georgia's face two problems that easily could interact to increase prison use. First, in states that lack presumptive sentencing guidelines, it is exceedingly difficult to be sure that a purportedly prison-bound ISP offender really would otherwise have gone to prison. Of offenders receiving ISP in Georgia in 1983, half got there by amended sentence and half by direct sentence. In the latter case, judges were asked to sign a certificate that the offender would have been imprisoned had he not been sentenced to ISP; Billie Erwin, the primary Georgia evaluator, notes that "this was a formality that could hardly be considered proof." Even in the former case, it would shock few observers of courts if judges, who wished to justify sentencing a probation-bound offender to ISP, would first announce some other sentence and then "amend" it to specify ISP. . . .

The second complexity that undercuts the effectiveness of front-door ISP programs at reducing prison populations is that they, like many ISP programs, have high revocation rates. Partly this results from the intensity of programs that involve 20 to 30 contacts per month compared with programs involving one or two contacts per month; inevitably the case officers know more about their clients. Partly also it stems from the avowedly punitive, intrusive nature of ISP programs; they are claimed to be tough, and low tolerance of violation of conditions is the best way to show probationers, prosecutors, and judges that they *are* tough.

In Georgia, 40% of ISP offenders in an evaluation of people sentenced to ISP in 1983 were rearrested. As of September 1986, 18% of ISP clients to that date had absconded or had their status revoked. By one calculation, only half of Georgia's ISP offenders successfully completed the program. . . .

When these two problems of front-end ISP—use for offenders who were not prison-bound, high revocation rates—are combined, it becomes apparent that the net effect of a front-door ISP program may be to increase prison populations. Depending on the proportion of an ISP program's caseload diverted from prison, and the proportion imprisoned following revocation, it is possible that some ISP programs fill more prison beds than they empty.

Back-door ISP Programs

On first impression, back-door ISP programs should not suffer from the same problems as the front-door variety. After all, if the aim of the program is to release people from prison early and it is available only to offenders who apply for admission from prison, it must reduce prison crowding. However, it is not so simple. T. Clear, S. Flynn, and C. Shapiro suggest that "there is a growing concern that some judges are 'backdooring' cases into ISP by sentencing borderline offenders to prison while announcing they will 'welcome an application for intensive supervision.'" This is not as far fetched as it may appear; a reasonable judge might well decide to create ad hoc "shock probation" sentences by imprisoning marginal offenders on the rationales that ordinary probation is a slap on the wrist, a short stay in prison will get the offender's attention, and the offender's marginal nature will assure early release to ISP. The problem, however, is that the eligibility screening is very rigorous and at the last of seven stages entirely subjective. Less than one-sixth of the prisoners who apply for New Jersey ISP are selected. Thus the creative judge may miscalculate: The prisoner whom he sentenced on the assumption of early ISP release may not be released. . . .

It will vary from case to case but, in some jurisdictions, either front or back-door ISP may increase prison crowding. By definition this will happen with case management ISP, like that in Massachusetts. The heightened surveillance experienced by the high-risk offenders assigned to the ISP program should, in the nature of things, uncover more technical violations and new crimes which, in turn, should send more people to prison. Most people would presumably regard this as a desirable result of the more efficient use of probation resources.

If the case for ISP as a prison population reducer is weak, the case for cost savings must also fail. . . .

Many analyses that purport to show that a new program billed as a "sentencing option" or an "alternative to incarceration" will save the state money do not withstand scrutiny. The biggest problem is that evaluators nearly always compare average per-capita costs for prisoners and, for example, ISP probationers, factor in the number of days the average offender would have been imprisoned and the number of days on ISP, do some multiplying and comparing, and conclude that the ISP project will save the state a substantial sum. A fundamental problem with this kind of analysis is its use of average costs. The reality is that one more prisoner costs the state only marginal costs—a bit of food, some disposable supplies, some record keeping. Only when the numbers of people diverted from prison by a new program permit the closing of all or a major part of an institution or the cancellation of construction plans will there be substantial savings. . . .

[Furthermore], some percentage of the ISP offenders have been diverted not from prison but from ordinary probation. Erwin's best guess is that 80% are diverted from prison [in the Georgia ISP]; I would guess half. For those not diverted from prison, ISP costs per day are six times higher than the cost of ordinary probation, the sanction from which they were diverted, not less, and that has to be taken into account.

[In addition], whatever sentences they were diverted from, many ISP offenders will commit new crimes or technical violations, have their ISP revoked, and be sent to prison. New Jersey's revocation rate was nearly 40%. In Georgia, 40% of the 1983 ISP offenders were arrested for new crimes, and roughly half of those terminated from the program by December 1985 suffered revocations. This seems to suggest that 40 to 50% of ISP offenders will be returned to prison; that additional time incarcerated must be included in any cost estimates. . . .

Crime Prevention and Recidivism Reduction

Two conclusions stand out about the crime-reduction properties of ISP. First, if ISP programs really divert offenders from prison, it is inevitably at the cost of increased crime in the community. Study after study demonstrates that released prisoners have nontrivial recidivism rates. In the nature of things, diverting offenders from prison or releasing them earlier results in crimes and victims in the community that would not exist if those offenders had not been diverted or released. Most of the research compares the recidivism rates of ISP clients with those of comparison groups of offenders released from prison; this is, however, like comparing apples and oranges. The truest crime reduction analysis would compare crimes in the community that would have occurred if the offenders had not been diverted or released (none) with those that did occur. By that measure, all ISP programs that divert offenders from prison should increase crime victimization. Second, insofar as the ISP evaluation research is reliable, it has consistently failed to show any crime reduction effects. . . .

Thus it now appears that those ISP programs that have been evaluated do not reduce recidivism rates, significantly reduce prison crowding, or save much (if any) money, though they do seem often to deliver the punitive, intrusive sanctioning experience that their proponents promise. . . .

ISP's Latent Functions

If ISP programs do not accomplish their stated goals, and yet continue to proliferate, they must be serving some other purposes of value to someone. My hypothesis is that a combination of latent institutional, professional, and political aims are being well-served by ISP programs, and that their proliferation is attributable to their effective achievement of those aims. . . .

Which Prisoners for Intensive Probation?

Intensive supervision programs in Georgia, Washington, Texas, and New York allow judges to sentence an offender directly to the programs, opening the possibility that intensive supervision will be applied to offenders who would otherwise receive routine probation. New Jersey, on the other hand, imposes so many requirements on offenders that they have difficulties locating enough prison-bound offenders who qualify. In short, as Kay Harris recently noted, "Reformers have not yet developed alternative programs that clearly avoid net-widening while maintaining an effective impact on incarceration."

Joan Petersilia, *Controversial Issues in Crime and Justice*, 1988.

ISP has served to increase the institutional credibility of probation, and therein lies much of its allure. Under the pressures in many places of staggering caseloads, and everywhere of disillusionment with probation's ability to achieve its traditional rehabilitative goals, probation was a demoralized institution. Many people saw probationary sentences as token punishments. One veteran probation executive observed that most people see probation "as a slap on the wrist." A veteran prosecutor has observed that probation has become "just something you slap on people when you don't know what else to do with them. We waste a lot of resources on probation, which means absolutely nothing in most places." The "slap on the wrist" rap may be a bad rap, but it was and is commonly believed. ISP has given probation administrators a chance to rebuild probation's credibility, influence, and, not incidentally, material resources. . . .

Everyone wants to feel useful and important. For probation officials and officers in Georgia, for example, ISP must have made them feel both more useful and more important. Their agency was seen to be in the middle of things and performing crucial public services. Personally and politically, probation officials were probably accorded more visibility, acknowledgment, and respect than before ISP became part of Georgia's criminal justice system. The substantial national attention, the media coverage, the invitations to discuss Georgia's program at national meetings must all have been flattering and reinforced probation officials' self-esteem. It would not be astonishing to learn that more Georgians chose careers as probation officers and that recruitment became easier. . . .

One last, more speculative, benefit deserves mention, though I realize I am stumbling ever deeper into the realm of pop psychology. Winds of reduced public and political tolerance of crime and criminals have been blowing across the United States for at least fifteen years. There is no reason to suspect that probation professionals have been unaffected by those social and cultural trends. ISP, especially in its hybrid helping and hurting form symbolized by paired probation and surveillance officers, permits probation simultaneously to reflect tougher attitudes toward crime and to carry out probation's traditional commitment to provision of social services and humane support to the disadvantaged who have committed crimes. . . .

A Role for ISP in the Future

Whatever the justification of the existence of ISP in particular states today on the basis of the existing evidence, there is a place for ISP and other intermediate punishments in the future. Most states lack meaningful punishments that are more severe than ordinary probation or less severe than imprisonment. A moment's reflection should teach that some offenders deserve punishments that are more than nominal but less than all-encompassing. ISP is one of these. But until the time comes, as it will, when sentencing guidelines or other approaches to structuring judicial discretion are implemented in most states, including within their scope a full range of punishments of graded severity, it is unlikely that these mid-range punishments will be preponderantly used for the mid-range offenders for whom in principle they are designed. Until that day, judges who are frustrated by the lack of rigor of ordinary probation are likely to use newer intermediate punishments for the more villainous among the probation-bound rather than for the less villainous among the prison-bound for whom, in public declaration, they are designed.

a critical thinking activity

Determining Punishments

Determining appropriate punishment for crimes is particularly important today because of the problem of prison overcrowding. Every criminal simply cannot be sent to prison. Growing recognition of this reality has aroused great interest in developing suitable alternative punishments to prison. Among recommended alternatives are house arrest, victim restitution, community service, and intensive probation supervision.

Deciding which offenders should be sent to prison and which offenders should receive alternative punishments is not easy. There are many questions to consider, including:

1. How serious is the offense?
2. Is the criminal a danger to society?
3. Would the punishment fit the crime?
4. Will the punishment deter the criminal from future criminal activity?
5. Will the punishment deter other criminals from committing similar crimes?
6. Will the punishment satisfy the community and crime victims that justice has been done?

Instructions:

With these questions in mind, consider the crimes and punishments described below. Assign what you believe to be the most appropriate punishment for each crime. If you are doing this activity as a member of a class, work in a small group and attempt to reach a consensus on each punishment before moving on to the next crime. Be able to explain the reasoning behind your sentencing. The punishments listed are meant to be rough guidelines. You may use punishments more than once or not at all, combinations of punishments, or punishments not listed here.

punishment	crime
_____	**child abuse** male offender sexually abused a seven-year-old girl in his neighborhood while on probation for a similar offense.
_____	**child abuse** female schoolteacher, who was abused as a child, sexually abused two of her male kindergarten students. No prior record.
_____	**murder** wife murdered her husband after being mentally and physically abused by husband throughout their marriage of sixteen years. No prior record.
_____	**murder** husband murdered his ex-wife who had a restraining order barring him from any contact with her. Husband has one prior conviction for an earlier assault on his wife.
_____	**murder** male offender murders nine women over a two-year period. He claims the women were prostitutes and that the devil told him to kill them. No prior record.
_____	**murder** male offender kills policeman during a raid on a crack house. Five prior convictions for possession of crack cocaine.
_____	**kidnapping** childless female offender impersonates a nurse and kidnaps a newborn baby from a hospital. No prior record.
_____	**rape** college freshman raped his date. No prior record.
_____	**rape** man rapes a woman stranger. He has two prior convictions for sexual assault.
_____	**drunk driving** female offender crashes her car into another car while driving drunk. The driver of the other car is killed. Offender has one prior conviction for driving while intoxicated.
_____	**drunk driving** male offender pulled over by police while drunk. Three prior convictions for driving while intoxicated.
_____	**shoplifting** woman stole cosmetics from supermarket. No prior record.
_____	**theft** female accountant embezzled $50,000 from her employer. One prior conviction for theft.
_____	**robbery** male offender robbed a convenience store. Prior convictions for theft and possession of cocaine.
_____	**bank robbery** male offender robbed two banks while on parole for a similar offense.

punishments

intensive probation supervision

house arrest with electronic monitoring

victim restitution

drug/alcohol treatment

psychological treatment/counseling

community service

one to twelve months imprisonment

one to five years imprisonment

five to ten years imprisonment

ten years or more imprisonment

life imprisonment

death penalty

other (be specific)

Periodical Bibliography

The following articles have been selected to supplement the diverse views presented in this chapter.

James Bennet   "Sentences That Make Sense," *The Washington Monthly*, January 1990.

Celestine Bohlen   "Lessons for Prisoners and Prisons," *The New York Times*, July 30, 1989.

Charles Colson   "Why George Bush Should Break His Promise," *Christianity Today*, April 7, 1989.

John J. DiIulio Jr.   "Conflicts of Criminal Interest: A Program for Streets and Jails," *Los Angeles Times*, October 1, 1989.

John Dillin   " 'Shock Incarceration': Hardship, Help for Drug Dealers," *The Christian Science Monitor*, November 10, 1989.

Michael Gartner   "I Hereby Sentence You to Help Others . . . and to Help Yourself," *The Wall Street Journal*, October 12, 1989.

Mike Goss   "Electronic Monitoring: The Missing Link for Successful House Arrest," *Corrections Today*, July 1989. Available from the American Correctional Association, Inc., 8025 Laurel Lakes Court, Laurel, MD 20707.

Richard Greene   "Who's Punishing Whom?" *Forbes*, March 21, 1988.

Joseph J. Kane   "A Dose of Discipline for First Offenders," *Time*, October 16, 1989.

David A. Kaplan and   "A New Era of Punishment," *Newsweek*,
Clara Bingham   May 14, 1990.

Stephen Labaton   "Glutted Probation System Puts Communities in Peril," *The New York Times*, June 19, 1990.

Cal Thomas   "Unlocking the Prison Doors," *The Washington Times*, May 14, 1990.

Scott Ticer   "The Search for Ways to Break Out of the Prison Crisis," *Business Week*, May 8, 1989.

Andrew von Hirsch   " 'Creative Sentencing': Punishment to Fit the Criminal," *The Nation*, June 25, 1988.

Organizations to Contact

The editors have compiled the following list of organizations that are concerned with the issues debated in this book. All of them have publications or information available for interested readers. The descriptions are derived from materials provided by the organizations. This list was compiled upon the date of publication. Names and phone numbers of organizations are subject to change.

American Bar Association (ABA)
Section of Criminal Justice
1800 M St. NW, 2nd Floor, South Lobby
Washington, DC 20036-5886
(202) 331-2260

Founded in 1921, the American Bar Association's Section of Criminal Justice is comprised of attorneys, law students, judges, law professors, and law enforcement personnel interested in the quick, fair, and effective administration of criminal justice. The association maintains over twenty committees, including one for prison and jail problems. Publications include the quarterly *Criminal Justice* magazine and various reference guides, books, course materials, and legal analyses.

American Correctional Association (ACA)
8025 Laurel Lakes Ct.
Laurel, MD 20707
(301) 206-5100

The American Correctional Association, founded in 1870, is committed to exerting a positive influence on national and international correctional policy and promoting the professional development of people in every aspect of corrections. ACA offers its members, corrections professionals, educators, and others a variety of books and correspondence courses on corrections and criminal justice. The association publishes the periodical *Corrections Today*.

Americans for Effective Law Enforcement (AELE)
5519 N. Cumberland Ave., No. 1008
Chicago, IL 60656-1471
(312) 763-2800

Americans for Effective Law Enforcement is a nonpolitical organization that seeks to arouse public concern for the nation's crime problems. AELE helps police, prosecutors, and courts promote fairer, more effective administration of criminal law. Its publications include three monthly magazines, *Jail and Prison Law Bulletin*, *Law Enforcement Legal Liability Reporter*, and *Security Legal Update*.

Contact Center, Inc. (CC)
PO Box 81826
Lincoln, NE 68501-1826
(402) 464-0602

The Contact Center is an international, nonprofit agency founded on the premise that all communities have the basic ingredients necessary to meet human needs, including those of prisoners. The center specializes in human service and criminal justice and publishes *Fact Sheets* on a variety of related topics.

One of its publications, *Corrections Compendium: The National Journal for Corrections Professionals*, describes current aspects of the nation's prisons, jails, and juvenile penal institutions.

Correctional Service Federation-U.S.A. (CSF/USA)
436 W. Wisconsin Ave., Suite 500
Milwaukee, WI 53203
(414) 271-2512

Correctional Service Federation is a group of voluntary agencies, bureaus, and departments of agencies devoted to rehabilitating criminal offenders. The federation produces public information material on crime prevention and rehabilitation of offenders and serves as a clearinghouse for public information about volunteer correctional service agencies. Publications include the periodic *Directory* and the quarterly *Newsletter*.

Federal Bureau of Prisons/U.S. Department of Justice
320 First St. NW
Washington, DC 20530
(202) 514-2000

The Federal Bureau of Prisons is responsible for the administration of the nation's federal prisons. The bureau publishes and distributes numerous reports, publications, and pamphlets regarding prisoners and the current federal prison system.

Fortune Society (FS)
39 W. 19th St., 7th Floor
New York, NY 10011
(212) 206-7070

The Fortune Society is comprised of ex-convicts and others interested in penal reform. The society seeks to create a greater public awareness of the prison system and of the problems confronting inmates before, during, and after incarceration. Publications include the quarterly *Fortune News*, which is free to prison inmates and society sponsors.

Friends Outside (FO)
2105 Hamilton Ave., Suite 290
San Jose, CA 95125-5900
(408) 879-0691

Friends Outside consists of staff and volunteers seeking to stop the perpetuation of crime and poverty. The group assists prison inmates in assuming responsibility for their own successful reintegration into society. FO also conducts educational, recreational, and social programs for adult and juvenile offenders and their families. Publications include a monthly *Newsletter* and various pamphlets.

The Heritage Foundation
214 Massachusets Ave. NE
Washington, DC 20002
(202) 546-4400

The Heritage Foundation is a conservative public policy research institute dedicated to the principles of free enterprise, limited government, individual liberty, and stiff prison sentencing policies. The foundation's Heritage Resource Bank provides information on one thousand academic studies. The foundation publishes the monthly *Policy Review*, and the *Backgrounder* series of occasional papers that includes such articles as "Time to Deal with America's Prison Crisis" and "What Congress Should Do to Defuse the Prison Crisis."

John Howard Association (JHA)
67 E. Madison St., Suite 1416
Chicago, IL 60603
(312) 263-1901

Founded in 1901, the John Howard Association has worked for humane, cost-effective policies for the criminal justice system. Its ultimate objective is the reduction of crime. The association is comprised of knowledgeable citizens, attorneys, judges, former members of the Illinois General Assembly, and criminal justice experts with extensive public policy-making experience. The association publishes policy statements and various *Update* pamphlets.

Mennonite Central Committee (MCC)
21 S. 12th St.
Akron, PA 17501-0500
(717) 859-1151

The Mennonite Central Committee is a relief and service agency of the North American Mennonite and Brethren in Christ churches. The group administers and participates in a number of public assistance programs, including one for prison ministries. Publications include the *Crime and Justice Network Newsletter*, *Life After Prison, Who Belongs in Prison?* and others.

The National Association of Chiefs of Police
3801 Biscayne Blvd.
Miami, FL 33137
(305) 891-1700

The National Association of Chiefs of Police is a tax-exempt, educational group that takes a conservative stance toward prisoners' rights and freedoms. The association's eleven thousand members include people from all aspects of law enforcement, including police chiefs, sheriffs, and others. The association publishes *Chief of Police* magazine and various pamphlets. It also conducts regional seminars for police officers.

National Coalition for Jail Reform (NCJR)
1828 L St. NW, Suite 1200
Washington, DC 20036
(301) 290-5814

The National Coalition for Jail Reform works to reform the nation's jails by educating the public on the unnecessary incarceration of individuals such as the mentally ill and retarded, public inebriates, juveniles, and pretrial detainees. It publishes a number of brochures, position papers, and proceedings on inappropriate confinement.

252

National Council on Crime and Delinquency (NCCD)
77 Maiden Lane, 4th Floor
San Francisco, CA 94108
(415) 956-5651

The National Council on Crime and Delinquency is comprised of social workers, corrections specialists, and others interested in community-based programs
to prevent, control, and treat crime and delinquency. Publications include the
monthly magazine *Crime & Delinquency*, among other works.

National Criminal Justice Association (NCJA)
444 N. Capitol St. NW, Suite 608
Washington, DC 20001
(202) 347-4900

The National Criminal Justice Association is comprised of state and local justice
planners, police chiefs, judges, prosecutors, defenders, corrections officials, and
others. One of the association's goals is to promote innovation in the criminal
justice system through the focused coordination of law enforcement, the courts,
corrections, and juvenile justice. Another goal is to improve the states' administration of their criminal and juvenile justice responsibilities through the development and dissemination of information to and among the states. Publications include the periodic magazine *Justice Alert*, the monthly *Justice Bulletin*, and the bimonthly *Justice Research*.

The National Prison Project (NPP)
1875 Connecticut Ave. NW
Washington, DC 20009
(202) 234-4830

The National Prison Project is a tax-exempt, foundation-funded project of the
American Civil Liberties Union. The project seeks to strengthen and protect the
rights of adult and juvenile offenders, improve conditions in correctional facilities, and develop alternatives to incarceration. The project publishes a prisoners'
rights magazine, *The Journal*, a quarterly report, a prisoners' assistance directory, and various pamphlets.

The Police Foundation (PF)
1001 22nd St. NW, Suite 200
Washington, DC 20037
(202) 833-1460

The Police Foundation is committed to increasing police effectiveness in control-
ling crime, maintaining order, and providing humane and efficient service. The
foundation sponsors forums that debate and disseminate ideas to improve personnel and practice in American criminal policing. It publishes a number of books,
reports, and handbooks regarding all aspects of the criminal justice system.

Prison Fellowship Ministries (PFM)
PO Box 17500
Washington, DC 20041
(703) 478-0100

Prison Fellowship Ministries encourages Christians to work in prisons and to assist communities in ministering to prisoners, ex-offenders, and their families. It works toward establishing a fair and effective criminal justice system and trains volunteers for in-prison ministries. Publications include the monthly *Jubilee* newsletter, the quarterly *Justice Report*, and numerous books, including *Born Again* and *Life Sentence*.

Prisoners Rights Union (PRU)
1909 6th St.
Sacramento, CA 95814
(916) 441-4214

The Prisoners Rights Union is comprised of convicts, ex-convicts, and others interested in improving conditions for those incarcerated in California's prisons. Goals include seeking redress for convict grievances, ending economic exploitation of prisoners, establishing a uniform sentencing procedure, and restoring civil and human rights to prisoners. The union publishes the bimonthly magazine *The California Prisoner*.

The Rand Corporation
1700 Main St.
Santa Monica, CA 90406-2138
(213) 393-0411

The Rand Corporation is an independent, nonprofit organization engaged in research on national security issues and the public welfare. It conducts its work with support from federal, state, and local governments, and from foundations and other philanthropic sources. Its books on prisons and prisoner sentencing include *Prison vs. Probation: Implications for Crime and Offender Recidivism* and forty-three other reports related to America's prisons.

The Sentencing Project (TSP)
918 F St. NW, Suite 501
Washington, DC 20004
(202) 628-0871

The Sentencing Project is a national, nonprofit organization that promotes sentencing reform and the development of alternative sentencing programs for prisoners. Its publications include *Americans Behind Bars: A Comparison of International Rates of Incarceration* and various other books and pamphlets regarding prisoners and prisoners' rights.

Bibliography of Books

The American Correctional Association *The State of Corrections.* Laurel, MD: The American Correctional Association, 1990.

Richard A. Ball, C. Ronald Huff, and J. Robert Lilly *House Arrest and Correctional Policy: Doing Time at Home.* Newbury Park, CA: Sage Publications, 1988.

Dean J. Champion *Corrections in the United States: A Contemporary Perspective.* Englewood Cliffs, NJ: Prentice Hall, 1990.

Charles Colson and Daniel Van Ness *Convicted: New Hope for Ending America's Crime Crisis.* Westchester, IL: Crossway Books, 1989.

Bertha Davis *Instead of Prison.* New York: Franklin Watts, 1986.

John J. DiIulio Jr. *Governing Prisons: A Comparative Study of Correctional Management.* New York: The Free Press, 1987.

John D. Donahue *Prisons for Profit: Public Justice, Private Interests.* Washington, DC: Economic Policy Institute, 1988.

Ralph D. Ellis and Carol S. Ellis *Theories of Criminal Justice: A Critical Reappraisal.* Wolfeboro, NH: Longwood Academic, 1989.

David Farrington and John Gunn, eds. *Reactions to Crime: The Public, the Police, Courts, and Prisons.* New York: John Wiley, 1985.

Mark S. Fleisher *Warehousing Violence.* Newbury Park, CA: Sage Publications, 1989.

Lynne Goodstein and Doris Layton McKenzie, eds. *The American Prison: Issues in Research and Policy.* New York: Plenum Press, 1989.

Stephen D. Gottfredson and Sean McConville, eds. *America's Correctional Crisis: Prison Populations and Public Policy.* Westport, CT: Greenwood Press, 1987.

Robert Johnson *Hard Time: Understanding and Reforming the Prison.* Monterey, CA: Brooks/Cole Publishers, 1987.

Robert Johnson and Hans Toch, eds. *The Pains of Imprisonment.* Newbury Park, CA: Sage Publications, 1982.

Jack Katz *Seductions of Crime: Moral and Sensual Attractions in Doing Evil.* New York: Basic Books, 1988.

Nicola Lacey *State Punishment: Political Principles and Community Values.* London: Routledge, 1988.

Roger J. Lauen *Community-Managed Corrections and Other Solutions to America's Prison Crisis.* Laurel, MD: The American Correctional Association, 1988.

Charles H. Logan *Private Prisons: Cons and Pros.* New York: Oxford University Press, 1990.

Belinda R. McCarthy, ed. *Intermediate Punishments: Intensive Supervision, Home Confinement, and Electronic Surveillance.* Monsey, NY: Criminal Justice Press, 1987.

Douglas Corry McDonald *Punishment Without Walls: Community Service Sentences in New York City.* New Brunswick, NJ: Rutgers University Press, 1986.

Thomas Mathiesen *Prison on Trial.* Newbury Park, CA: Sage Publications, 1990.

Roger Matthews, ed.

Privatizing Criminal Justice. Newbury Park, CA: Sage Publications, 1989.

Karl Menninger

The Crime of Punishment. New York: Viking Press, 1966.

Norval Morris and Michael Tonry

Between Prison and Probation: Intermediate Punishments in a Rational Sentencing System. New York: Oxford University Press, 1990.

John W. Murphy and Jack E. Dison, eds.

Are Prisons Any Better? Twenty Years of Correctional Reform. Newbury Park, CA: Sage Publications, 1990.

Paul B. Paulus with Verne C. Cox and Gavin McCain

Prison Crowding: A Psychological Perspective. New York: Springer-Verlag, 1988.

Joan Petersilia

Expanding Options for Criminal Sentencing. Santa Monica, CA: The Rand Corporation, 1987.

Igor Primoratz

Justifying Legal Punishment. Atlantic Highlands, NJ: Humanities Press International, 1989.

Graham Rickard

Prisons and Punishment. New York: Bookwright Press, 1987.

Ira P. Robbins

The Legal Dimensions of Private Incarceration. Washington, DC: American Bar Association, 1988.

Edgardo Rotman

Beyond Punishment: A New View on the Rehabilitation of Criminal Offenders. Westport, CT: Greenwood Press, 1990.

Joseph E. Scott and Travis Hirschi, eds.

Controversial Issues in Crime and Justice. Newbury Park, CA: Sage Publications, 1988.

James R. Sevick and Warren J. Cikins

Constructing Correctional Facilities: Is There a Role for the Private Sector? Washington, DC: The Brookings Institution, 1987.

C.L. Ten

Crime, Guilt, and Punishment: A Philosophical Introduction. Oxford, England: Clarendon Press, 1987.

Antony A. Vass

Alternatives to Prison: Punishment, Custody and the Community. Newbury Park, CA: Sage Publications, 1990.

Nigel Walker and Mike Hough, eds.

Public Attitudes to Sentencing: Surveys from Five Countries. Brookfield, VT: Gower Publishing Company, 1988.

Glenn D. Walters

The Criminal Lifestyle. Newbury Park, CA: Sage Publications, 1990.

Neil Alan Weiner and Marvin E. Wolfgang, eds.

Violent Crime, Violent Criminals. Newbury Park, CA: Sage Publications, 1989.

Ann E. Weiss

Prisons: A System in Trouble. Hillside, NJ: Enslow, 1988.

James Q. Wilson and Richard J. Herrnstein

Crime and Human Nature. New York: Simon & Schuster, 1985.

Edward Zamble and Frank John Porporino

Coping, Behavior, and Adaptation in Prison Inmates. New York: Springer-Verlag, 1988.

Index